W9-AOP-982

PRAISE FOR *Value-Based Marketing for Bottom-Line Success*

"Any marketing book capable of generating real discomfort and inspiration in equal quantities (like this one does) has to be a 'must read.' A 'hands-on,' practical guide to help you improve your business and delight your customers."

Paul J. Snaith
Vice President Marketing
Shell Gas (LPG)

"*Value-Based Marketing for Bottom-Line Success* is a value-based book whose practical approach separates it from the plethora of theoretical marketing books. The treasure this book gives us is the template for building our own practical, proven marketing road map."

David L. Hilton
Director New Business Acquisition
Lockheed Martin Corporation, Systems
Integration

"*Value-Based Marketing* is a wake-up call not for just marketing executives but for all members of leadership in an organization who need to understand and deliver on the simple axiom—the company that creates the highest customer value and best customer experience wins. [This book is] a 'must read' framework for discovering and delivering on a unique and distinguishing value position in the market."

Jack Calhoun
CEO
Accelare

"A refreshing change from the usual literature on marketing. The authors address the challenges of creating and sustaining value through an innovative, practical, and pragmatic 'blue print.' A must read for any corporate executive frustrated as to how to translate theory into practice that delivers value."

Omar M. Shamma
Chief Executive
Al Gurg Fosroc LLC, a division of BP Plc

Value-Based Marketing for Bottom-Line Success

Value-Based Marketing for Bottom-Line Success

5 Steps to Creating Customer Value

J. NICHOLAS De BONIS, ERIC BALINSKI & PHIL ALLEN

AMERICAN MARKETING ASSOCIATION

McGraw·Hill

New York   Chicago   San Francisco   Lisbon   London   Madrid   Mexico City
Milan   New Delhi   San Juan   Seoul   Singapore   Sydney   Toronto

Library of Congress Cataloging-in-Publication Data

De Bonis, J. Nicholas.
    Value-based marketing for bottom-line success : 5 steps to creating customer
value / J. Nicholas De Bonis, Eric W. Balinski, Phil Allen.
        p.   cm.
    ISBN 0-07-139656-X
    1. Consumer satisfaction.   2. Customer services—Management.
3. Marketing—Management.   I. Balinski, Eric W.   II. Allen, Phil, 1953– .
III. Title.

HF5415.13.D378   2002
658.8—dc21   2002026490

1 2 3 4 5 6 7 8 9 0   DOC/DOC   1 0 9 8 7 6 5 4 3 2

ISBN 0-07-139656-X

McGraw-Hill books are available at special quantity discounts to use as premiums and
sales promotions, or for use in corporate training programs. For more information, please
write to the Director of Special Sales, Professional Publishing, McGraw-Hill, Two Penn
Plaza, New York, NY 10121-2298. Or contact your local bookstore.

This book is printed on acid-free paper.

Dedicated to my Susan, Andrew, and Gabriela, my best friends and patient supporters, without whom this book would not have become a reality. For my coauthors, Eric and Phil, thank you for being part of my life's journey.

—*J. Nicholas De Bonis, Ph.D., Peachtree City, Georgia*

For all those people in business who passionately believe the best business is one that makes a meaningful contribution to the lives of other people. For my coauthors, Nick and Phil—together we stretched our minds and relationships to prove that, with pain, there is also substantive gain in many ways. And of course to my mom, Marge, and dad, Tony, who provided the kind motivational support during the writing process that only parents can. Finally, for the women in my life—Ana, Sarah, Lauren, Megan, Katie, and Luanne, who drive me crazy, but make our life together special.

—*Eric W. Balinski, Sparta, New Jersey*

Dedicated to Ingrid and Daniel; without their love and support I would not survive. Dedicated to Sonia and Reg; without their love and support I would not be. To my coauthors: thank you for the experience—I hope it will be repeated.

—*Phil Allen, Wädenswil, Zürich, Schweiz*

CONTENTS

ACKNOWLEDGMENTS

July 2002

This book and our value-based marketing model wasn't the result of an overnight epiphany we three authors had individually or collectively. They have been years in the making; an integration of our experiences, interactions with the thinking of others and other models, discussions with professional colleagues, and insights in prewriting collaborative sessions over the past three years and in several locations around the world.

Among the companies we've worked for and with are AlliedSignal (now Honeywell), BASF, Boehringer Ingelheim Vetmedica, Dow Chemical, English China Clays, GE, Hilti, Lonza, Schlumberger, Shell, Sprint, and W. R. Grace & Co. Each of these companies and their business environments afforded us—in the truest sense—real-life labs to advance innovative thinking and practices in understanding customers' needs and to explore and put into practice ideas that impacted business, people, processes, and systems.

The work of people like Roger Best, Jim Collins and Jerry Porras, Steven Covey, George Day and David Reibstein, Philip Kotler, Michael Lanning, George Lucas, Malcolm MacDonald, Roger Nagel, Michael Porter, Jagdish Sheth, and Michael Treacy and Fred Weirsema provided challenges, perspectives, and foundations on which to build.

This book is the coalescence of our backgrounds, skills, and experiences. We hope that it's enlightening and practical for you and that you gain as much by reading it as we have by writing it.

In addition, we need to recognize and profusely thank those people who helped, guided, or motivated us during the writing process—Danielle Eagan-Miller and Kathy Dennis at McGraw-Hill; Mark and Paul Balinski, George Biltz, Arie de Boer, Mike Crosswell, Marc Fermont, Paul Goldner, Paul Hague, Niki

Heimann, Bob Jenkot, Laura Jones, Bernard Kaminker, Terry Kendrick, Peggy Malnati, Kathy McCreedy, Bob Mitchell, Carol-Ann Morgan, Dan Murphy, Bill Pine, Henry Proctor, Scott Ravech, Amy Rosborough, Anne Seline, Diane Skorina, Ken Spero, Greg Stevens, Bob Szladek, Bob Thorley, James Thorne, John Zoetjes, and Volker Württenberger.

INTRODUCTION
THE BUSINESS WORLD
WE HAVE COME TO KNOW

It's easy for a company to believe that it is doing what's best for its customers. It's another matter entirely for the customer to believe it!
—De Bonis, Balinski, Allen (2002)

Over time, this maxim became an ever stronger focus for our life's work and the basis for this book. As we witnessed companies struggling to improve their business performance, we grew passionate about learning, testing, validating, and applying key business practices that create superior customer performance, healthy organizations, and sustainable business results.

Our passion, though, has not been focused on searching for the next big business idea. We fought to avoid finding a rare idea that worked once by some stroke of luck and then generalizing it to every business situation. Rather, we focused on finding the repeating clues, themes, and principles that worked most consistently throughout time and across situations. Personal performance and motivational guru Anthony Robbins always stresses that "success leaves clues." We think so, too.

First, we sought to identify ideas, practices, methods, and principles that had and hadn't worked in our own businesses. Then we sought to examine why these aspects either worked or didn't work. In many cases, we found that we did what we knew worked, but we couldn't communicate to someone else why these aspects worked. This led us to analyze and then structure frameworks and tools that others could use. Finally, we explored the thinking and practices of other people and businesses. Over several years, a strong framework began to emerge that could be used with great success to face just about any market or customer or business challenge. We have refined these practices and applications to speed implementation and improve results performance.

This book enters the market where there is no shortage of new business ideas or lack of advice on how to better run businesses. The market for such business books is composed of a tough audience of battle-weary business readers who have heard too many ideas that never worked and failed to outlast their hype. Yet there has never been a greater need for ideas and practical methods that can make a difference to a business.

In 2001, there were 257 public companies with $258 billion in assets that declared bankruptcy in the United States. This beat the previous worst year in bankruptcies, 2000, which saw 176 companies with $95 billion in assets declare bankruptcy. In the bear market of 2001–2002, 26 of the Fortune 100 lost at least two-thirds of their market value. In 2002, 67 companies went bust in the first quarter alone.[1]

There is plenty written to explain this phenomenon of business prosperity followed by a painful decline. Explanations include loss of focus, loss of leadership, spending too much, losing sight of customers, competitive response, weakening market forces, lack of process, bad systems, wrong employees, employee shortages, arrogance, and complacency. While all of these can be contributors, we believe the decline often has a simpler explanation.

As it grows, a business loses sight of its value commitments and customers. The business focuses on capturing the growth available to it. As the business grows, it fails to give deliberate reflection on whether customers require more and more modifications to the value it offers and the way it conducts business. And with a business's success, new attitudes and behaviors arrive to help propel the business confidently forward. These attitudes and behaviors often hide what's really happening inside many companies:

1. They grow disconnected from what really matters to customers.

2. They lose vision, lose sight of what the company is really in business to accomplish.

3. The cost of doing business changes.

4. The people working in the business change.

In a world where capitalism has emerged as the economic and customer model on which to build a business or a country, more companies are likely to struggle and many will still fail. The question remains, "Is there a way for business to *succeed today and to sustain that success* using good business practices, or has the marketplace become so crazy that success is merely by chance?"

We've learned that part of the answer lies within the character and the ambitions of people running a business. The recent behavior of Enron, WorldCom, and many Wall Street investment firms reminds business people that character is still an important component of a business's culture and value system. But were these failures triggered by a defect in their culture or value systems? Or did the leaders lose sight of what the business was created for in the first place, thereby setting in motion their own demise through the emergence of other cultural values and norms? If many of these failures are really rooted in losing track of what the business is created for, then we think that business (and capitalism) has a very bright future.

This optimism assumes that the majority of business people want to operate with integrity and honesty. They just need an approach they can count on to guide their thinking and behavior to accomplish the fundamental mission of any business: to bring together a group of talented people, resources, and capital in order to provide other people (customers) with something that will make everyone's lives better. Not surprisingly, the power of this simple concept of capitalism is easily lost when money, power, and prestige start to guide the business.

Where Have the Clues Led Us?

- If you were asked today, "Who are the greatest value-creating businesses in the '90s," what would you answer?
- If you were asked today, "Which company have you most admired in the past 10 years," which company or companies would you name?
- If you were asked today, "Which companies do you think are managed the best," who would you name?
- If you were asked today, "Which business leader(s) do you admire most," who would you name?
- If you were asked today, "Which companies' practices and ideas are you trying to benchmark and introduce into your own firm, and whose are you trying to emulate," what would you answer?

In the past couple of years, most people arguably would name Jack Welch as the best leader and say that GE had the best business performance. Welch has been called one of the greatest and most influential business leaders of our time, and as a result has spawned a dedicated following of me-too Jacks and GEs. Clearly his leadership was impressive, and GE's performance appears to bear out his effectiveness. Part of GE's success can be attributed to the fact that each of its business units was indoctrinated with GE's own point of view about successful business characteristics. Its continued success has led to a wealth of explanations from the business media examining GE's "secrets." One might even wonder if anyone other than GE could succeed today.

But if you're sitting there thinking your company is no GE and you are not Jack Welch, you need to read further. While their performance has been consistently impressive, the reality is that there will be very few companies who will ever be able to duplicate GE's approach. To be just like them, another business must do everything GE does *and* have three other things working for it. First, it needs a world-class financial/capital operation to be able to manage money flows. Second, it needs to be an expert at acquiring many other companies and efficiently integrating these acquisitions to extract earnings and reduce costs quickly. Third, it must be world-class in managing public relations. These three capabilities, often overlooked, are a critical part of their business approach and will be needed if you plan to build your business into a highly valued stock the way GE does it.

We have also found strong evidence by leading thinkers that many less idolized companies are very successful today. In *Good to Great*, Jim Collins identifies twelve firms whose average financial performance outperformed such companies as GE, Merck, Intel, Walt Disney, Wal-Mart, and Coca-Cola by 2.5 times.[2]

Our work isn't a research study. Rather, we have taken a "get-your-hands-dirty" approach to discovering the things that will guide any business to become a high performance business. For the past 10 years, our goal has been to develop and apply practical ideas, approaches, and tools that any company could use regardless of its current market position. The quest was to focus on those things that were well within a company's ability to control. This both increased the reproducible results and reduced the excuses of why the approach didn't work for X, who was *unique and different* as a business, team, product, or market. Fortunately, many of the companies we worked with applied these approaches in complex market environments where the companies faced significant challenges. Over time we noticed that there were similar and common themes to most challenges. The idea emerged that some common principles are at the core of running a business and achieving great performance with customers.

These core principles then became the compass which not only guided practical implementation of work processes and improvements, but was also to judge magnetic North when it came to evaluating the latest new management idea. This may have become one of the more powerful spin-off benefits of developing this approach. There was now a commonsense way to validate the potential use of new ideas.

For example, the popular management idea currently being pursued by many companies is to build a business based upon Six Sigma. While Six Sigma is in our view a good process improvement tool, most companies need to do more to find success with customers than just apply Six Sigma. As we discuss later in the book, the Six-Sigma tool, *Voice-of-the-Customer*, is based on the questionable assumption that customers can tell you how you can help them improve their businesses. This may be true in some cases, but we have found that it is far better to assume that the customer will never be more knowledgeable about what a product, technology, or service can do for them than the company selling it. We also warn against just letting the customer decide what the value-creating component of your product, technology, or service is. A company needs to discover on its own how to make its customers more successful by knowing more about the customer than the customer might know about his or her own business or life.

One company that discovered what really mattered to customers is Southwest Airlines. Southwest may represent the best example of a value-based marketing company in action. Southwest Airlines has consistently implemented what it discovered about customer value by simply offering the best value commitment and backing it up with a solid organizational alignment that enabled it to deliver the chosen value commitment to a precisely targeted group of travelers.

What has struck us about Southwest is its ever increasing success in one of the toughest industries in the world. The airline industry has high fixed and variable costs and large capital requirements, and airline customers are brutally demanding. It is a fiercely competitive industry, led by the biggest players, sometimes irrationally. In fact, the airline industry over time tends to make no profit because of competitive and financial pressures.

Despite these industry constraints, Southwest historically has had the best financial performance of any airline and is the only airline in the world that has made money consistently every year. Southwest's performance from 1990 to 2000 averaged a total return to investors of 34.8 percent. By 2000, Southwest had become one of America's most admired companies, returning 37.7 percent from 1995 to 2000, with a whopping 108.2 percent in 2000. In comparison, GE delivered 28.6 percent from 1990 to 2000, a 34 percent return from 1995 to 2000 and a total return of −6.1 percent in 2000.

As Southwest Airlines CEO Herb Kelleher stated in the June 1999 issue of *Money Magazine*: "When we started out, the people of Texas weren't willing to settle for peanuts either. You have to establish a different value system. What do people really want from air transportation? They want to get there safely, on time and with pleasant people."[3] Of course, Southwest will get you there quite economically as well. Another interesting insight about great value creators was subtly expressed by Kelleher. *"You have to establish a different value system."*[4] This suggests that there is a proactive element to implementing a better value for customers. At first, customers may not completely appreciate the new value, since they have been conditioned by past business offers companies have made. Southwest Airlines discovered what the best value was and has consistently made money for investors after its initial six-year start-up phase. How you can determine the best value for your customers is one of the key steps in this book.

Equally intriguing beyond Southwest's shareholder performance is its high customer satisfaction level and great safety record while maintaining the lowest cost structure in the industry. In addition, it has well-paid and highly motivated employees, and airport authorities aggressively lobbied Southwest to come to their towns.

The real demonstration of Southwest's effectiveness as an organization and as a business worthy of emulation came in the wake of the World Trade Center tragedy. Southwest didn't call for government bailouts or start lay-offs, as did its industry peers. Neither option fit with its commitment to its people nor were they necessary for the airline's well-being. "Nothing would devastate Southwest Airline Co.'s arm-around-the-shoulder chairman, Herb Kelleher, more than a lay-off," Michelle Conlin wrote in *BusinessWeek*. "Through jet fuel spikes, recession, even the Gulf War, Southwest has never in its thirty years downsized a single employee."[5]

"We are willing to suffer some damage, even to our stock price, to protect the jobs of our people," said Southwest CEO James F. Parker.[6] Can't you feel the stock analysts and business leaders grimacing when they read this? How committed do you think Southwest's employees will be now and in the future? And how many people would love to work for a company like Southwest?

It is perhaps tempting to turn this into a case for better employee practices to achieve better business performance. But better business performance is never sustainable if the business value to customers is weak. Our belief is that superior value for customers, with the appropriately aligned organizational structure, creates the most successful business that can ultimately foster great employee practices. This is really the secret that Southwest Airlines figured out, a secret it's practiced diligently for thirty years. It's the same value commitment you can use to achieve great business performance.

Two European airlines—Ryanair and Easyjet—have also turned in record-breaking market and business successes by emulating Southwest.

Ryanair began operations in 1985 with the launch of a daily flight on a fifteen-seater turboprop Bandeirante aircraft between Waterford Airport in the southeast of Ireland and London Gatwick. In 1986 it began offering Dublin-to-London flights, challenging the dominance of government-owned Aer Lingus and British Airways.

When CEO Michael O'Leary arrived in 1991, he inherited a $30MM loss. The airline redesigned its service to target underserved segments and target business and leisure travelers with low price guarantees over the Internet. It cut unprofitable routes, inefficient planes, and frills. Passengers grew from 4MM in 1998 to 7.4MM in 2001, with a 2002 target of 10MM. Ryanair's 2001 profits grew 37 percent over the previous year to €123.4MM on revenues of €487.7MM and increased margins to the highest in Europe, 25 percent in 2001. Ryanair's costs per employee are purportedly half British Airway's.

Started in Luton, UK, in 1995, Easyjet targets business travelers who would normally fly the main flag-carriers. Initially the airline flew to smaller airports, but has recently added Schiphol and Gatwick. Operating on an 11 percent margin in 2001, Easyjet's profits grew 81 percent in 2001 over the previous year to £40.1MM on revenues of £356.9MM. Its passenger load grew to 7.1MM in 2001 from 5.6MM in 2000.

The value-based marketing approach described in this book—instinctively developed and consciously practiced by Southwest, and now Easyjet and Ryanair—reflects a reality for any leader at any level in the organization; the real game is delivering superior, meaningful value impact to target customers.

While it may seem like there aren't any good answers today for achieving sustainable business success, don't give up just yet. *Value-Based Marketing for Bottom-Line Success* has been built on 10 years of applied knowledge and practices. Our Value Commitment to you is that *Value-Based Marketing for Bottom-Line Success* will both change the way you look at customers and your business, and give you the knowledge and tools to really make a difference to your performance.

We've written the book so that you can read it from cover to cover and follow the logic of our 5-step value-based Pentadigm marketing model. *Or* you can familiarize yourself with the Pentadigm model in Chapter 2 and then dive into the stage that is most important to your company or is most in need of development, updating, modification, or repair. Depending on your needs, either approach will help you extract maximum value.

THE VIEW FROM
PENTADIGM'S WORLD

"Cheshire Puss," asked Alice. "Would you tell me, please, which way I ought to go from here?" "That depends a good deal on where you want to get to," said the Cat. "I don't much care where," said Alice. "Then it doesn't matter which way you go," said the Cat.
                              —Lewis Carroll, *Alice's Adventures in Wonderland* (1865)

T he business marketing mantra from the mid-1950s was the marketing mix, the 4Ps of marketing—Product, Placement, Price, Promotion. In the 1980s it was Michael Porter's competitive forces. The decade of the 1990s saw sales and marketing respond to the buyer's demands for more cooperative relationships with relationship marketing. As companies headed to the twenty-first century, "solutions" became the buzzword in the marketing lexicon as "value" replaced products and services in suppliers' offerings. Contribution Margin or bottom-line profitability usurped top-line revenue management.

Read through your annual report or visit your own company's website. Review the same information sources for your customers or your competitors. Count the number of times you see the word "solutions" or "value-added" solutions or "value."

A content analysis of a broad spectrum of public domain materials produced by the top 150 companies in the chemical industry in 2001 found that 65 percent announced that they are customer focused. But according to an analysis of what these companies actually *do* in the marketplace or how they deliver against what customers value, only 10 percent are even close to being customer focused. It's easy to say that the customer is the center of your business strategy. It's more difficult to behave that way.

- If you claim to be customer focused, you need to read this book with a critical eye on your company.

- If you shout your customer focus from the rooftops, you need to read this book with an open mind.
- If you don't profess to be customer focused, you need to read this book at least twice.

In the years prior to writing this book, the question we've been asked constantly by clients has been, "How can our business better succeed?" There is no shortage of answers. Like you, we've been exposed to many exciting ideas and theories; business strategies such as Strategic Intent and Value Migration; financial management approaches such as Economic Profit or EVA;[1] core competencies; business reengineering in organizational effectiveness; operations systems such as Lean Manufacturing and Six Sigma; and customer focus and satisfaction practices like one-to-one and permission marketing.

Most business improvement ideas seem to be one-dimensional—they propose a business focused on one central idea, like becoming lean or developing the best competencies or becoming competitive or focusing on leadership. While these can help you and your business, they often do so in isolation or in a vacuum that fails to consider the entire supply chain, the extended value chain, or the business ecosystem in which your business is operating.

Our own thinking, behavior, and practices have evolved over the years based upon what we've experienced, learned, and seen succeed or seen fail. These collective experiences challenged our thinking, and shaped ideas we applied and practiced as we ran our own businesses or helped other people manage theirs more profitably.

The more we began to organize our thoughts, the more we became convinced of the wisdom of a multi-dimensional view of the marketplace and an enterprise-wide sense of change and customer focus. As a result, our Pentadigm value creation model relies on those characteristics always associated with great business success: focus and discipline, alignment, commitment, intellectual decision making, determination to the point of doggedness, inspiration, innovation, and implementation. These aren't characteristics that are endemic to an organization or easily developed, but they must become intricately nurtured and embedded into the personality of the organization.

The business paradigm on which this book rests is the integration of business strategies, processes, and practices to deliver a superior customer value commitment to your chosen target customers while making a profit. It's a win-win approach to conducting business that results in mutual value for your customer value segments and you the supplier. We define mutual value in terms of the difference between a long-term relationship driven by value exchanged or shared between buyer and seller and a short-term transaction that focuses on revenue and costs.

This is Pentadigm, a term we have coined to describe the complete picture of business thinking that we are urging business people to adopt from this book. Pentadigm is the quickest way for us to integrate and convey what we need to say throughout the book. Pentadigm is an innovative new paradigm—an advanced new way of thinking about business from the customer perspective—and Pentadigm is a simple 5-step model enabling any business person to approach managing or building his or her business from the customer perspective. Pentadigm thinking and behavior ensures that business people recognize their fiscal role in managing a business. So Pentadigm is shorthand for the title of our book, *Value-Based Marketing for Bottom-Line Success: 5 Steps to Creating Customer Value.*

The Value Paradigm

The ancient business axiom is "Build a better mousetrap and the world will beat a path to your door." That doesn't work anymore. In the mutual value paradigm, you have to ask the following questions.

1. Does anyone need a better mousetrap? If the answer is "yes," you have to ask the next question. If the answer is "no," don't build it anyway.

2. What does the target customer want the mousetrap to do? Define this explicitly, thoroughly, completely. Then ask the next question.

3. How much value does the world associate with the benefits of a better mousetrap? What are the customers willing to pay for?

4. The final question is this: Are you willing and profitably able to deliver a trap that does what the target customer wants it to do?

These four questions will help you determine whether you provide value at a cost that enables your business to make a return greater than what the investment costs are, that is, make an economic profit. One of the core insights of Pentadigm is that successful value creation requires, first and foremost, understanding what really constitutes customer value and secondly, understanding how your business subsequently aligns its resources to deliver that value to its chosen value segments.

This requires an outside-in, market-focused, customer-driven commitment, which addresses whether or not your company's customer value commitment is the best value for the customer relative to anything else in the marketplace. It is not asking your business to be foolhardy and do anything and everything to delight customers. Rather, you must figure out what will make a difference to your customers, even to the point of not doing certain things you currently do. In this way, then, you can profitably afford to do the things that make the biggest difference to customers. Making the biggest difference to your customers is how you will win and then retain them for the long term.

In one of our consultative projects a number of years ago, our task was to help a large multi-divisional, technically driven business comprehend key elements of value delivery. Simply telling this business about key ideas and practices wasn't going to get it over the threshold of letting go of its traditional ways of doing business and embracing the concept of customer value commitment. Case studies provided a more influential tool. We needed an unusual case for this client to demonstrate how a technically oriented company could think about its business and customer value.

One of the companies we studied was RĒVO, a maker of high-performance sunglasses. RĒVO was founded by former NASA scientists who had been part of developing and using specialized technology for glass surfaces on spacecraft to protect highly sensitive instruments exposed to the extreme sunlight conditions of outer space. From a start-up position, RĒVO created a new category of very expensive high-performance sunglasses priced at $150 to $300 per pair. The company grew quickly and was ultimately purchased by Bausch & Lomb, which sold RĒVO to the Luxottica Group S.p.A. in 2002.

Visionary thinking led RĒVO's founders to believe that there could be an application for the technology in protecting the human eye. But what made the company unique was how the scientists studied specific consumers and created customer value segments based upon unique insights—the value of the glass technology for each segment. The insights RĒVO developed about potential sunglass customers were achieved studying the lives and activities of these customers to determine how the glass technology could provide unique value for these people and their activities. The entire RĒVO operation was aligned around the customer value segments. Rather than focusing on the technology, behavior you might expect from scientists, the focus was on the customer.

RĒVO could have chosen to translate its technology story into a feature-rich promotional message focusing on how its technology achieved distortion-free 100 percent UV and IR ray protection for wearers. This could have been backed up with plenty of light-wave charts to prove the key selling points.

Instead, RĒVO's actual customer approach to developing its business started with going to ski slopes, and fishing and boating locations to watch and interact with people who wore sunglasses. They were trying to learn what their potential customers faced while skiing, fishing, or boating. What was it about coming down a mogul field, for example, that made it difficult for skiers to see, which affected their ability to navigate the run for maximum fun? Or how could seeing better help someone catch more fish? Even more specifically, RĒVO focused on those customers in these activities they considered innovative within the activity—the people who had to have the latest, best gear for the activities in which they passionately engaged.

For maximum customer value, RĒVO came to realize that not only did the customers need RĒVO's superior sunglasses to make the ski run easier or to see more fish, but they also needed lens frames that provided superior fit, comfort, and style. RĒVO found that its customer value segments tended to participate in their chosen activity for long periods. The best technology would be useless to customers if the frames made the customer uncomfortable when worn for a long time.

During an interview for the case study, RĒVO CEO Carol Montgomery was asked why we were interested in documenting her company's business model. Before we could respond, she finished her question with, "Doesn't everyone run his or her business this way?" as if the approach was just common business sense.

The answer for her then and even today is "no," the majority of businesses aren't run with a customer value focus. While many businesses claim they are customer focused and provide value, the actual corporate behavior and financial results belie the claim. And explaining away performance shortfalls as "it's the new economy" or "the global market has become so competitive" prevents these businesses from adopting a customer value approach to business.

Other sunglass suppliers look at business through the eyes of their own organizations and not the eyes of their customers, an appropriate metaphor that explains why competitors couldn't see the opportunities RĒVO did. To extend the metaphor, one of us is a brand loyal RĒVO wearer, primarily because the glasses not only protect his eyes, but help him see the fish better. While there are at least two dozen sunglasses brands from which fishermen and women can choose, RĒVO provides its customer value segment with the best value, even at more than $200 per pair.

Many respected companies are less customer value focused at times than the market demands. Nikon, the renowned Japanese camera and optics manufacturer, entered the market, for example, to compete directly against RĒVO in the mid-'90s. Like RĒVO, Nikon also had a very strong heritage of technological leadership in its field. Nikon customers also tended to reward its superior technology and quality with a willingness to pay premium prices for its products. The RĒVO market seemed like a great fit for them, yet Nikon withdrew a few years later after entering. A quick examination of Nikon's strategy execution may help explain why.

Nikon did produce a superior lens and good-looking glasses. It also studied and segmented customers. Nikon entered the marketplace at a time when numerous other "cool" brands were entering or expanding into the high-end sunglasses market.

However, the Nikon sunglasses which competed with the RĒVO H20s were heavier, the frames were less comfortable, and the lens coloration reduced visibility when looking for fish in the water. For a price tag of more than $300, one of the primary value needs for a fisherman wasn't met, even if the sunglasses did carry the Nikon brand. In addition, Nikon's products were first made available through its traditional channel—camera shops. This channel had little value for sunglass buyers.

Many businesses have some appreciation of customers' needs, their operating costs, and their product/service benefits and investor expectations. Most firms, however, tend to misunderstand which of these drives performance and which follows as a result. We believe that the most important aspect to long-term success is providing superior customer value, and this is supported by substantial evidence from those companies who tend to be the leaders in their respective markets—Nike,

Home Depot, Hilti, Starbucks, BMW, Southwest Airlines, Dell Computers, and Toyota, to name but a few.

Related to this is where competition and the competitive environment fit. Amid the growing intensity of doing business globally, beating the competition has become the main strategic thrust for some organizations. Competition is relevant in the Pentadigm model, but it should not be the basis of your strategic thrust. You need to consider the implications of competition: Do the customers believe that the competition is or will be capable of delivering a superior value?

Your reason for existing as a company should not be to crush the competition. It should be to create value for your chosen customer value segments, to make your customers more profitable and thereby gain profitability for your company, and to do this better than the competition. Two reasons for *not* focusing on beating your competition are:

1. Great value creators understand that it's the customer who ultimately is the final judge of value, not the competition. One of the consistent Pentadigm themes is that all of your strategic efforts, thoughts, insights, and actions need to be working on figuring out how to win with customers. Interestingly, you are more likely to beat the competition when you deliver the best value to your customers.

2. Every single dollar, every hour of a person's time, and every piece of equipment or relationship with suppliers and customers is extremely rare and precious, and is becoming more so every day. These need to be focused where you will have the most impact—and that's with delivering superior customer value.

It's been our experience that, to be successful in business and achieve excellence, you must focus on what really matters to your customers. Don't let your competition be your arbiters of value. Don't let your competition drive your performance by what could likely be noncustomer value metrics and strategies. And don't claim in your annual report to be a market leader when you are just focused on beating the competition. Great market leaders bring to the customer something that redefines what customers can do or achieve today. Beating the competition only makes companies more efficient in what customers can already do today.

Business success isn't just about providing customer value. You're not a charity; you're in business to make a profit. You can become so focused on customer value that you become myopic and lose sight of your own long-term profitability needs. The dynamic tension between satisfying your customers and managing your costs distinguishes the gap that exists between most marketers and successful Pentadigm marketers. The latter combine the disciplines of customer focus and profit orientation to sustain their business growth profitably. The Internet was plagued with good marketers, some great customer value stories, and lousy businesses. Remember, no matter how great the customer value commitment is, if there isn't a sustainable profit model underpinning the business, there is no business.

While customers will often want more and more value from you, what they are willing to pay for is another story. Pentadigm marketers focus on those benefits that have the most impact to their customers and for which their customers will pay. Eliminating the lower priority benefits controls costs and is critical to your own ability to make and sustain economic profit. In so doing, your business success attracts new customers, and your business is able to maintain a leading edge in the value committed to customers. This will be particularly important as your success draws the attention of competitors.

Pentadigm: Five Steps to Creating Customer Value

Broadly paraphrasing Mark Twain's assessment of the weather, "Everyone talks about value, but very few companies know how to recognize, quantify, and deliver it." Pentadigm is our innovative, practical approach to understanding, creating, and capturing customer value. It's innovative because it's driven entirely by customer value. It's practical in its simple five-step approach. It's a value delivery model that enables your company to become truly driven by customer value, to implement value-based processes, and to capture your appropriate share of that customer value as a profit.

A significant contributor to business failure is poor implementation. This book provides both the tools and insights to practically implement value-driven thinking and behavior both within your company and with customers. Pentadigm provides simple, practical tips and commonsense approaches based on our firsthand experiences of creating customer value and on our experiences helping clients develop and implement customer value commitment.

Pentadigm has some beneficial consequences or side effects, if you will. It communicates a unique message to those customers who are judging your ability to continually deliver meaningful value. It builds an enterprise-wide, customer-focused culture and teamwork that enables your resources and processes to zero in on delivering customer value.

More importantly, Pentadigm provides a foundation for building trust between you and your customers by demonstrating that you understand and will fulfill customer needs and value expectations. You may not have the best new product, but customers can place their faith on your Pentadigm model to continually deliver the best value over time.

Think for a moment about the number of times that companies tried to sell to you personally something that they have claimed is the best product. The message might have sounded great, but you didn't buy from them because you weren't quite sure you could trust them to deliver the expected value. Your continued loyalty to your current product or supplier is likely based upon meaningful value you gained in the past and your current provider's consistency in meeting your needs over a long period of time.

Is this value commitment too far-fetched in today's cutthroat business-to-business (B2B) world? Too naïve? We've heard the arguments. Who has time to worry about building relationships and trust? Get that fast nickel today because who knows what tomorrow will bring. You have to sell to generate revenue and you have to generate revenue to stay in business. Besides, customers don't really care about building a relationship if they can get a better product or better price.

Several years ago a large automotive industry supplier we'll call Cutting Edge developed a new and highly innovative system for one of the large automotive manufacturers. The auto engineers evaluated the system and said it was clearly superior to any other supplier's system. There was no question in anyone's mind that Cutting Edge should get the contract because of its cutting-edge technology and its cost-effective approach. Cutting Edge was given the word that they would be awarded the contract valued in the tens of millions of dollars per year.

Shortly before the contract was to be signed, Cutting Edge was notified that auto executives had decided to award the contract to a rival supplier we'll call Constant Performer. Cutting Edge and the automotive company's engineers and purchasing and manufacturing departments were all disappointed that the superior product had lost out, but chalked it up to company politics.

As we began to evaluate the situation with Cutting Edge, it became apparent that the automotive company's decision was a good one after all. The automotive executives did recognize that Cutting Edge's product was superior in features, benefits, and price. But what they also recognized was that Constant Performer, to whom the contract was ultimately awarded, had established a long track record of continually delivering a series of value-creating ideas, products, and innovations. Constant Performer made sure the auto executives understood this by quantifying how much this had represented in financial worth to the automotive company.

Faced with a decision of buying the latest innovative idea from Cutting Edge with no track record or buying from Constant Performer who had a proven history of demonstrating the ability and the commitment to continually deliver new value, the auto executives understood what really mattered to the ongoing vitality of its business, and what gave its company the most cumulative financial and innovation impact.

Something good came out of this experience for Cutting Edge as well. Rather than turn around and bemoan the automotive company's decision, it learned the lesson about the need to build a value-creation process and to build a track record of performance in what value it delivered to its customer. The automotive company was impressed with Cutting Edge's innovation and was open to evaluating whether this was a one-time event or a sign that this company had some unique capability that could help it long term.

Cutting Edge continued to develop great products and systems, proving its ability to continually bring value. Today, the automotive company trusts in the ability of Cutting Edge to consistently deliver both innovation and value. The result is that Cutting Edge has usurped Constant Performer's position as the supplier of choice whose business is most committed to delivering value to customers.

There's another important reason why you should view Pentadigm value creation as a dynamic model. A dynamic model is something that is continually improved. When innovation, for example, is viewed as a continuous, interactive process, it will make you far more effective at product development.

Pentadigm is a more productive path to transforming your business into a dynamic value-creation model by transforming your culture and processes into ones that continually scan for market insight about customers' behavior and future needs. At times this insight results in simpler product and service improvements that help you maintain your value position; at other times it presents truly large opportunities for change. This enables your business and innovation efforts to offer future value that customers will be more likely to pay for because it's connected to what really matters to them.

Breaking a Few Eggs

You can't make an omelet without breaking a few eggs is conventional business wisdom. We're going to challenge you to break some eggs, to break with some common and popular business ideas and practices. If successful, by the end of this book you should reach the conclusion that Pentadigm makes a lot of sense intuitively and practically.

The changes Pentadigm proposes require you and your company to challenge its traditional product mind-set, which says, "Build a better mousetrap and the world will beat a path to your door." Too often a company puts so much effort into striving for improvement that it forgets about first learning what really matters to customers and what customers will pay for. These businesses tend to focus on:

- providing more value-added quality products/services to customers
- finding a new point of differentiation with current products
- improving cost efficiencies of current products
- creating new products for customers
- cutting price

While potentially beneficial for customers, this perspective puts the focus back on internal thinking, products, and goals. These efforts tend to send the message internally and externally that product and price drive the business. But it more often tends to blind the business from seeing critical value-creating insights that surround the business every day.

We're not splitting hairs on this point. We've seen this pattern play out frequently in many different organizations because this type of thinking and behavior seems to make sense, at least until you've seen a lot of "value-added" that never gets added to the business's bottom line. A Pentadigm business builds a better mousetrap because it *knows* that customers really need and want a better mousetrap, it *knows* what "better" means, and it *knows* how much the customer will pay for the improvement. The Pentadigm model offers insights to realize true customer focus, frameworks for how your organization must function, and some essential tools to set up and implement Pentadigm thinking within your business.

We realize challenging popular business practices may not be the safest thing to do in your organization. Many practices, such as corporate restructuring, customer satisfaction, and Six Sigma, have become so much a part of the management toolbox that any alternative views could be treated as subversive. Most popular management tools have their fit and are a benefit to running a business. But the focus is introspective. Even most customer satisfaction programs run on an internally generated set of criteria rather than a model giving customers the opportunity to speak their minds. Six Sigma and its voice-of-the-customer tool seduces a company into thinking it's listening to the customer, which it might be. This tool also presupposes that customers have enough insight about their own business to accurately describe their needs.

But what's missing is the proper "guidance system" that links the essence of your business (EOB), the fundamental core purpose of your business, to these tools in such a way that sustainable profit and organizational performance are created. The essence of what business is about hasn't changed through the years. EOB remains figuring out what customers need, delivering products and/or services to fulfill their needs, and making a profit doing so. Any tools should enhance the EOB. Of course you should always be concerned with how efficiently your business is run. However, when efficiency of processes and organization become the driving focus, you have lost sight of your EOB. Pentadigm is the way to maximize both your EOB and efficiencies.

For example, Customer Relationship Management (CRM) is often driven first to maximize your profitability with customers. In many cases, CRM rates customers based on their profit stream to you. The lower rated customers, those with small or no profit, are then eliminated from your customer base. In seems to make sense, but it misses the opportunity that might be derived from real discovery. Though the more profitable customer base could be an indication that it values you more so it is willing to pay you higher prices, this is only the case until the customer base has been discovered by a Pentadigm-driven competitor.

This represents an inherent conflict between CRM and our dynamic Pentadigm model. It was once conventional wisdom that money could no longer be made in PCs, steel, airlines, or manufacturing, but Dell, Nucor Steel, Southwest Airlines, and Solectron have proven otherwise. It was once conventional wisdom that money couldn't be made in groceries, paper goods, plastics, or small cars. But the success of Kroger, Kimberly-Clark, GE Plastics, and Toyota belies that belief.

In fast-moving consumer markets, this fallacy of unprofitability is exacerbated by the speed of change and the swiftness with which competitors copy or improve on your offering. This phenomenon is also becoming increasingly prevalent in many business-to-business markets as protection becomes more difficult and the speed of catching up accelerates. Branding provides one of the most powerful ways of differentiating your value offerings by linking the value offering to the brand.

Your customers brand your company and its value offerings, whether you intend for that to happen or not. Just by virtue of being aware of you, you are "branded" in customers' minds. Fundamentally, your brand is a mental representation of your value. A proactive branding strategy enables you to assume and exert control over branding to make certain customers' perceptions match your intentions. If you don't manage the branding, you run the risk of losing control. Never forget, ignore, or underestimate the impact of branding.

Our Biases

We're not academic researchers. We're practitioners who have experienced and observed business performance that couldn't be explained by a company being in the right place at the right time with the right wind at its back. Southwest Airlines, Nucor Steel, Nike, Home Depot, and Dell operate in what are considered to be lousy industries, but they perform well year after year. As we began this book to explain value-based marketing for bottom-line success, we pooled our observations about the best behaviors, practices, and leadership of companies we encountered or worked with who were exceptional or ineffective in providing value.

These observations led us to recognize some biases that have shaped the Pentadigm model and our thinking. You may agree with some of these while others may strike you as absurd. Arguing each of these isn't the point. After reading this book, we believe you'll understand that successful businesses happen when there is a well-executed implementation of a meaningful customer value commitment—meaningful to the customer and meaningful to the supplying company. With this understanding, these biases—which aren't listed in any order of priority—should make more sense.

1. *Conventional wisdom:* Being fast in time-to-market is critical.
Our bias: Delivering a winning Customer Value beats speed every time. Fast-to-market and a bad Customer Value Commitment = big fat losses quickly.
2. *Conventional wisdom:* The customer is the domain of sales and marketing.
Our bias: The customer pays the wages of everyone in the company. It is a combined and inextricable responsibility of everyone in the company to ensure that a

profitable commitment to chosen target customers is created, implemented, and sustained.

3. *Conventional wisdom:* Ask the customer what improvements we need to make and match them to our capabilities.

Our bias: Constantly and proactively strive to improve the value commitment to the customer. "Dollarize," that is, quantify those improvements that delight the customer at every opportunity. Do not let the competition get better at quantifying customer value than you are.

4. *Conventional wisdom:* The "old economy" manager was poorly prepared, but the "new economy" graduate has the right skills to figure out how to succeed.

Our bias: Both have poorly understood the implications of economic profit when making investments to pursue opportunities in the new economy. According to the Gartner Group, the total net return on information technology investment from 1985 to 1995 was only 1 percent. The $500 billion spent by the United States alone in 1996 exceeded the combined corporate profits in 1995 by $175 million. If we did the math since 1996, we would be willing to bet there is still little improvement. While the productivity claims might be correct, attaining high productivity with a weak Value Proposition doesn't generate profit because the buyer response is likely to be weak. All too often, information technology investments are driven by an overriding desire to cut people and costs without a clear connection to how customers benefit. Being faster, easier, and better needs to be measured for the relevant and meaningful impact to customers.

5. *Conventional wisdom:* The new E-business economy is creating a new list of new rules for business success.

Our bias: All the best examples of business success stories, such as Dell, Nucor, Southwest, Home Depot, Solectron, and so forth, are companies that didn't exactly make up their own rules. They understood their essence of business (EOB) and how it related to customers, and they drove it forward to the marketplace. They delivered a superior customer value commitment to a targeted set of customers with an aligned business organization. And they excelled at aligning their organization and business systems to most economically deliver a superior customer value commitment. This is Pentadigm—and the new economy, including E-business issues.

6. *Conventional wisdom:* The new economy requires getting eyeballs over profits, which means that Amazon.com is the future.

Our bias: Eyeballs are easy to get. But eyeballs are attached to a brain that can determine quickly if the customer isn't deriving the value it needs or expects or was promised. Winners will be those companies that bring a superior, meaningful value to customers. Amazon.com has a good customer value commitment, but it has difficulty creating economic profit. Amazon.com could have made economic profit, but the math doesn't work in its favor. Now its cost of equity and debt is excruciatingly high, and its background channel and inventory systems costs outweighed its returns. In addition, Amazon.com has made no attempt to recognize and deliver to customer value segments. It has one model and one strategy, which leaves large amounts of money on the table. Businesses had better make economic profit or else investors will place their money where they get a positive return.

7. *Conventional wisdom:* Implementing the latest systems, software, devices, and partnerships to deliver a superior customer experience (what some call customer relationship management, or CRM) is critical to winning.

Our bias: There are costs associated with every one of these efforts. Winners select those activities that have the most significant impact on their targeted customers that the customers are willing to pay for and eliminate everything else. Even for their targeted customers, leaders don't do everything. Typically less profitable businesses write off the Information Technology (IT) investments as sunk cost and a necessary investment in today's competitive climate. But they don't account for the costs associated with getting more productive, hoping these costs can be recovered from leaner and more responsive operations. The question is, leaner and responsive for which customers?

The year-to-year listings of corporate economic profit performance tend to be topped by companies who are better at creating exceptional customer value. In those companies, every dollar spent is linked to a specific and relevant value-creating activity for customers for which the business has confirmed the customer is willing to pay. Surprisingly, often there are great customer ideas that customers will tell you to invest in, but which they don't want to pay for in the end. Sure, 24/7/365 customer service centers are great for customers, but what if it added to your cost of operation? Would customers pay for the attendant price increase, or are there other value drivers that are even more significant for them for which they would be more willing to pay first?

8. *Conventional wisdom:* If the margins aren't high enough, cut the costs.

Our bias: Get the customer value commitment right and you can create more value for your customer, which they *will* pay for. A 1 percent increase in price on the same cost base converts to a 10 to 30 percent increase in profit, depending on your average Return on Sales (ROS).

9. *Conventional wisdom:* The Internet changes everything.

Our bias: The Internet only enables new channel approaches. If your customer value commitment is unappealing to buyers, it doesn't matter whether it's offered over the Internet or through another channel. The Internet could be a powerful new way to deliver value to both existing and new customers if it's a channel to which they will respond. For example, the U.S. Department of Commerce reported in early 2002 that the amount of Internet retail sales had increased by 20 percent over 2001. This sounded significant until the second statistic was offered: for each retail dollar spent in the United States in 2001, only one cent was spent via the Internet. And just because Dell can be successful on the Internet doesn't mean your business can.

Dell's customer value segments and in-place operations, such as call centers, set the stage for Dell to upgrade to Internet-based operations.

10. *Conventional wisdom:* Understanding customer needs revolves around regular customer surveys.

Our bias: Discovering customer value demands regular, multi-level, interactive dialog and analysis with the customer at every customer interface. Five key questions frame the dialog:

- How does the customer do things today?
- What is the customer's cost picture and where does our customer value commitment figure in those costs?
- What's wrong with how the customers are doing things today?
- What would be the "dollarized" value of improvement?
- What will change for the customer over the next three to five years?

Customer satisfaction research must abandon the use of predefined checklists and provide an open format for customers to express their real views. Additionally, customer satisfaction must be done with a business team that can interpret what the customers are not telling you. This team needs to intuit what customer behavior, market trends, and your capabilities could mean for customers.

Our Objectives

We considered calling our book *The Art of Avoiding the Wabashi* based on a favorite "shaggy dog" story of one of our grandfathers.

During the final days of colonialism, a missionary visited a remote African village. Addressing the village people, he told them about the wonderful things he and his group were going to do for the villagers. They would build sanitation and irrigation systems, teach the children to read and write, and help the farmers become more productive by introducing new crops and livestock. After each of his pronouncements was translated by an elder who understood English, the people raised their arms in praise and shouted, "Wabashi. Wabashi." Later, while touring the village, the elder pulled the missionary away from a large pile of bull dung he was about to step in and advised him, "Be careful not to step in the wabashi."

Pentadigm is a very practical, "no Wabashi" guide for understanding, creating, and capturing customer value. Our litmus tests for value-based marketing as defined by the Pentadigm model are quite simple. Does it deliver desired value that customers will pay for? Does it improve a company's business profitability, what we've referred to as the Essence of Business?

Pentadigm stresses practicality, process, and measurable outcomes in committing customer value profitably. It challenges current concepts, precepts, and business and marketing biases. For example, we believe the concepts of commodity products or markets need to be challenged; every product or service can be value differentiated on some basis other than price, even in a mature market. The task is to discover unique value needs and expectations important to targeted customers who would respond to the value offering.

What was once a head of lettuce is now a package of pre-cut, washed, ready-to-serve salad greens that costs two to three times more. What was once a two-inch-by-ten-inch wooden floor joist is now a stronger, quieter, "engineered beam" at a premium price. What some might consider just a quarry with sand, rock, and gravel is now run like an ATM money machine offering 24/7/365 availability of Six Sigma quality materials to allow road builders to schedule around traffic jams, not quarry schedules.

Developing a consciously chosen value mind-set can allow your company to offer value differentiation that really matters to your targeted customers. Practicing Pentadigm will help your company create and capture value.

You may believe that you already have a customer-value–driven business, but our experience is that most companies who *say* they're customer focused actually are not. In fact, the louder they say it, the less they do it. Pentadigm provides a framework and a process flow methodology to make certain that there is a logical order of steps and priorities to turn what you say you want to do into action, creating value for customers and generating profits for your business.

Our expectation is that many of you will initially acknowledge Pentadigm's precepts—value-based marketing for bottom-line success—as obvious business common sense, which you already practice. Only those who really challenge current practices critically against the contents of this book are likely to be awakened and refreshed by Pentadigm insights. We hope that our practical tools will help you to become Pentadigm practitioners who can convert these realizations into reality for your customers and your businesses.

INTRODUCTION
TO PENTADIGM

. . . customers make their choices based (not on) how good the product or service being offered is, but rather, how good a value it is (compared) to the competitor's offering.

—Day & Reibstein[1]

Assume that a favorite restaurant you frequent is Ziroli's Italian Ristorante, and that between your house and Ziroli's there are at least four other Italian establishments. Why do you drive past the others to have dinner at Ziroli's? It's because Ziroli's meets or exceeds your value expectations and offers you more value than the others. Value is a tangible concept that can be defined and quantified. This is a major premise on which Pentadigm is based.

Our view of value-based marketing is an integrated view of the entire business process that focuses on the value needs and value expectations of the customer, so it's more than a traditional functional marketing approach. It's an enterprise-wide leveraging of powerful market concepts we refer to as Pentidigm or how we use the term value-based marketing. Pentadigm is the optimized combination of business processes, people, capabilities, resources, and capital that are focused and implemented in five continuous, dynamic steps that help you create value for both you and your customers. Exhibit 2-1 shows a road map of these five steps.

Step 1: Discover—Understand the customer.
Step 2: Commit—Commit to the customer.
Step 3: Create—Create customer value.
Step 4: Assess—Obtain customer feedback.
Step 5: Improve—Measure and improve value.

EXHIBIT 2-1

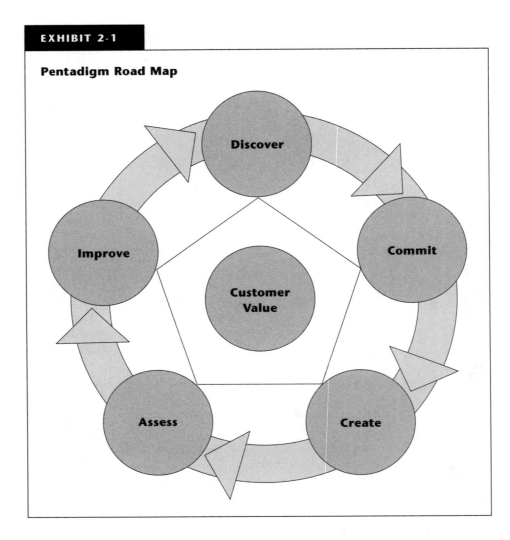

Pentadigm Road Map

Pentadigm is a framework around which you can organize your business, make decisions, develop your people and processes, and allocate capital in line with the value set of your customers. Pentadigm is the way your company can compete profitably in its marketplaces by focusing on and maximizing the right Essence of Business (EOB) offer with customers. You can enter the Pentadigm model at any stage, but as a continuous improvement process, you will eventually go through all five steps.

Wherever you enter the five steps, your value-based marketing should start with a visit to the optician to dispose of your Intra spectacles and get your Value spectacles fitted. Intra specs are the dark spectacles (glasses) through which a traditional business looks from the inside out at its markets and customers. Value specs are the glasses with clear lenses through which a company sees its markets and customers from an enlightened perspective. Without Value specs you're blind to the true views, perspectives, opinions, and behaviors that build your customer's value set.

To support your Pentadigm transition, there are a number of key concepts that appear throughout the book.

- *Customer value* comes first and foremost. This should be the heart of your EOB. Customer value is the single most important concept your business needs to comprehend and build itself upon. Starting anywhere else is myopic.
- The *fundamental principles* of a customer value commitment are that it must (1) provide *real* value to the customer, (2) be *superior* to competitor value offers, and (3) be *profitable* for you.
- *Form follows value.* In 1896, American architect Louis Sullivan proposed that "form follows function" in successful architectural design. Paraphrasing Sullivan, Pentadigm is grounded in the premise that form follows value in business. Organization design, processes, utilization of capital, and human and other corporate resources are determined by your customer value commitment to your target customers. There isn't one right answer to organizing and utilizing your company's resources, but we suggest that this is one governing principle that needs to be followed. Your customer value commitment must be aligned with your customers' value needs and expectations. And since the value expectations are different for each value segment, many different customer value commitments may be required to be successful.
- *Sustainable value creation.* A successful value-creating organization thinks and breathes value commitment and behaves in ways that deliver what really matters to its customers. The goal is to embed this thinking and behavior into your organization to capture value from market dynamics.
- *DTS* and *DTC*. Develop your value delivery around Dominating the Segment (DTS) or Dominating the Cycle (DTC). In DTS, you stay focused on a particular customer segment you have chosen, as Southwest Airlines does with short-haul business travelers. In DTC, you dominate a group of customers as the customer value changes over time, as Toyota does with car buyers. In either case the customer's success is your success.

The biggest and most difficult shift to Pentadigm is looking at the world through Value spectacles. In fact, as long as you continue to wear Intra specs, you'll never truly integrate Pentadigm behavior. Value specs may seem like an odd metaphor at first. Most companies tend to be internally focused, spending more time trying to figure out how to improve their own bottom-line performances. The thinking is, "Let our customers worry about their own bottom lines. We have our own profitability issues and obligations to shareholders."

Successful firms determine what brings real impact to their customers. For example, an internally focused quarry can run efficiently and make a profit. But as Granite Rock Quarry in California has proven, a rock quarry run on a value-driven basis understands that idle manpower and equipment has a far greater impact on a construction company's bottom line than the cost of the raw materials. The contractor's profitability is affected by on-time delivery of sand, rock, and gravel. The customer value commitment should be focused on eliminating costly downtime for the contractor customers.

Granite Rock's simple but powerful customer insight came because it looked at its business through Value specs. Perhaps more interesting is why the entire industry missed what everyone could see driving down any highway under construction—idle manpower and equipment waiting for sand and gravel to show up. Granite understood that business success comes from making its customers' businesses run more profitably, that *the best way to make your numbers is to help your customers make their numbers.*

If your daily mission is to generate more revenue by selling product, your outcomes are going to be very different than if your daily mission is to help your customers become more profitable. Positively impacting customers' profitability makes you a valued and valuable supplier. Regardless of what your customers make or sell or what you sell to them, the ultimate deal maker is demonstrating tangibly how you impact their profitability better than your competitors.

Consider the rise of EMC from a $380 million dollar corporation in 1992 to one valued at more than $6 billion by the end of the decade. EMC's first breakthrough came when CEO Mike Ruettgers and his team realized that a super-fast data storage system to access critical information would be of significant value to customers' operations. EMC customers like Delta Airlines saw the value of fast data mining and "went so far as to waive a freeze on capital expenditures so that it could chuck its old IBM and Hitachi" equipment and spend $8 million to acquire faster, more reliable, more cost-efficient EMC machines.[2]

Fundamental Principles of Value-Based Marketing for Bottom-Line Success

Value-based marketing is the optimized combination of business processes, people, capabilities, resources, and capital that are focused and implemented in five continuous steps so that your business is able to understand, commit to, create, and capture value with customers and sustain its own profit growth.

First, Pentadigm is a model driven by customer values and impacting all aspects of your organizational dynamics. Second, Pentadigm is a business ethic that focuses on the needs and values of the customer. Third, Pentadigm is a practical toolkit to enable you to implement the model and the ethic in your organization. Fourth, Pentadigm is a new integrated view of the entire business process driven from the source of demand, which is customer value expectations. Fifth, Pentadigm is a dynamic model that you can enter at any stage.

The fundamental principles of customer value commitment cited in Chapter 1 provide the basis for three key questions when committing to creating value:

1. Is your customer value commitment providing *real* value to the customer?

2. Is your customer value commitment *superior* to competitors' customer value commitment?

3. Is your customer value commitment *profitable* for you?

The basis of this thinking is rooted in management training for New Product Development nearly twenty years ago. Managers were trained to figure out if (1) their product was real for customers, (2) the product could win versus competition, and (3) the product was worthwhile financially for the company. The attribution for this paradigm has been lost with time, but the idea behind the question grew much broader and deeper for us than just for applying to new products.

Over time we came to realize the limitations of such product-centric views, and gradually started to craft the logic around value for customers and the supplier organization's ability to understand, create, and capture that customer value. This led to a fundamental principle of Pentadigm—value must be predicated on what really matters to your customers, where your value is superior to any other options the customer has, and where you can provide what-really-matters profitably. These three Principles of the Customer Value Commitment depicted in Exhibit 2-2 should drive all your value thinking, behavior, and decisions.

While in the short term you may satisfy only one or two of these principles, no business can sustain performance if it doesn't excel at balancing all three principles (see Exhibit 2-3). In some new-business scenarios, profit may slip short term, but this loss is acceptable only if you have a distinct advantage in the first two parts—real value and superior value. If you don't, you're building a business based upon a cracked and leaky foundation. The ultimate goal of Pentadigm is to help you create, implement, and sustain your customer value commitment. Arguably, Amazon.com offered real and superior value. But once the company lost sight of profit, it invested in expensive infrastructure that could have been achieved more economically through partnerships.

Defining Value: The Value Ratio

An exchange occurs when two parties get and give up something of value.[3] What each party expects to give and get constitutes their value expectations. Give and get are value drivers; they drive the buyer's purchasing behavior with the objective of satisfying the value expectations. As Day and Reibstein suggest, the basic founda-

EXHIBIT 2-2

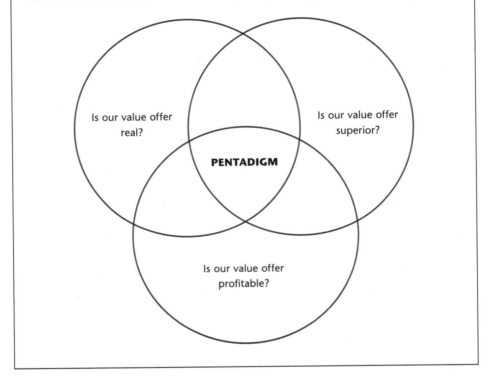

Three Fundamental Principles of a Customer Value Commitment

THE PENTADIGM PRINCIPLE: Pentadigm—where customer value commitment and business value are created and sustainable performance is grounded.

Is our value offer real?

Is our value offer superior?

PENTADIGM

Is our value offer profitable?

tion of any successful business exchange is that the customer obtains value, not products or features. A customer relationship is based on the ability of the supplier to consistently provide value and to provide more value than can be derived by the customer from the competitors' offerings.

In seminal work done by Lanning and Philips and others in the early 1980s, value (V) was defined as the equation: End-Result Benefits (B) minus Price (P) or $V = B - P$. [4] Value is a quantification of what the customer will get minus what the customer has to pay.

Benefits are frequently confused with features, to which anyone who's ever worked in sales can attest. Benefits are desirable consequences or specific advantages sought from an offering by a customer to satisfy a need. It's always a creative challenge to take a product or service, its features, and the outcomes of those features and derive a benefit. For example, the viscosity of ink—the feature—permits consistent application of a legible product time and date information on a package—

EXHIBIT 2-3

Developing and Sustaining Enterprise Value Creation

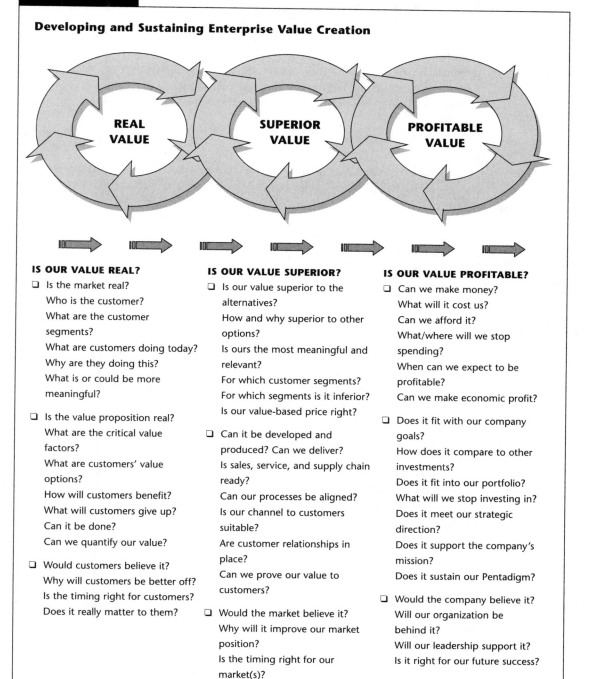

REAL VALUE

SUPERIOR VALUE

PROFITABLE VALUE

IS OUR VALUE REAL?

☐ Is the market real?
  Who is the customer?
  What are the customer segments?
  What are customers doing today?
  Why are they doing this?
  What is or could be more meaningful?

☐ Is the value proposition real?
  What are the critical value factors?
  What are customers' value options?
  How will customers benefit?
  What will customers give up?
  Can it be done?
  Can we quantify our value?

☐ Would customers believe it?
  Why will customers be better off?
  Is the timing right for customers?
  Does it really matter to them?

IS OUR VALUE SUPERIOR?

☐ Is our value superior to the alternatives?
  How and why superior to other options?
  Is ours the most meaningful and relevant?
  For which customer segments?
  For which segments is it inferior?
  Is our value-based price right?

☐ Can it be developed and produced? Can we deliver?
  Is sales, service, and supply chain ready?
  Can our processes be aligned?
  Is our channel to customers suitable?
  Are customer relationships in place?
  Can we prove our value to customers?

☐ Would the market believe it?
  Why will it improve our market position?
  Is the timing right for our market(s)?
  Does it really make a difference?

IS OUR VALUE PROFITABLE?

☐ Can we make money?
  What will it cost us?
  Can we afford it?
  What/where will we stop spending?
  When can we expect to be profitable?
  Can we make economic profit?

☐ Does it fit with our company goals?
  How does it compare to other investments?
  Does it fit into our portfolio?
  What will we stop investing in?
  Does it meet our strategic direction?
  Does it support the company's mission?
  Does it sustain our Pentadigm?

☐ Would the company believe it?
  Will our organization be behind it?
  Will our leadership support it?
  Is it right for our future success?

what the feature does. The benefit is that the production line experiences no costly downtime, which is the real benefit to the manufacturer, and which is quantifiable.

Home Depot's 2002 Winter Olympics advertising campaign, for which the company was a corporate sponsor, focused on the number of Olympic athletes who work for the company and the medals they had earned. As Home Depot Olympians won medals, the ads had a rollover counter at the end, which increased the total. The ads were engaging, but having Olympic athletes for employees may not be perceived as being a benefit to a building contractor. The buyer, not the seller, defines benefits.

Price in the original value equation was defined as what's paid for the product or service.

Benefits and Price are delimiting terms. And since the purchasing decision is a trade-off, it makes more sense to us to treat the Value (V) as a ratio of Desired Benefits (DB) over Relative Costs (RC) or $V = DB / RC$. Value is a quantification of what the customer will get divided by what the customer has to give up in the exchange.

The terms *Desired Benefits* and *Relative Costs* are used deliberately as more efficient descriptors in describing value in an exchange. Exhibit 2-4 illustrates this concept. A Desired Benefit is something the customer really wants, something that matters to them and for which they're willing to pay. The Desired Benefits you expected Ziroli's Ristorante to provide the first time you ate there ranged from, perhaps, ambience and delicious food to a well-stocked wine list and great service. The Desired Benefits sought from an automotive paint by a body shop that specializes in high-quality refinishing of BMWs could be ease of application, a single application to achieve the desired quality, a consistent color match, and technical assistance to achieve the desired quality.

Relative Costs is more than price. Cost is what the customer has to give up to acquire the Desired Benefits derived from your products or services, which is more than the price of the product or service. A professional purchasing department or buying center knows what it costs to acquire the products and services it's buying and how much it costs to spend each purchasing dollar. And costs are relative: ordering costs could be lower for a centralized purchasing function for one global customer, higher for another.

The three basic components of Relative Costs are:

1. Acquisition costs: for example, net price; ordering costs; time, energy, and effort in the purchasing process; cost of mistakes in order; prepurchase evaluation costs; risk; and trade-offs.

2. Possession costs: for example, storage costs; shrinkage and obsolescence; taxes and insurance; materials management and inventory; transportation; and maintenance.

EXHIBIT 2-4

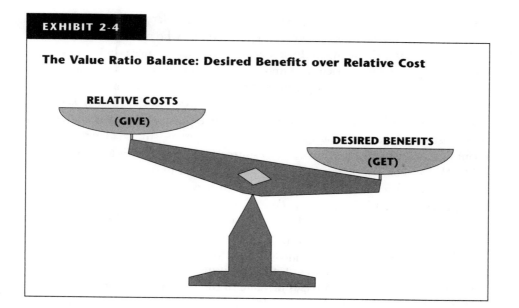

The Value Ratio Balance: Desired Benefits over Relative Cost

3. Usage costs: for example, user labor costs; process costs; product shelf life costs; replacement costs; and disposal costs.

A fourth, often overlooked, component of cost is opportunity cost—what is traded off or forfeited by the spender deciding to incur the cost. The trade-off could be foregoing quarterly sourcing and negotiation for a long-term supplier contract. Cost can also include the perceived level of risk; failure to use substitute products; the time, energy, and effort required to make the purchase decision, among other situations.

Your Relative Costs when deciding to make a reservation at Ziroli's perhaps included the risk of an unknown dining experience, the time it would take you to drive to the restaurant and wait for a table, and the price of the meal. For the BMW auto body shop, cost might include not only the price of the paint and credit charges, but the skill level required by the employees applying the paint, special equipment, storage costs, and so on.

A product or service is perceived to have value when the customer perceives the value ratio to be $\geq 1.0/1.0$. This value really does make a difference to the customer, and so it is more likely to prompt a buying decision. If the ratio is $\leq 1.0/1.0$, then you haven't created value or the perception of value for the customer. To increase a value ratio, you have to either increase the Desired Benefits and/or decrease the Relative Costs.

Buyers of the same product will have different value ratios. The high-quality automotive shop described earlier is more focused on the Desired Benefits component of the value ratio and is less concerned about the Relative Costs. Conversely, a small-town mom-and-pop auto body repair shop may be more of a price buyer.

And looking through the Pentadigm Value specs, a price buyer *is* a value buyer. For a price buyer, price is an important value driver and is a big component of the Relative Costs denominator in the value ratio. The price buyer sees no differentiation in physical product nor in the basic services of each supplier. Typically, price buyers are sophisticated and knowledgeable users of what they are buying. If these customers are chosen as target customers to pursue, the challenge becomes forming the organization's processes, resources, and people to serve them profitably. We've seen only a few pure price buyers. Even in some large markets for undifferentiated products, we have discovered new value drivers for what were regarded as "Lowest Price Buyers." For example, the ease of doing business can be more valuable to such customers than pure lowest price, which raises an issue worth discussing.

In the customer value ratio, price is just one factor of Relative Costs. This means that, rather than thinking of price in terms of supplier costs plus margin, Pentadigm perceives price in terms of value to the customer. The more value you deliver in terms of Desired Benefits to Relative Costs, the more price is impacted. The less value you deliver, the more price is commoditized.

If you can't establish a positive value ratio for the customer in any aspect of the offering, price is irrelevant. Instead, you must challenge whether that element of the offering is relevant or appropriate. As customers' needs change over time, you must either make regular checks with customers to maintain your understanding of their value set and how that affects price, or you must proactively develop new value offerings based upon your knowledge and insights about customers.

In any market segment and to any customer there is a lowest price offering. In understanding and setting price, start with this offer, as this is the low-point benchmark against which to compare and contrast your offering. Once you've described the lowest price offering, you need to be able to build a logic and an argument to justify the scale of difference in your price compared to that low point. Then determine how the customer benefits from additional elements of your offering and what those elements are worth to the customer.

Every customer value segment has specific elements of its value set which—if fulfilled—will attract a non-price-sensitive response. The key is to identify these elements. This forms the basis of your pricing decision and your price argument/justification.

Any idiot can compete on price. But only the supplier with the best-cost position based on the principle of "form follows value" can sustain such a policy long term and hope to remain profitable. Others must find the true basis of value in their customers' value set, and position and price accordingly. A key principle in understanding price sensitivity is the age-old concept of price elasticity, summarized in Exhibit 2-5.

Understand that, in the supplier value ratio, pricing is the only element of the marketing mix that generates income; all other elements incur costs. A common perception is that value-added brings value. That's not true. Value-added is usually defined from the supplier's perspective. You've "added" something to a product or service offering which you think has "value." But if the customer doesn't care about that something, it's not value-added. It's critical in your Pentadigm pricing strategy that you understand how important Relative Cost is in relation to Desired Benefits for the customer value segment and how much value the customer assigns to or associates with that element of the offer.

The Value Ratio Chain

In reality, there are three value ratios relevant to the customer and integral to Pentadigm: the Expected Value (V^E) ratio, the Value Proposed (V^P) ratio, and the Actual Value Derived (V^A) ratio. In the prepurchase stage, a need drives buying behavior. Consider the situation when a global sales manager needs a way to connect his or her virtual sales force in real time. Specifications—a list reflecting Desired Benefits and Relative Costs concerns—are drawn up. This list is the user's Expected Value ratio that drives the purchasing behavior to the next stage.

The sales manager asks purchasing to see what products and services are available in the market that will satisfy his or her needs and meet or exceed the expected value. Purchasing sources potential suppliers, who are asked to respond to a Request For Quotation (RFQ) or tender containing the specifications with products, brand options, and prices. Potential suppliers respond with their respective value propositions, explanations of what Desired Benefits will be delivered at what Relative

EXHIBIT 2-5

Factors Affecting Price Elasticity

FACTORS AFFECTING PRICE ELASTICITY	Demand Will Be More	
	ELASTIC	INELASTIC
Product is perceived as unique		X
Many substitutes are available	X	
Product has low switching costs	X	
Product is easily compared with competition	X	
Price is used as an indicator of quality		X
Expenditure is significant investment for the customer	X	
Product forms only part of total costs		X

Costs. This is the buyer's value proposition ratio that helps the buyer decide which supplier to use.

A customer buys value, not the product or the service. The customer's purchase decision is motivated by the belief that it will get more value than expected, that $V^E \leq V^P$. If the expected value to be derived from your product or service is greater than what the customer is promised it will receive—$V^E \geq V^P$—the likelihood that a transaction will occur is very small.

Postpurchase, a customer has either a formal or an informal evaluation process to assess the value actually delivered from the transaction and, ultimately, the relationship. This result is in the Actual Value Delivered ratio. After your first dining experience at Ziroli's, you evaluated the actual value derived based on what you'd expected to receive and decided that the value was equal to or better than any of the other Italian restaurants in your area. It's that value that you continue to buy each time you have dinner there.

Customers must obtain at delivery a value greater than or equal to what they were promised they would receive—$V^P \leq V^A$. This leads to repurchase behavior. If customers fail to obtain the value they thought they would based on your communications and representations prior to the sale—$V^P \geq V^A$—there might be problems with payment on the purchase order, expectations for adjustments to the purchase agreement, and almost certainly no repeat business.

The value ratio chain that ultimately leads to a relationship over time is $V^E \leq V^P \leq V^A$. This means the actual value delivered (V^A) by the supplier must equal or exceed the perceived value (V^P) promised to be delivered. And that the perceived value (V^P) promised to be delivered must equal or exceed the expected value (V^E) the customer is seeking in a transaction with a supplier. A key Pentadigm axiom is that those companies that consistently provide this value ratio chain for customers gain a sustainable competitive advantage in the market.

What happens when customers reduce the number of suppliers? What's your experience in terms of who the first suppliers are to be cut? Is it the suppliers who have the least quantified impact on the customer's bottom line or the most? What happened when you were absolutely convinced you had the best deal for a customer and lost the business? Was it the best deal with the greatest profit impact from the customer's perspective? Are you really sure what the key drivers are of your customer's bottom line relative to your product and your competitors impact on it? The foundation for your business in any market—whether it's business-to-business or consumer markets—is having a superior customer experience that touches the buyers in ways that are most meaningful, relevant, and specific to what is important in their world.

The evaluation and adjustment of the customers' value expectations become easier to do as trust builds during the lifetime of the customer relationships. The result is the ability to partner with customers and proactively anticipate what their Desired Benefits and Relative Costs are going to be. This powerful relationship position creates a long-term sustainable competitive advantage.

It's also important to understand that you as a supplier also have a value ratio defined as the Desired Benefits derived from doing business with a customer or value segment divided by the Relative Costs of acquiring, maintaining, and retaining that customer or $V = DB / RC$.

The value ratio should consistently be above 1.0 for a customer or a customer segment to qualify as a target. A preferred customers' list with attendant criteria defining what makes a customer a desirable target helps keep the sales and marketing effort focused. Other useful tools include calculation of customer (discounted net) lifetime values for customers or target market segments and development of economic profit models for products and segments. Both of these are discussed later in the book.

The 1-2-3 Strategy for Customer Segments

In the mid-1980s, one of us worked for the GE Plastics business unit where he had the opportunity to work on a cutting-edge innovation program to advance building products in the housing market. The project, *Living Environments*, was more popularly referred to as the Plastics House or the House of the Future. At that time, GE's dominant customer segments focus was on Innovators and Optimizers. Its industry focus was the home building industry, one the group saw as positioned in the mature stage of the product-market life cycle (PMLC) curve. Though GE Plastics recognized that there was innovation occurring within the industry, the influence of the code and regulatory environment "controlled" innovation to protect homeowners, builders, and the industry itself.

Given this environment, GE needed to develop some way to help its customers, who were conservative by nature, become comfortable with the potential innovation that plastics could bring to the industry. What this market needed to know was what was possible with plastics right then, what could be done with plastics in the near future, and what the future might hold in store. From this simple idea grew the 1-2-3 Strategic Value Plan approach, which is a timeless way to develop a business's strategy and drive the customer value game plan.

While most companies spend a fair amount of time waiting for customers to tell what they want or studying trends, the GE Plastics group figured that it could create the trends or at least play a significant role in influencing them. The premise was that GE's customers would never invest time or energy in learning what GE Plastics and its products, services, and technology could do for them today or in the future. The objective became to proactively educate GE Plastics customers by showing them the future. Living environments became the working laboratories to explore the future and shape respective destinies with 53 leading home products companies, including Sony, Kohler, Bose, Johnson & Johnson, Masco, Carrier, Weyerhaeuser, and Matsushita Electric Company.

The parallel Pentadigm lesson is that, once you've decided who your target segments are and whether to be a DTC (dominate the cycle) or DTS (dominate the segment) player, you need to create a 1-2-3 Strategy Value Planning diagram, illustrated in Exhibit 2-6.

Strategy 1 is the most relevant meaningful value that you can deliver today, this year. Strategy 2 starts you thinking about what's likely to matter next with your customers one to two years in the future. Strategy 3 is your vision for your customers two to four years down the road. Strategies 2 and 3 don't need to be and won't be perfect, but they do need to help you suggest possibilities or prototypes that your customers can dialog with you on.

The point of the Plastics House wasn't intended to convince home products companies that people would be living in all-plastic houses. Rather, it was to find the best opportunities to provide customer value with present capabilities and expertise, and to involve customers in an ongoing dialog to help them envision what the future could be.

If you're always one step ahead with superior customer value commitment, you'll be one step ahead of your competition. Competition will surely come, but

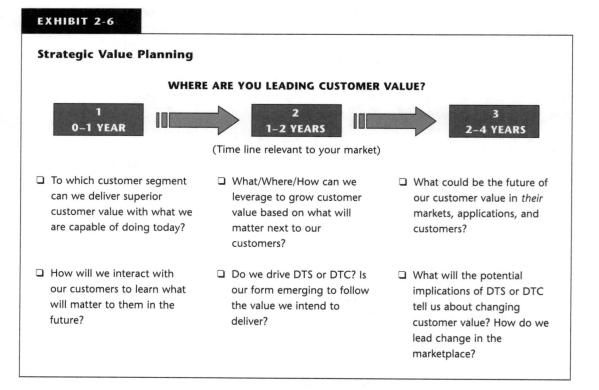

EXHIBIT 2-6

Strategic Value Planning

WHERE ARE YOU LEADING CUSTOMER VALUE?

| **1** 0–1 YEAR | ➡ | **2** 1–2 YEARS | ➡ | **3** 2–4 YEARS |

(Time line relevant to your market)

❏ To which customer segment can we deliver superior customer value with what we are capable of doing today?

❏ What/Where/How can we leverage to grow customer value based on what will matter next to our customers?

❏ What could be the future of our customer value in *their* markets, applications, and customers?

❏ How will we interact with our customers to learn what will matter to them in the future?

❏ Do we drive DTS or DTC? Is our form emerging to follow the value we intend to deliver?

❏ What will the potential implications of DTS or DTC tell us about changing customer value? How do we lead change in the marketplace?

once the Pentadigm momentum has gathered within your organization, you'll have created a significant competitive weapon.

Understanding the definition and calculation of value is critical to each of the five Pentadigm steps. You have to *discover* your customers' value expectations and value ratios to understand the Desired Benefits sought and the Relative Costs concerns. You must decide whether or not to *commit* to providing the expected value. You have to *create* the value by making sure that the Desired Benefits and Relative Costs are implemented and delivered. You need to *assess* the customer relationships you've acquired by measuring the actual value delivered. And you have to constantly *improve* your customer value commitment as the value ratios for the customer value segments change.

One question you may have right now is, "Is Pentadigm something our business can do?" You may be thinking that your situation is different from any example we have used so far. And that's probably true, to a point. The companies in our examples all had their own unique and different challenges.

What Pentadigm helped us realize is that it doesn't matter so much what your current position or difficulties are. Businesses like $\overline{\text{REVO}}$ and IBM start or turn around, as IBM has done in the past decade, when customer value needs and expectations are connected with and aligned to the business's EOB. That's the challenge and promise of Pentadigm.

KEY INSIGHTS

1. The biggest and most difficult shift to Pentadigm is looking at the world through Value spectacles. In fact, as long as you continue to wear Intra specs, you'll never truly integrate Pentadigm behavior.

2. The best way to make your numbers is to help your customers make their numbers.

3. The fundamental principles of a customer value commitment cited in Chapter 1 provide the basis for three key questions when committing to creating value:

   • Is the customer value commitment providing *real* value to the customer?

   • Is the customer value commitment *superior* to competitors' customer value commitment?

   • Is the customer value commitment *profitable* for you?

4. Since the purchasing decision is a trade-off, it makes more sense to us to treat the Value (V) as a ratio of Desired Benefits (DB) over Relative Costs (RC) or V = DB / RC. Value is a quantification of what the customer will get divided by what the customer has to give up in the exchange.

5. The value chain that ultimately leads to a relationship over time is $V^E \leq V^P \leq V^A$. It's axiomatic that companies which consistently provide a superior value ratio for customers gain a sustainable competitive advantage in the market.

CHECKLIST

❑ Step 1—Discover: Understand the customer.

❑ Step 2—Commit: Commit to the customer.

❑ Step 3—Create: Create customer value.

❑ Step 4—Assess: Obtain customer feedback.

❑ Step 5—Improve: Measure and improve value.

CHAPTER 3

STEP 1: DISCOVER— UNDERSTAND THE CUSTOMER

Be it furniture, clothes, or health care, many industries today are marketing nothing more than commodities—no more, no less. What will make the difference in the long run is the care and feeding of customers.

—Michael Mescon[1]

The marketing landscape is littered with the carcasses of products and services launched by companies who didn't understand their customers and, as a result, were caught in the trap of "if we build it and sell it, they will buy it." In the mid-1980s, Coca-Cola spent $4 million to develop a new Coke, failing to understand that the new formulation wasn't good enough to overcome buyer loyalty for the "classic" Coke taste. Buyer loyalty was predicated on something in classic Coke valued by buyers and absent in the new Coke, which Coca-Cola failed to assess or realize. What Coke had seen and focused on was the Pepsi product that was gaining customers.

In 1987, GM launched the "Not your father's Oldsmobile" campaign targeting younger buyers. Focused on improved styling and features, the campaign featured famous parent-child pairs like Ringo Starr and his daughter, Winona and Naomi Judd, William Shatner and Leonard Nimoy and their kids, Harry and Shari Belafonte, and Roger Moore and his daughter. Even with its new features and design, Olds didn't meet the needs and expectations of the younger drivers in the Olds target market. The campaign slogan has become part of the vernacular, what one pundit described as a phrase "synonymous with marketing desperation." GM is now closing its Oldsmobile division.

In the late 1990s, Webvan launched a home grocery delivery service. The assumptions were that the grumbles in the tiresome line at the grocery store would translate into online behavior grocery buying. That parents with small kids would appreciate having to make fewer trips to the store, always a challenge in child management and control. That the graying population would be physically safer not going out to shop. That the newness of online ordering would trigger a trial that would lead to a change in grocery-buying behavior.

Webvan had an efficient website and on-time delivery system at comparable prices to what consumers would find in the stores. Webvan was ranked first among all Internet grocery stores when it went out of business. What Webvan failed to understand was customer needs and behavior. Online grocery shopping isn't a convenience buying activity like stopping at the store on the way home for a loaf of bread; it requires advanced planning of a shopping list, which consumers don't do often. Online grocery shopping behavior was primarily for stocking up on staples or heavier and larger items that are difficult to carry to and from the car and then into the house. And even with a quick online interface, online ordering was still more of a hassle than pushing a cart up and down an aisle. Buyer behavior doesn't change in Internet time.

From these cases it might seem like we're advocating an anti–new-product development stance; we're not. But think about product development for a moment from the perspective of value-based marketing for bottom-line success. Reexamine the terms new *product* development or *product* innovation. The focus is *product*. The objective for product management is to make new or existing products profitable. We understand that product can mean offerings broader than the physical product, such as service, information, and relationships. But your product/service is often only one, and perhaps the least important, value driver for your customer. Value-based marketing is less about product and more about a customer value creation and commitment model, which may occasionally require a new product to be developed.

One of our favorite examples of a product whose manufacturer thought it had discovered a value-added, differentiated offering but which missed the target market by not understanding its value expectations was the smokeless cigarette. Touted as a new, differentiated, value-added cigarette, it was intended to change the fortunes of R. J. Reynolds.

The cigarette was almost smoke-free and the smoke emitted was supposed to be cleaner than the smoke from a regular cigarette. Given smoking trends and the national antismoking sentiment in the United States, the smokeless cigarette should have been a winner. After more than $500 million invested, have you ever seen a smokeless cigarette? The benefits of a smokeless cigarette weren't desired by smokers and didn't offer enough value to result in a change of behavior. The benefits of a smokeless cigarette were immense for nonsmokers, but they weren't benefits for the target buyer.

What's your company's best marketing *faux pas* or disaster story, and how much of the failure is attributable to not understanding the customer and the customer's value needs and expectations?

Five Actions in Pentadigm Step 1: Discover

Understanding the customer is the first step in achieving bottom-line success by applying value-based marketing using the Pentadigm model. Discover what your customers' needs and value expectations are. Discover what the business relationship looks like through their eyes. Discover who the players are in the value chain, from the end user of your value commitment to all channel members. Discover and quantify the value that flows between the value chain members. Discover which customer value segments exist, based on their value needs, expectations, and choices.

Discovery demands a much greater proactive commitment than merely surveying customers or listening to them. Resistance at the start of discovery may even be desirable. Your cynics will keep the process grounded. Discovery requires attentiveness, creativity, imagination, and even speculation. Discovery should be one of the most exciting adrenaline rushes your team gets. Discovery is as unpredictable as it is exciting; you must constantly be alert to new discoveries that may challenge or change your original ideas. Listen for signals like, ". . . if only . . . ," ". . . but what I really need . . . ," or ". . . it would be worth . . . to me."

You only have to look around at some of the really successful offerings in the marketplace to realize that this is true. If Michael Dell had listened to the traditional channel partners in the PC industry, he wouldn't have invented his highly successful direct offering. People and companies who anticipate or fuel market needs and exceed the customers' value expectations are the market makers.

Discover includes five major actions.

1. *Define and map the market.* The customer's buying process examines the underlying value drivers that guide the buyer's decision making and links the drivers to the evolution of customer value (Customer Value Cycle). Look at your market and the offerings in the market through the eyes of the customer. Understand customer choices and the reasons for those choices. Define the market by the needs of the customer.

2. *Understand customer value expectations.* Identify benefits sought by the customer and quantify the value to the customer of that benefit. Understand buyers' willingness to give up certain things in order to get what is most important to them.

3. *Discover customer value segments.* Value-based segmentation identifies groups of customers with the same or similar value ratios, that is, what drives and triggers their buying decisions. Seek unmet needs relentlessly.

4. *Assess competitive position.* Know how customers in a customer value segment perceive and value your offering versus that of your competition. Assessment of your competitive position evaluates the customer's judgment of your customer value commitment in comparison with those of your competitors.

5. *Select target customer value segments.* This is based on their attractiveness and your ability to compete effectively in that customer value segment by delivering

superior customer value. Target only those customer value segments that are attractive, and where you have or can build a competitive advantage that the customer recognizes and values. Selecting target customer value segments leads to a value-based strategy where you as a supplier make a conscious choice about which customer value segments you choose to serve. Only serve customers whose Customer Lifetime Value (CLV) is positive and high.

Define and Map the Market

Until 1965, Harley-Davidson was the dominant player in the U.S. motorcycle market. Company analysis showed that Honda wasn't a significant threat, that lightweight motorcycles would not be popular and that little market growth could be expected. However, from 1964 to 1981 while motorcycle registrations in the United States quadrupled, Harley-Davidson's market share dropped to 3 percent. Part of that was attributable to major quality and cost issues.

A bloc of Harley-Davidson executives and stockholders bought the company in 1981, and made it the company's mission to improve the bike's battered quality image. To emphasize its after-sales service commitment, Harley-Davidson established the HOG (Harley Owners Group). And it "pressured dealers who they felt perpetuated a 'bad-guy image' . . . to clean up their acts, to stop treating owners of Japanese motorcycles (hence potential Harley owners) with contempt, and to reach out to new customers through (Harley-Davidson's) new product lines and 'boutique'-quality clothing."[2]

But a major hurdle remained in the public's perception of a HOG—Harley Owners Group—member as a ". . . pot-smoking, beer-drinking, woman-chasing, tattoo-covered, leather-clad biker."[3] Market research suggested that an unexpected customer value segment was developing an interest in big motorcycles. Dubbed "the Rubbies," shorthand for Rich Urban Bikers, this customer value segment included lawyers, doctors, businessmen, and other nontraditional HOG-types looking for a prestigious "all-American" item. Focusing on the Rubbies, Harley-Davidson had 20 models of huge bikes available for the market by 1991 and began to license its distinctive Harley-Davidson shield logo on T-shirts, cologne, pajamas, caps, and other products. "The biker image was sanitized in an effort to make it safe for 'rubbies' and wannabe bikers."[4] The company was back in the black by 1983. From 1989 to 2000, HOG membership rose from 90,000 to 200,000. Sales revenues almost quadrupled and profits increased from $35 million to $350 million.

The Harley-Davidson story has three key learning points relevant to defining and mapping your market.

1. Think about customer value expectations in innovative ways. Motorcycle buyers weren't all just looking for transportation; some just needed the big,

attention-getting, distinctive throb of a Harley motor—the all-American toy.

2. Use market research, but merge and combine it with intuition and gut feeling, to understand customer behavior, trends and unmet needs.

3. A new value segmentation strategy can help reposition or reinvent a product, a brand, or a company.

Understanding customers' value ratios and being able to quantify them requires the resource commitment of a mix of people who believe in the value delivery paradigm, who like to interact with customers and who are naturally curious, comfortable with the ambiguity of customers' needs, and are objective, factual, analytical, and data driven. They should be from a number of functions, some of which currently interact with customers like marketing, sales, and customer and technical services, while others may not currently have direct customer interface like finance, production, or IT.

Defining and mapping the market seems self-explanatory. The objective is to chart what the market looks like in terms of behavior, needs and expectations, channel players, and solution providers to discover customer value segments. In its simplest form, it's altering your mass market to a segmented one composed of clusters of customers with homogeneous behavior and needs. It's changing a random aggregation of target buyers to a linear plot from those most likely to respond to your customer value commitment to those who will never respond.

A good way to think about defining and mapping a market is to consider using the Product-Market Life Cycle (PMLC) and turning it into the Value Life Cycle (VLC). The PMLC maps the four stages a product goes through in its life: Innovation, Growth, Maturity, and Decline. One might argue at great length about details and descriptors of the PMLC, but we have found some remarkable patterns and common denominators of value across many markets.

For now, consider the key theme of the traditional look at PMLC. Most business people can accept that over time an innovation's relative relationship with customers will change as the market grows and new competitors enter. Ultimately, businesses tend to believe that they will need new products in their pipeline as over time the product will reach maturity and become a "commodity" in their markets. Before that time, though, if you're product-centric in your strategy, you will develop another innovation and start a new PMLC curve. The top of Exhibit 3-1 illustrates this pattern of strategic thinking.

However, there is a more effective approach to understanding the market and developing a strategy, choosing to Dominate the Segment (DTS) or to Dominate the Cycle (DTC).

The PMLC represents a dynamic model of customers as well as product markets. Customers with different value drivers buy in different stages of the

EXHIBIT 3-1

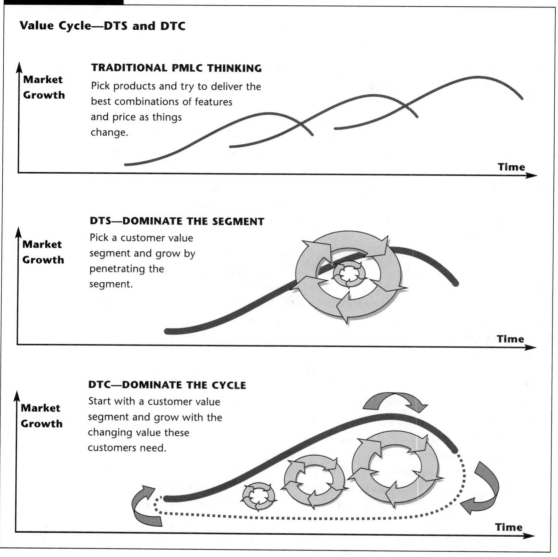

Value Cycle—DTS and DTC

TRADITIONAL PMLC THINKING
Pick products and try to deliver the best combinations of features and price as things change.

Market Growth / Time

DTS—DOMINATE THE SEGMENT
Pick a customer value segment and grow by penetrating the segment.

Market Growth / Time

DTC—DOMINATE THE CYCLE
Start with a customer value segment and grow with the changing value these customers need.

Market Growth / Time

PMLC and many of these customers demonstrate consistent behavior over time. Yesterday's economizer customer, for example, will likely be an economizer customer today, tomorrow, and the next day. A paper mill that buys several thousand tons of processing additives is likely to show very consistent buying behavior as an economizer or an operationalizer.

But there are also buyers who, because of the nature of their markets, change buying behavior, which you can count on happening just as consistently. An example might be an automotive company like GM, Ford, Toyota, or DaimlerChrysler. It initially looks for innovation and optimization, but as a vehicle model matures, it rewards suppliers less and less for the original innovation, and more and more for behaving like economizer and operationalizer suppliers.

In DTS, the middle diagram in Exhibit 3-1, you focus on one segment, such as Innovators. Your entire business is focused and aligned to deliver valuable innovation to buyers who themselves are focused on providing leading-edge innovation to their customers. You grow your business based upon growing innovation with existing customers and adding new customers who are also looking for an innovative edge. This was exactly the approach Intel used in chip development and GE used in growing its plastics business. The trick is to be able to discriminate between customers who are only looking to create one innovation and then decide to ride their own PMLC curve into maturity from customers who use constant innovations as their primary source of profit generation. It's also important not to be seduced into following the former.

This has been the brilliance of Southwest Airlines—it targeted one segment and kept on growing by looking for more airport markets with the same customer type. It also explains why the other airlines fail to compete successfully against Southwest. While the other airlines kept thinking Southwest wasn't a real airline, they never considered Southwest's simple insight of just looking for more of the same customers in other geographic areas.

In DTC, the bottom diagram in Exhibit 3-1, you recognize that customer needs will change over time, and you build the ability to manage and drive customers through the cycle. This is a far more complicated strategy to pull off. Many companies think they do this today, but we think there are some powerful implications most overlook. Let's again consider suppliers to automotive companies. Once a supplier sells an innovation, the supplier knows it will be down-engineered as an automotive company gets more experience with their product or system. Rather than proactively moving customers to a more cost-effective, down-engineered value specification, most suppliers will spend considerable energy and resources trying to justify the original value. This is the same strategy you see with many pharmaceutical and software companies. They have a tendency to wrap themselves in expensive branding campaigns to prevent the customer from being able to purchase a product or service more cost-effectively, even when the original product may be overspecified or overpriced relative to its current marketplace position on the VLC.

In DTC, a business uses to its advantage the natural cycle that buyers and markets go through. Your goal is to not build artificial customer value barriers and thereby add costs, but to build velocity to get customers through the cycle. Think of it as the inventory turns for customer value. The other traditional downfall to doing this has been in building cost structure that gets spread across all segments and customers. To sustain doing this, a firm must consider separate operating value units or change its cost accounting practices.

Dell computer has successfully managed both its customer segments and changing technology innovations in the marketplace. Look through Dell's website at www.dell.com. Dell has segmented its customers and has given them the option to choose which level of technology sophistication fits their needs and priorities. Catalog and Internet retailer, the TireRack, also has aligned its business to manage changing customer value over the cycle.

You're probably thinking we've oversimplified the reality of your business. We recognize that you may be playing all over the PMLC with all four customer segments and your business is base loaded with customers you can't give up. But you're not ready to make the DTC and DTS decisions until your segmentation work is done anyway.

In most cases there will be an evolution between your budgetary cycles to get to either DTC or DTS. In some cases your business may have the ability to successfully manage several DTS markets. But you won't know this until you understand your existing customer segment mix. Pentadigm market maps need to be developed at different levels of detail.

We recommend you start with a "high-level" map describing all the needs, all the value expectations, all the value chain members and their behavior. From this knowledge, you can "drill-down" to deeper levels of detail, depending upon what you discover to be relevant and appropriate to developing your understanding of the customer value set. Always start with the customer and work back up the value chain.

It's important to quantify the customer expectations and customer value commitments at each level in the chain.

- Who pays how much for what? Why are they paying for these things?
- What customer value do they create?
- What do they get back in profit from the next value chain member?
- What customer value are they seeking themselves?

Often the market map is only a first step in understanding customer needs. Further analysis and questioning may be needed, such as:

- Why customers choose certain solutions and/or sources of supply?
- What are their current cost and drivers of their behavior? What would cause them to change behavior?
- What unmet or poorly met needs do they have?

These questions and their answers may lead to a redrawing of the market map to discover groups of customers with similar needs or behaviors.

Understand Customer Value Expectations

A client once asked, "Should we develop a geomarket strategy first and fit that into a global market strategy or vice versa?" Our response was, since the subject of the question was "we," the wrong question was being asked of the wrong people. The question should be, "What would best fulfill our customers' needs and expectations?"

Each customer has a different set of values that it uses as a basis for reaching a buying decision. Discovering and understanding the purchasing behavior and value drivers of individual customers is the first step in value segmentation. This provides a meaningful basis for targeting those customers who are most likely to value your offering and to enable you to calculate whether you can serve those customers profitably.

In Pentadigm, a customer is any member of the value chain who directly or indirectly purchases or influences the purchase of your customer value commitment. In some cases this can be one or more individuals at one or more levels in the buyer's organization. Or it could be one or more members of the value channel. The more complex the purchasing decision or the greater the value of the purchase, the more likely there is to be a decision-making unit comprising several individuals. In such cases, it's crucial to understand the different needs of each individual, how much weight each has in making the decision, as well as identifying who will make the final decision. These criteria could determine the choice or preference of supplier.

For example, criticality and value of the purchase, as illustrated in Exhibit 3-2, can help define buying behavior. For the Low Critical/Low Value buyer, an EDI interface for order placement could be critical, where a Low Critical/High Value buyer would be driven more by price. For a High Critical/Low Value, guaranteed availability of a just-in-time (JIT) supply would be a key value driver compared to long-term supply, R&D, finance, and marketing partnership for a High Critical/High Value customer or customer value segment.

Submitting a tender or request for a quotation (RFQ) are both strategic indications of benefits sought and cost concerns. An analysis of a customer's RFQs can establish a clear checklist of what value the customer will buy. One of the best tools for understanding a customer's value needs and expectations is its Preferred Supplier List (PSL), which is discussed in the section on proactively seeking customer feedback in Chapter 6.

Make sure that your understanding of the customer isn't too myopic. Customers don't make buying decisions based on a single desired benefit like 24/7 technical support or a single relative cost like finance charges. Customers want as much value as they can get and will make trade-offs when forced to do so. A buyer may like the technical service responsiveness of Supplier A, but selects Supplier B based on the R&D support it provides, despite the fact that technical service responsiveness is slower. For the buyer, R&D support is more important; it has a high utility value for the buyer. Low price should be preferable to a high price. But a buying

EXHIBIT 3-2

Value Drivers Based on Criticality and Value of the Purchase

	LOW CRITICALITY OF THE PURCHASE	HIGH CRITICALITY OF THE PURCHASE
Low Purchase Value	Programmed rebuys	Security of supply
High Purchase Value	Price buyers	Partnership with supplier

decision isn't made based on price alone. The buyer's value set consists of a series of criteria, usually associated to a value and organized into a priority order. This value set is used by the buyer to compare and eventually select offerings based on a trade-off of benefits and value versus cost.

Customer preferences should be analyzed in terms of these trade-offs that then shape your company's customer value commitment. Trade-off analysis is a widely used customer research technique that can help determine:

- The relative importance of each of the desired benefits and relative costs of a given offering
- The desirability of each benefit and cost option
- The optimum combination of benefit and cost options that results in the most value

One popular trade-off analysis method is conjoint analysis, which is effective in many situations, to help you understand the combination of benefit and cost values to which your customers will respond. Conjoint analysis helps determine the relative importance of each desired benefit or relative cost, the importance of every option within each combination of benefits and costs, and the value expected from each possible combination. "Conjoint" means *factors presented together*. Conjoint analysis involves the measurement and analysis of customer preferences for benefits and costs. Preferences are driven by "utility functions" that influence customer preferences. Utility functions can differ among markets or customer value segments. Conjoint analysis provides an estimate of the value or utility placed on each level of a value driver or preferences for combinations of benefits and costs. Combining the utility score of various value drivers helps identify product preferences for optimal benefit-cost combinations.

By quantifying customer preferences for benefit-cost combinations and the trade-offs, conjoint analysis can also provide valuable information for new-product development and forecasting, pricing decisions, and market segmentation. And customer value segments can be defined according to how they are differentiated by their preference for specific offerings.

Discover Customer Value Segments

Customer value segmentation is where you jump-start your value-based marketing for bottom-line success. To fully understand customers, you should be familiar with the concept of market segmentation, which incorporates patterns of customers' unfilled wants and needs and their resulting value expectations and purchasing behavior. You can use this understanding to organize customers into discrete customer value segments or clusters or groups according to similar value expectation (V^E).

Segmentation is based on the idea that markets are not randomly aligned but can be defined by groups of customers with homogeneous needs and value drivers called *customer value segments*. Segmenting is a crucial step in organizing your understanding of customer value that is not only the basis for choosing target customers, but the building block of your customer value commitment. It not only permits you to concentrate your customer value commitment efforts, but allows you to concentrate your strength against the value commitment weaknesses of your competitors.

Once you understand the customers' value needs and expectations, you can discover the customer value segments. The word *discover* is used intentionally; the customer value segments already exist, but haven't been defined. Customers are behaving, thinking, and making decisions. Your challenge is to discover what drives this behavior. Remember that the customer is any member of the value chain who directly or indirectly purchases or influences the purchase of your customer value commitment. For many market opportunities, this can mean segmenting at more than one level in the value chain.

Unmet or poorly met needs are the most powerful way to define a customer value segment, and these should be targeted as a first priority. If you don't find any unmet or poorly met needs on a first pass, look again. Give every customer the opportunity to *create* a need by helping them see needs and expectations they didn't know they had. Our experience has been that predictable and discoverable customer value segments exist within all markets.

Take the simple example of a producer of insulation products. These products are sold via a distributor to a building contractor who installs the products in a building to provide a certain level of comfort, warmth, and energy efficiency for the building owner or occupier, described in the value chain in Exhibit 3-3. The choice of the insulation will be made or influenced by an architect who is not directly part of the purchasing process and, as such, is an influencer. There are also building codes that must be satisfied. At the beginning of the value chain is the insulation producer's raw material supplier.

Each of the members of the value chain has needs and value expectations, sets of desired benefits and relative costs, which need to be fulfilled by one or more value chain members. For the distributor, the value drivers could be the brand, availability, and margin to be earned. The contractor's value drivers might be ease of instal-

EXHIBIT 3-3

Value Chain from Raw Materials Manufacturer (RMM) Through an Insulation OEM to a Building Occupant

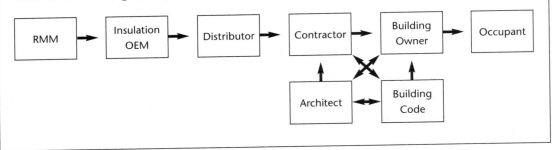

lation, availability, local codes satisfied, and no health risk for the crew. Value drivers for the architect might be no risk for specifying the brand and exceptional environmental performance, which enhances the architect's reputation. The building owner would also be interested in the efficiency of the materials that would impact energy costs and maintenance required. If the owner isn't the person living in the building, warmth and comfort would be value expectations for the occupant, who we'll call the Warm and Comfortable Building occupant. So, who are the customers for the insulation producer?

The insulation producer needs to discover

- what the value drivers are at each step in the value chain
- what needs it can deliver profitably at each step in the value chain
- who really calls the shots in this value chain—the channel captain

The insulation producer's final marketing strategy would have to address and fulfill the value drivers as far down the value chain as it can, which could mean having up to six different customer value commitments to exploit the market opportunity, one each for the distributor, contractor, architect, owner, occupant, and building codes regulators.

The insulation producer also sells its insulation to companies that specialize in creating cold-storage facilities for food retailers, depicted in Exhibit 3-4. The value drivers for the members of this value chain will be different. For the occupant in the first value chain, the key expectation is building warmth. For the food produce consumer, it's not suffering food poisoning. It's the same insulation product with different channels and different value expectations for the members of those channels. Selling the product based on standard features and benefits limits the ability to differentiate and to capture profit from the value being delivered.

EXHIBIT 3-4

Value Chain from Raw Materials Manufacturer (RMM) Through an Insulation OEM to a Food Produce Consumer

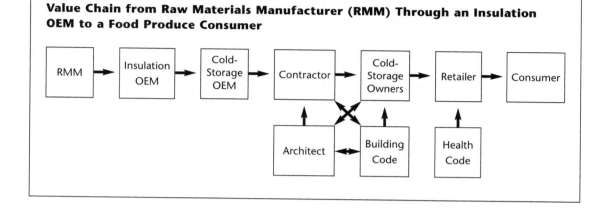

In searching for customer value segments, start at the deepest level in the value chain where the value or benefit of your offering is still recognized and work back from there, discovering customer value segments at each level up to the direct trading partner. In order to develop a winning marketing strategy, you will have to target customer value segments at each of these levels in the value chain.

It's crucial to start at the last level in the value chain where the real value and benefit of your customer value commitment is still recognized. It's here that the greatest value in your offering is likely to be acknowledged and here that it can have the most impact on the member. In many cases, particularly where you are serving the final customer through one or more channels or intermediaries, those intermediaries may not fully or accurately communicate the needs of the final customer. This means it's important to either have a regular dialog with those customers directly or do your own independent market research.

It's equally essential to discover customer value segments at each level between you and the final customer. You must target each relevant customer value segment at each level in the value chain with an offering that is compelling to them, and these customer value segments will be driven by different needs that also require managing.

Many companies divide their customers into some continuum within two basic customer value segments—price buyers and premium buyers. Premium buyers are so-called because they pay you more; therefore, you claim they value you more or are value-buyers. Suppliers tend to feel they can differentiate themselves in some way to premium buyers more than price buyers. The higher the amount of differentiation these customers pay for, the more premium they get classified. We consider this simplistic and not a sound basis for value-based marketing for bottom-line success.

We would always recommend that you conduct thorough research into your customers' needs and value ratios as a basis for segmentation. But recognizing that time doesn't always permit that step, the Pentadigm model has a basic, generic customer value segmentation that may be helpful as a starting point for need- and behavior-based customer value segmentation: Innovators, Optimizers, Operationalizers, and Economizers. Each customer value segment buys according to a unique set of needs and uses the value ratio to make a purchasing decision.

For the *Innovator* customer value segment, the primary value driver is the need to maintain a leading-edge competitive advantage in the customer's market and to be perceived as an innovator in its industry by creating value with leading-edge products, technology, markets, and processes. A highly knowledgeable risk taker, the Innovator focuses on the Desired Benefits and offsets the Relative Costs with a higher priced offering, which means an innovator tends not to be price sensitive, but *innovation* sensitive.

The *Optimizer* customer value segment is not a pioneer like the Innovator, but its most important value driver is the need to reach full market potential by being able to fulfill demand and avoid the loss of opportunity. This segment wants to capitalize quickly on the emergence of new market opportunity that someone else pioneered. Less of a risk taker, the Optimizer customer value segment focuses on a balance of Desired Benefits and Relative Costs around the need to ramp-up production of tried and tested product and service solutions.

The need to optimize profits is the main value driver for the *Operationalizer* customer value segment. The market is nearly mature and this segment recognizes the need to drive operational effectiveness to gain share with customers. The Operationalizer seeks desired benefits to optimize total cost of acquisition and use. This customer value segment expects Relative Costs to be satisfied by achieving operational efficiency.

The final generic Pentadigm customer value segment is the *Economizer*. The essential value driver for this group is the need to buy from the low-cost supplier in its value chain. Purchase decisions are made on the basis of price alone, when no further cost advantages are perceived overall.

The case for and against market segmentation has been a hot topic in the past decade. There are those who suggest that to be successful today, you have to treat every customer as unique and special, the customer of one. In some markets, customers are so big it makes sense to do this. Ironically, much of the customer-of-one thinking has been with consumer goods, mirrored in many B2B markets by the practice of Key Account Management, so it's certainly not a new idea. While treating every customer as an individual might be an ideal to be strived for, often the cold hard facts of business economics make it prohibitive. Customer value segmentation at least helps you to get as close to 1:1 (one-to-one) marketing as you practically and profitably can by grouping together and targeting customers who at least share many values. The weakness of one-to-one marketing has been its lack of critical consideration on costs and explanation of how to leverage scarce resources, suggesting instead that prices of customized solutions will be justified by buyers to cover any costs for the customization.

Assess Competitive Position

Sun Tzu wrote in 500 B.C., "If you know yourself but not the enemy, for every victory gained you will also suffer a defeat."[5]

Most of us were taught early in our youth how to compete, to beat our opponent, sometimes at any cost, to win. While understanding the competition and your competitive position is relevant, your strategic thrust shouldn't be to crush the competition. This is a fundamental precept of the Pentadigm value-based marketing model, which focuses on creating value and sustainable performance by delivering what really matters to your customers while being profitable. Whether the competition will be able to deliver superior value now or in the future is relevant, but it should not be the foundation of your business philosophy.

Most companies, including yours, conduct some type of competitive assessment, ranging from informal to very sophisticated. The primary objective? Fundamentally, you're looking for ways to grow your business and improve your profit, to try and figure out how you can sell more. You want to know where you have a competitive advantage. You want to know where you're not as strong as you need to be, where you need to improve relative to the competition.

And all of this must be judged and measured from the customers' perspective, since they are ultimately the arbiter of the purchase. You're looking for the places your competitor is weak and you can exploit. Unfortunately, the presumption underlying most competitive analysis is that, in figuring out how to beat the competition or gain a competitive advantage, you will gain something that will matter to your customers. This is a flawed *more is better* or *better is better* logic.

The effect is a very product-centric exercise. Most of the tools, graphs, and matrices that your business probably uses in the competitive analysis are designed to show where you can leverage strength to increase market share. Often these assessments are used to justify business decisions that have already been made, to support a compelling story for your business on why your competition is going to get clobbered by your new strategy.

Should the objective of competitive analysis be to figure out where and how you can beat the competition? The answer to that question depends on your fundamental business perspective. Are you in business to sell products or to create and deliver value? Do your customers really care if you beat your competition? The customers care if you provide them with a superior customer value commitment. Is the customer better off if you beat the competition? Same answer.

In most cases, a business strategy bent on beating the competition sets in motion a costly, brutal, long-term no-win game. When competition becomes too much of the orientation and focus for a business, three things happen.

1. Your improvement becomes driven by the competition, often giving that competitor credit for knowing what really matters to customers. This is a dangerous assumption.

2. The competition is also conducting competitive assessments, so they are improving based upon what they see you do. The competitors' customer satisfaction studies are telling them the same things your studies are. While you think you're outsmarting them, savvy competitors are implementing the same operational improvement ideas you are.

3. You and your competitors become focused on each other, ignoring what really matters to your customers. Rather than figuring out a unique customer value commitment for customers, you focus on improving what you have, what you already know, and what your investments already are doing. Did you ever notice every competitor in your market is working to become the low-cost and high-value producer?

Michael E. Porter, the guru of competitive strategy in the 1980s, later lamented the inordinate attention paid to competition by businesses. ". . . a focus on operational effectiveness alone tends to create a mutually destructive form of competition. If everyone's trying to get to the same place, then, almost inevitably, that causes customers to choose on price. This is a bit of a metaphor for the past five years, when we've seen widespread cratering of prices."[6]

There is a need for competitive analysis and assessment, which can be one of the most formidable undertakings in which a business can engage. This may be true in some cases, but, as Pentadigm suggests, there is a better way to both improve your business and deliver better value to your customers than your competition without engaging in the zero-sum game.

Since it's the customer who is the final arbiter of value, not the competition, every single effort, thought, and insight needs to discover how to win with customers. You are more likely to beat the competition when you deliver the best value. Superior value for customers wins and keeps customers and befuddles the competition because most companies are focused on their own products first. A clearly superior customer value commitment means you can compete and succeed without it being a blood sport.

The competitive behavior of Southwest Airlines, in our Pentadigm analysis, suggests it practices this mind-set. Unlike most traditional airlines whose leadership is intent on driving competitors out of business, Southwest has historically avoided engaging in these death matches. Southwest knows that head-to-head price wars are costly. It lets competitors beat up one another and then moves into a market, usually at the invitation of a local airport authority, when it can better serve the customer on its own terms. As a result, the airline preserves precious resources, energy, and talent until it's able to satisfy the customers' expectations. Not a macho business strategy, but smart.

Most of Southwest's competitors focus on justifying within their own minds why Southwest isn't a real airline, on their own business operations, or on how to achieve the lowest cost per passenger mile. They fail to grasp the link between the value Southwest delivers to its targeted customer value segments and Southwest's success.

When Pan Am tried to reemerge in the late 1990s, its self-described competitive strategy was to emulate Southwest, but with its own unique perspective on how to reach a broad market spectrum of customers through a variable cost organizational structure. Further, it believed that the historical Pan-Am brand was an asset which could be leveraged to gain customers in this new strategy.

The reality was that the new Pan Am tried to be the old Pan Am in the belief that the customer would respond to its variable cost structure, a cost structure that was supposed to enable it to provide value-added benefits to different customers in different seats on the plane. But because Pan Am wasn't targeting specific customer value segments, it had no customer value commitment with which any of its customers could really identify.

If nothing else, your current competitor analysis approach should confirm that your competition is working just as hard and as smart as you are on the same things. There are few businesses consciously looking to perform more poorly. Some may be better at improving themselves, but everyone is working to improve operations in the same fundamental ways: cutting costs, improving productivity, restructuring to be faster, simplifying processes, and getting better at satisfying customers. While operations and short-term profitability may improve, where do the real breakthroughs in your customer value commitment come from when your competition is doing the same to improve their business? See Competitive Assessment in Appendix 4.

Select Target Customer Value Segments

When asked what the return on investment (ROI) was for a $30,000 golf weekend with clients and potential clients, the national sales manager of a Fortune 100 company told us that he didn't know. Challenged about the justification for the cost, he replied that he didn't know what business was derived as a result of hosting the golf events, but was sure that business would be lost if he didn't.

Value-based marketing isn't mass marketing and it's not about market share. It's laser-targeted marketing that identifies customer value segments to pursue. You not only have to decide whether or not the company has the critical processes and desire to meet the customers' value expectations, but whether or not those relationships result in value that's important to customers. Answering those two questions helps select viable target customer value segments and ignore others. You must conduct analysis and exercise judgment to decide whether you can do business more meaningfully and profitably with any customer as a single customer or as part of a customer value segment. The greater the share of your profit and/or sales from one customer, the greater the justification for individualizing these customers as their own customer value segments.

A basic question that needs to be answered for each customer value segment and sometimes even each account within it is, "What does it cost us to acquire, maintain, and retain those customers?" This must be compared against the value captured from the customer value segment. Most organizations can't measure either side of this equation at the customer or customer value segment level.

Most often there are more opportunities than you either can or want to exploit. So you must make choices. You as a supplier have a value ratio just like customers do. Your desired benefit is a profit stream over time divided by the cost of that profit. Your relative costs are the acquisition, maintenance, and retention costs associated with your customer relationships.

There are some customer value segments where the Relative Costs are greater than the desired profitability of those customer value segments. Long-distance telecommunications providers have paid $50 or $75 or $100 to acquire six-week consumer relationships with a revenue stream of less than $25 per month and negative profitability.

Many tools have been tried and tested over the years to help decide which customer value segments should be targeted and which shouldn't. There are two that are helpful: the Target Customer Value Segment Tracer and the Pentadigm CLV calculation.

The *Target Customer Value Segment Tracer*, calculated in Appendix 2, is a tool that helps identify quality customer value segments to target based upon your ability to fulfill the needs of that customer value segment better than your competition, and at a profit.

Customer Lifetime Value (CLV), described in Appendix 3, is variously referred to as Net Present Value (NPV) or Life Time Value (LTV). It's a calculation of the profit that can be anticipated from a customer or a customer value segment over a specified period of time, a financial metric that is relevant to corporate budget planning and forecasting. CLV answers the basic question about whether or not a customer or a customer value segment is worth selling to based on the anticipated profitability of the relationship. By knowing the worth of customers in terms of profitability, the acquisition cost of relationships can be calculated.

And remember, not choosing to serve a segment today only means you haven't yet figured out what constitutes a value to the segment and or how to provide a superior value to the segment and make a profit.

KEY INSIGHTS

1. Map the market from the customer end of the value chain. Map at all relevant levels of detail from broad product-market to customer value segment. Name the customer value segments according to benefits sought.

2. Customer value set. Everything can be quantified somehow. In a recent workshop, participants were exploring the unmet needs of hotel guests and one participant—a tall gentleman—highlighted his unmet need for a guaranteed longer bed. When asked how much this would be worth, he initially estimated $10-20 per night, which the group felt might not be so attractive to a hotel. We explored the value further to define and map his value expectations. Several questions and their answers helped define and map the respondent's value expectations and the trade-offs he might be willing to make.

   - *When do you stay in hotels?* During the week.

   - *Why?* On business, to visit customers.

   - *What happens if you don't get a room with a longer bed?* I don't sleep so well.

   - *What is the upshot of that?* I may not be 100 percent on the ball the next day.

   - *What happens if you're not on the ball at the customer's location the next day?* I could make a mistake, even lose a contract.

   - *What are the implications for you from that mistake?* It could impact my performance bonus, jeopardize my career progress, or, in an extreme case, I could lose my job.

   - *So, what is the* real *value to you of the longer bed?* Well, having considered all this, maybe more like $50-100 per night!

3. Pentadigm "generic" customer value segments can kick-start your value-based marketing for bottom-line success: Innovators, Optimizers, Operationalizers, and Economizers. Each customer value segment buys according to a value commitment and the use of the value ratio to make a purchasing decision.

CHECKLIST

☐ Have you defined and mapped the market? Look at your market and the value offerings in the market through the eyes of the customer. Understand customer choices and the reasons for those choices.

☐ Have you developed a clear understanding of your customers' value needs and expectations? Identify the value sought by the customer value segment and quantify the value to the customer.

☐ Have you discovered customer value segments built around similar values? Seek unmet needs relentlessly and segment according to customer needs.

❑ Do you know how customers in a customer value segment perceive and value your customer value commitment versus that of your competition? Base your assessment of your relative competitive difference on the customers' perception and judgment of your customer value commitment and competing offerings.

❑ How have you targeted customer value segments? Target only those customer value segments where you have or can build a customer-competitive advantage that the customer recognizes and values and for which the customer is willing to pay. Only serve customer value segments whose lifetime value is positive and high.

STEP 2: COMMIT — COMMIT TO THE CUSTOMER

Unless commitment is made, there are only promises and hopes, but no plans.
—Peter Drucker[1]

Early in the 1990s, a start-up Taiwanese company we'll call Taiwan Industrial Products (TIP) started marketing and selling its products to big-name manufacturers of consumer electronics, appliances, and computers who purchased large quantities of limited range plastics. Three Global 500 companies based in North America and Europe dominated this mature market.

TIP targeted the price-sensitive Economizer customer value segment with its tight margins and offered prices 20 percent lower than the Big 3, a strategy that appeared to reinforce the stereotype of cheap Taiwanese products.

At first, the Big 3 ignored TIP, thinking it was just another cheap, low-price supplier using a penetration strategy to buy share, but which would eventually raise its prices. From their perspective, Economizers were big, "bad" customers who demand unrealistically low prices because of their volume purchases. They tried to look for ways to "sell" value to these companies while sustaining their prices and margins, but the Economizer customers defected to TIP in hordes.

What the Big 3 didn't comprehend was that—from a customer value perspective—TIP was the high value supplier to the price-driven Economizer customer value segment. TIP became an enormously successful and highly profitable business in a mature market. Its profitability was up to 2.5 times better than the Big 3. What TIP clearly understood was that there was considerable value to be captured with Economizers.

Large manufacturing operations are price sensitive, but they also require high-quality product suppliers—defined by consistency and predictability of performance at Six Sigma level—as well as on-time delivery as important value drivers. Without quality and on-time supply, these large manufacturer customers that sell into fiercely competitive markets could suffer downtime in their plants, wiping out profits.

While the Big 3 continued to invest time, effort, and money in search of ways to sell value, TIP committed itself to helping the Economizers become profitable. It discovered what mattered most to the Economizer customer value segment and eliminated the added-value costs that didn't matter. TIP turned the industry's traditionally "bad" customers into great customers and did so profitably by offering superior value and creating an enterprise form that was aligned to the superior value. See Appendix 5 for the value commitment rating tool.

The TIP case flies in the face of much of today's Customer Relationship Management (CRM) thinking, in which customers are classified based on their profit stream to you, the supplier. The lower rated customers, those with small or no profit, are eliminated from your customer base. This seems to make sense on the surface, but it can lead to missed opportunities that might be derived from real discovery. Most CRM approaches fail to reflect the insight needed to turn bad customers into great ones, like TIP was able to. Often, under the CRM model, a more profitable customer might be misconstrued as one that values you more and is willing to pay you higher prices. However, this may only be true until the customer has been discovered by a value-driven competitor. If a customer value analysis, like we describe in Pentadigm, is not part of your CRM package, you won't realize this until the business is lost.

The TIP story exemplifies the inherent conflict between CRM and Pentadigm. CRM focuses a company on profitable customers in the current way a company conducts business; the five-step Pentadigm model focuses a company on creating superior value for customers first and then achieving profit through the right resource alignment. And this challenge is becoming increasingly common in many business-to-business and consumer markets as companies continue to try to gain competitive advantage through the same product-centric view of markets and customers.

Five Actions in Pentadigm Step 2: Commit

As the behavior of the Big 3 toward the Economizer customer value segment illustrates, just developing an offering doesn't necessarily offer value to the customer. Once you've understood the customers' needs and value expectations, you have to make a serious commitment to the customer to meet or exceed those expectations.

Customer value segments at different levels in your value chain impact the demand for your products and services to a greater or lesser extent. The key is to deploy the right customer value commitments for each customer value segment so that you're not deploying resources unnecessarily, and so that customers can appreciate the value they're receiving from you and appreciate the real value of your customer value commitments. If you are to capture the true value for your customer value commitments, you must commit to fulfilling the customer value segment's needs and expectations.

Commit includes five major actions:

1. *Define customer value segment strategy.* This must be based on choosing the customer value commitments on which you're going to compete in your target customer value segments.

2. *Develop superior offering.* Your customer value commitments have to embody superior values and benefits for the respective customer value segment and link the customer value commitments to the brand.

3. *Create the right organization.* This requires assessment of your current capabilities against the capabilities needed to deliver the customer value commitments competitively and effectively to the target customer value segment and a plan to fill the gaps.

4. *Define Key Performance Indicators (KPIs).* Include the key measures and benchmarks customers use to track your value performance.

5. *Communicate internally and externally.* The customer value commitments must be communicated to the target customer value segments and within your own organization. This means managing both the sales, the marketing communications, and the internal communications processes to provide a clear, consistent message.

Define Customer Value Segment Strategy

What TIP understood in committing to its target customers, the Economizers, was that it could dominate the customer value segment by providing the superior price value expected. It then created a business organization that was completely aligned to deliver that value; that is, form follows value. After your value discovery is complete and you understand the customer, you need to assess your customer objectives in each customer value segment. There are four objectives that can be adopted.

The first is *growth*, through expanding the size of the customer value segment, expanding your average share of customer demand, taking customers from the competition, or a combination of all three. The second is *maintenance*, designed to protect and retain a growth position with customers and optimize your profitability for a given customer value segment. Third is *harvest*, in which you're making little or no investment in a customer value segment—simply extracting cash from the customer value segment for as long as it remains feasible and profitable to do so. The fourth is to not compete or to *exit* the customer value segment, especially if it's not profitable to enter or to remain.

Your customer value segment objectives are an evolution of strategic decisions. When first targeting a customer value segment, you would most likely pursue a growth strategy, investing in sales, expanding channels, and offering incentives to penetrate the market. As your relationship with the customer value segment matures, your strategy shifts to maintenance, consolidating the customer interfaces and channels; investment is made in this customer value segment only to protect your position or resist competitive threat and only until the position is no longer sustainable. Given the opportunity, you take advantage of your position with the customer value segment and harvest it to generate cash for investment in the next growth opportunity. Finally, you may exit the customer value segment when it no longer represents a significant source of value to you either in terms of cash or profit or when it has been superseded by another customer value segment. Exit is a strategy many companies adopt far too late for their own good!

Determining your position in a customer value segment as well as that of your competition provides needed insight about not only the customer value commitments and Customer Lifetime Value, but whether it's possible for you to dominate the customer value segment (DTS) or dominate the cycle (DTC). This was discussed in Chapter 2. It's most likely you will choose DTS where you have the most significant value advantage for a customer value segment, but it's not advisable for most companies to commit to pursuing DTS simultaneously for each customer value segment identified. The better strategy is to pursue DTS in a few chosen customer value segments. Next, reverse engineer your competition's ability to duplicate what you have discovered. While your discovered insight might be novel, the ability to imitate might not be so novel.

You're also better choosing one customer value segment to first establish your DTS position before tackling another customer value segment. The remaining customer value segments ultimately become part of your customer portfolio, each managed based on its own distinct value expectations. Your business may not be the dominant supplier until adequate resources and funding can be dedicated to the second prioritized customer value segment for DTS.

In considering DTC, the key is to determine whether you can create enough strength within each customer value commitment to sustain the hand-off that will occur between changes in customer value in the cycle As customers transition through each customer value segment in the cycle, they need to recognize that you have strong customer value commitments for the part of the cycle they are now entering. If the market is closed-loop in nature, customers will recognize your ability to transition them to any value in the cycle.

For example, a graphic design business we'll call Edgy Design may at first buy cutting-edge software and computers to develop edgy advertisements for clients. As it grows, edge is still important, but its client projects are also requiring more and more production by more and more people for less dramatic design output for clients. In time, competition has gotten wicked and Edgy Design has to manage its costs much more closely. The reality is that cheaper computers and software get the job done. During these transitions, if you're a supplier to Edgy Design, your objective is to lead it into each phase, recognizing the nature of how its business is changing, not trying to up-sell your latest, more expensive stuff.

If the cycle is closed-loop, Edgy Design will eventually realize that new cutting-edge graphics equipment is needed and your offering reflects cutting-edge again. In an open loop DTC, the original buyers eventually leave. The Edgy Design partners close shop to develop other business ventures. But new buyers are continually brought in to replace those that leave.

As the Edgy Design situation illustrates, DTC has customers transitioning through different segment values. Your critical concern needs to be whether you have the internal capability to be the leading value offer at each stage or whether you'll lose the cycle to stronger competitive customer value commitments. Once you lose the connection to the customer, you're no longer in a position to dominate the cycle.

The two choices from a business structure standpoint are whether (1) you create distinctive units to create and deliver the different customer value commitments with a Customer Value Manager (CVM) responsible for leading customer value transitions, or (2) the CVM role is the primary business structure with a network of alliances and partners who provide the distinctive customer value commitments through the central CVM capability.

Similarly, the overall mix of offerings in your value portfolio must optimize value fulfillment for the customer and value recovery for your corporation. You must have an effective and efficient portfolio management system that enables you to balance the customer value commitments against the profitability of target customer value segments.

Develop Superior Offering

The value customers receive from your customer value commitments should have a positive, meaningful impact on your relationship with them. Once customers' value drivers are known, your customer value segment strategy is set, and you've closed the gaps. The next step is to determine how these values can become the driving influence of your essence of business (EOB) by developing what is usually described as a value proposition. Developed by Michael J. Lanning of the DPV Group in 1983 while he was at McKinsey and Company, the term *value proposition* has been part of business vocabulary for almost two decades.[2] Many companies lack real appreciation of the business transformation capability a value proposition holds. In Pentadigm we go beyond value propositions and make commitments to the customer.

Following are five critical elements of a best-practice Customer Value Commitment.

- *Customer Value Segment:* Who specifically are you targeting with this customer value commitment? *Example:* purchasers of bulk and full truckloads of epoxy.
- *Customer Value:* What is the specific value in your offer that addresses the value set of the target audience? *Example:* convenient and easy to purchase; transparent pricing.
- *Superior Value:* What elements of value do you offer that are relevant to the target audience and are better than competing offerings, often expressed as a superlative? *Example:* cost competitive; easiest to do business with.
- *Profitable for the supplier:* How are you going to make a profit from the customer value commitment? *Example:* low cost to serve; adherence to clear rules; no confusion.
- *Banner Headline:* A good acid test is to be able to express your customer value commitments in a few chosen words. Imagine you have just met the customer in the elevator and you have 30 seconds to convince him or her of your compelling customer value commitment. *Example:* fastest and cheapest bulk epoxy; no nonsense.

Your customer value commitment provides a compelling reason for customers to buy from you. Your commitment is that, if the customer buys from you, this is the value it will derive—the Desired Benefits over the Relative Cost—and that your customer value commitments are superior to what the competition can offer. A successful customer value commitment leads to a long-term relationship, which provides value to your customer and value to your company. This relationship, defined as Supplier Value (V^s), is equal to CLV over the sum of your Acquisition, Maintenance, and Retention costs or $V^s = CLV / \Sigma$ (Acquisition + Maintenance + Retention).

All businesses have customer value commitments whether it's understood formally or not. When you don't actively discover what matters to customers, but merely market and sell the features of your products, your customers are left to decide what your value proposition is to them and whether or not it's valuable to them. This results in confusing and often contradicting value messages, which creates dissonance and risk for the buyer. See Developing Customer Value Commitments in Appendix 6.

The failure to manage and leverage customer value commitments happens because companies become so focused on internal needs, goals, and ambitions that customers have become a distraction and not the reason for doing business. Consistently successful companies are ones that have developed and implemented customer value commitments based on customer value expectations.

In Pentadigm, customer value commitments are distinctive, differentiated from, and superior to competitors' value propositions for a targeted customer value segment, and they are profitable over time for the supplier. *Distinctive* means it grabs the customer's attention. *Differentiated* means a unique commitment that is a combination of a different mix of Desired Benefits and Relative Costs for each customer value segment. *Superior* means that there are elements of the commitment that are identifiably and quantifiably better than the competing offerings. *Profitable over time* means that the supplier can achieve an acceptable economic profit from the commitment for a reasonable length of time. Customer value commitments are value-segment specific; there isn't a "one size fits all" attitude. *Targeted* means that customer value segments have been identified and selected as viable, that is, you can create customer value while making a profit and covering investment costs.

Crafting customer value commitments defines which business resources are critical to winning business in the targeted customer value segments. This enables you to focus on specific value-creating factors, resource accordingly, and achieve the superior value position with customers. Companies often struggle with the battle between cost management and value to the customer. Pentadigm isn't about choosing either cost management or value delivery. It's about understanding the growing gap between the two so that you can deliver superior value profitably. Providing superior value and managing costs are mutually attainable since you concentrate precious resources for which the customer is most likely to reward you. Where there is no reward, your costs are eliminated, so the gap gets bigger until value-cost equilibrium is reached.

Creating value for customers has a cost associated with it. Value-driven companies earn a profit by building their value upon the most important customer benefits and discipline themselves to not provide items of little or no value to the customer. If you offer all features and all services to all customers or if your customer value commitments to different customer value segments are not clearly different, you haven't gained enough insight about the customers' value expectations and your profit drivers.

It's important to reinforce the fact that one customer value commitment isn't enough even for a company with a single product. The Pentadigm definition of customer is "any member of the value chain who directly or indirectly purchases or influences the purchase of our offering." In many instances you may be confronted with a complex value chain in which you must address several value chain members, each with their own unique value set, demanding you to address that value set with a unique customer value commitment.

A computer chip manufacturer's customer value commitment for a computer user is based on power and reliability—*you can perform all the tasks you want to perform for the life of your PC*. The customer value commitment for computer distribution channel members is based on brand recognition and demand pull—*more customers demanding more computers with our chips means more sales and margin for you*. The customer value commitment for the computer manufacturer promises innovation and security of supply—*stay ahead of your competition with guaranteed supply of leading-edge chips*. The customer value commitment for opinion leaders like computer magazine technology journalists is based on being informed about leading edge technology and innovations—*we'll make you look good and increase your journal sales by giving you the lead innovation stories*. For investors, the customer value commitment is built around market or product leadership and value growth—*your investment in our shares will earn you higher returns than investments in our peers' or competitors' shares*.

In the Chapter 2 discussion about the inherent Pentadigm-CRM conflict, we talked about differentiating your customer value commitments. Branding is a powerful way of doing just that. Again, there is a plethora of material about branding, but a couple of comments about branding within the Pentadigm model are appropriate.

Your customers brand your company and its customer value commitments whether you intend for that to happen or not. Just by virtue of being aware of you, you are "branded" in customers' minds. In essence, your brand is a mental representation of your value. A proactive branding strategy enables you to assume and exert control over branding to make certain customers' perceptions match your intentions. If you don't manage the branding, you run the risk of losing control. Never forget, ignore, or underestimate the impact of branding.

The red Coca-Cola logo and patented bottle shape are global brand icons. Nike's "Just do it" was a globally recognized brand slogan. Brands not only have equity but, in some cases, there is brand liability. How quickly did Enron, World-Com, Arthur Andersen, *et al* go from darlings to devils?

Branding allows you to establish and associate your offering with a specific perception or idea that is relevant and attractive to your target customers. At a minimum, its function is to allow you to differentiate your offering from one target customer value segment to another. Akzo Nobel's automotive paints are marketed under the Akzo Nobel brand, but with different brand names that reflect not only a difference in quality, but different target customer value segments. The company developed a mid-range product and branded it as Lesonal so that it would be distinct from its established high-quality Sikkens product.

A strong brand also enables you to establish and protect price differentials between offerings to different customer value segments. Here the strategy is to have a different offering for each target customer value segment and to leverage the strength of the overall brand—setting price according to the benefits delivered to the customer value segment.

For example, a boat hull made with Kevlar means that a commercial fisherman will use less fuel, can get to the fishing ground faster, and can carry more fish. For an aircraft designer, a Lockheed 1011 engine is 807 pounds lighter because it uses Kevlar 49, which means better fuel efficiency, less stress on the structural design, and the ability to carry 807 pounds more in passengers, cargo, or on-board service items. But the Relative Costs of the Kevlar solution are totally different for each of these customer value segments and both sets of customers are satisfied because of the cost/benefit delivered. Both experiences reinforce the overall Kevlar brand.

STYROFOAM brand insulation board, manufactured by The Dow Chemical Company, is marketed under a number of application-related subbrands in order to differentiate what is essentially the same physical product—an extruded expanded polystyrene insulation board—from one application to another. ROOFMATE, WALLMATE, FLOORMATE, and PERIMATE are just four of the successful STYROFOAM subbrands in this range, each with modified properties or features targeted at a specific building application. Each is priced according to need fulfillment, benefit, and value delivered relative to competitive offerings in the respective application-based customer value segments. Branding enables Dow and its distributors to successfully position the different insulation boards with their customers and to obtain differential pricing.

While there's no limit to information about how to manage a brand available from myriad sources, there are a couple of key concepts that are relevant to Pentadigm. There is no "right" branding strategy to pursue; each strategy should be based on the customer value commitments made to the target customer value segments and whether or not branding supports or perhaps even diminishes that commitment, as described in Exhibit 4-1.

Create the Right Organization

Once you've worked out what your customer value commitments are and what it entails to deliver them effectively to the target customer value segment, you must ensure that you have the capabilities to do this. Capabilities are those people, resources, processes, and systems that you will need to produce, sell, deliver, and service the customer value commitments to the targeted customers. The key Pentadigm concept you need to employ here is "form follows value." As diagrammed in Exhibit 4-2, form follows value starts with choosing your customer value commitments. The *form* or business model or design is determined by this commitment and shapes your decisions, resource deployment, and all organizational capabilities and processes.

This challenges the popular notion of core competencies and doing what you do well. What you do well may, in fact, deliver little or no value to customers or deliver value that may not be superior from competitors' offerings. A business with great internal core competencies that the customer doesn't value incurs costs, lowered profitability, and sagging sales. It's counterproductive to concentrate on competencies that make no difference to customers.

In order for form to follow value, you have to link your identified customer value commitments to people, resources, processes, and systems as opposed to just saying, "Gosh, we have these people, resources, processes, and systems that we have to pay for, so how do we use these capabilities?" This will help you to avoid making investments in developing new people, resources, processes, and systems capabilities that can't be directly linked to your identified customer value commitments.

EXHIBIT 4-1

Key Pentadigm Value Branding Strategies

STRATEGY	POSITIVES	NEGATIVES
Single brand—enables strong brand building with multiple price points.	• stronger brand position • family of products under the single brand	• confused brand image at customer level • difficult to establish and maintain pricing differences across channels
Umbrella brand with sub-brands—facilitates differentiation while maintaining and reinforcing an overall brand image.	• greater potential to differentiate pricing through the subbrands • strong umbrella brand when supported by the subbrands	• possible weakening of individual brand because of different brand levels • confused brand image at customer level
Multiple brands—enables differentiation and facilitates differentiated channel and pricing strategies. One brand per channel.	• strong individual brand image within the channel • differential pricing more easily established and protected	• diffused brand position • weaker overall brand image
Third-party branding "own labels"—protects the manufacturer's main brand and enables differentiated channel strategies.	• lower risk of damage to manufacturer's brand • differential pricing more easily established and protected	• diffused brand position • weaker overall brand image

Once it's accepted that form follows value, the processes of developing capabilities and eliminating or filling gaps in your business become fairly straightforward. For example, if your customer value commitment is to provide your targeted customers with the latest innovations, then capabilities to look at are in

- Research and Development and Design for the capability to create the new ideas and develop the innovations;
- Account Management for the skill of creating open dialog and in-depth relationships with customer value segments; and
- Marketing for the ability to help translate customer needs into specific technologies or solutions to fulfill those needs.

If your innovator customer base buys a manufactured product from you, it may make sense to *not* develop your production capability internally. You would first need to understand the way innovation impacts your fixed asset capabilities. If

EXHIBIT 4-2

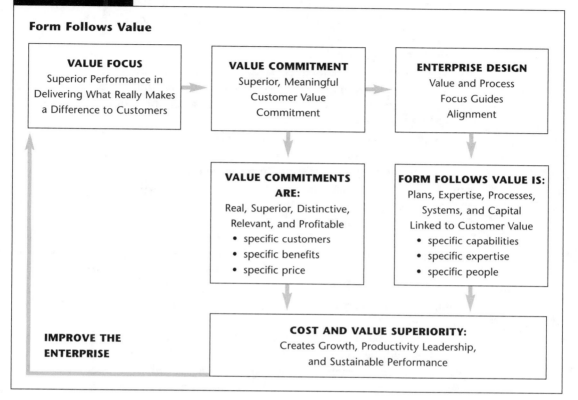

Form Follows Value

VALUE FOCUS
Superior Performance in Delivering What Really Makes a Difference to Customers

VALUE COMMITMENT
Superior, Meaningful Customer Value Commitment

ENTERPRISE DESIGN
Value and Process Focus Guides Alignment

VALUE COMMITMENTS ARE:
Real, Superior, Distinctive, Relevant, and Profitable
• specific customers
• specific benefits
• specific price

FORM FOLLOWS VALUE IS:
Plans, Expertise, Processes, Systems, and Capital Linked to Customer Value
• specific capabilities
• specific expertise
• specific people

IMPROVE THE ENTERPRISE

COST AND VALUE SUPERIORITY:
Creates Growth, Productivity Leadership, and Sustainable Performance

there are rapid effects on fixed capital, the question is whether this rate would deter you from making ongoing investments in capital to provide the continuous stream of new innovations for these customers. If the capital use financial needs exceed your ability to recapture your investment, then these capabilities should be outsourced or obtained through partnerships.

If your Pentadigm customer value segments, on the other hand, are operationalizer and economizer customers looking for high quality but more standardized offerings, your innovation capabilities become less important. Efficiency of your supply chain, cost management capabilities, more indirect sales capabilities, and speed and accuracy of transactional capabilities are more valued. In this case, you may be able to outsource the innovation of your product or service.

Your specific customer value commitments will define the exact capabilities you need to consider developing. The intent of "form follows value" is to provide you with the insight into which capabilities are directly linked to what the customer most values and, therefore, most likely to pay for and which capabilities are of lesser value and harder for you to get the customer to pay for.

Finally, using the customer value commitments as your compass to develop capabilities will change the nature of conversations and decision making within your business. The dialog and decisions should be less "global" in nature. It may sound sexy or politically correct to develop new capabilities to keep your business current. But the dialog and decisions now need to reflect the specific connection of any capability development to its contribution to your customer value commitments. If your team can't make the connections, the likelihood is you identified a feel-good capability, which is a cost for your business, but not a value for either you or your customers.

Gap analysis is a good tool for use in identifying competencies and capabilities that need to be acquired, developed, enhanced, or improved. This must be complete before moving into creating customer value. Gap analysis is a structured approach to defining what is needed to create, develop, sell, deliver, and service your customer value commitments. Once you have defined the people, resources, processes, and systems capabilities needed, you must evaluate your company's actual level of capability and competence on each of the key elements identified. Wherever a gap is identified you must define and decide how it can be filled, which may involve one or more of: develop internally; acquire; partner; or outsource. This must be complete before moving into creating customer value. The example matrix in Exhibit 4-3 can help you to decide the most appropriate route to competency development.

First, list the elements of your value commitment down the left side of the grid. There will be some elements that stand out as the core foundation of what customers really value and some elements that may be only a necessary standard to enter the market. The more the elements are directly linked to giving you the unique ability to create and deliver the superior value components, the more these will likely become competencies or done internally. For those elements that are part of standard business procedures, look more to partnering and outsourcing when forming the organizational model.

Define Key Performance Indicators (KPIs)

Pentadigm shouldn't result in conflicting goals or objectives. You must ensure that your value delivery objectives are consistent with the overall goals of your corporation or business unit and that they are consistent with each other.

Too often a company's marketing objectives are driven by profit, operations goals are driven by cost reduction, and sales objectives are driven by revenue growth. All of these may be desirable to a greater or lesser extent and, when managed holistically in the strategic framework, they can be consistent. Often this requires a greater level of detail to be entered into in the goal setting.

This also highlights the preoccupation of many business people with basic financial goals. In Pentadigm, KPIs are also based on nonfinancial goals and even

EXHIBIT 4-3

Simple Analysis to Help Identify and Fill the Credibility Gaps

CUSTOMER COMMITMENT	COMPETENCY	DEVELOP INTERNALLY	ACQUIRE	PARTNER	OUTSOURCE
Tight resin specifications for coatings formulators, which eliminates lot-to-lot production variances	Ability to create and make highly consistent quality products	Six Sigma manufacturing program launched across key functions and personnel			
One source responsibility for all components	Expertise in sourcing for customers all products and ingredients		Buy Internet sourcing company		
Process technical services at customer site	Ability to give comprehensive process control support			Alliance with equipment OEM or independent process consultant	
On-demand customer service	Capability to answer any question 24/7				Contract with call center provider

include customer-based KPIs. Some examples of nonfinancial metrics might include, but are by no means limited to:

- Share of customer value segment demand
- Brand position in a customer value segment
- Awareness of customer value commitments
- Acquisition of new customers
- Retention of existing customers
- Sales from new customer value commitments
- Proportion of total sales (or profit) from new customer value commitments
- Time to market of new customer value commitments

Goals should be established and evaluated at a customer value segment level. For example, it's quite possible for you to pursue a growth strategy with a product or service in one customer value segment, which means revenue growth, investment in sales, and channel infrastructure, but probably not optimized profit. In a second customer value segment where your position is more established, your objective with the same product or service may be to optimize profits with only regular or lower revenue growth. Taking out cost may be the overriding goal in a third customer value segment for the same product.

Having defined a unique customer value commitment for each value segment, you must define a specific set of goals relating to sales revenue, costs, and profit to reflect the customer value commitment, along with specific and relevant key performance indicators to track these. The rule here is to avoid generalization and to only aggregate up to higher level goals from these more meaningful levels of goal and target setting.

Once these goals and KPIs have been derived, they must be widely communicated and understood throughout the organization. Management must have a meaningful dialog with all members of the team(s) involved or impacted by any goal to ensure that they understand it and believe in it. Stretch goals are fine and should be encouraged, but ambiguous or secret goals are a demotivator and should be avoided. Linking goals to some part of variable compensation and to career development is also to be encouraged.

Be careful not to set goals using your favorite internal metrics and ignore the customers' metrics. Pentadigm insists that you understand your customer's scorecard and that you define goals and KPIs that reflect the customer's value set and metrics. A discussion of KPIs, goals, and metrics can be found in Chapter 7.

A number of years ago, a heated argument ignited in a global company between the sales organization and the supply chain organization concerning the record of on-time deliveries. The company's performance targets related to the number of shipments made On-Time, In Full, In Specification. The supply chain director announced proudly to a highly perplexed sales organization that more than 98 percent of deliveries in the previous quarter had met these targets. The sales director vociferously challenged this statistic, arguing that a figure of 70 percent was more accurate.

What you see depends on where you're standing in the forest. Both assessments were correct depending on which metric was used. The supply chain people measured when shipments left the plant; more than 98 percent of deliveries in the previous quarter had left the plant On Time, In Full, and In Specification. Salespeople measured when the shipments arrived at the customer—only 70 percent of deliveries in the previous quarter were received by the customer On Time, In Full, and In Specification. From the internal product-centric perspective, the supply chain operation was functioning at a very high level of efficiency. From the sales function perspective, customer expectations were not being met.

In addition to setting measures and KPIs according to customers' scorecards, performance should also be measured relative to your competitors' customer value commitment and relative to your customers' best-performing suppliers on their customer value commitments. This is one way to discover how to improve your own offering by performing beyond the limitations of your normal frame of supplier-customer reference.

Some external, independent signals that you are providing value to your customer value segments would include

- Customer satisfaction ratings, which lead to repeat purchases
- Acquisition of new customers, especially those defecting from other brands
- Improved status in the industry as a value company to benchmark
- Referrals from existing customers
- Positive press

You're familiar with normal goal setting, SMART goals, and so forth. But there are a couple of issues related to establishing some benchmarks or metrics to determine whether or not Pentadigm is meeting your objectives.

Customers' value expectations aren't static; they change as expectations are met or go away. An important unmet need that is fulfilled will at some point cause the next unmet need to surface. In practice, it's imperative that value-focused organizations constantly assess and understand what the customers' value drivers are and increase their ability to provide that value. Using continuous feedback and assessment through all five Pentadigm stages, your business can continually identify customers' changing value expectations and new value drivers that emerge in your customer value segments. These data will influence all of the Pentadigm value-based marketing stages, which results in your business planning and marketing being transformed into an uninterrupted dynamic system of business renewal and growth. This means that your KPIs need to be adjusted to reflect these changing needs.

Following are the most important questions to consider in measuring your performance on delivering needs to the target customer value segment with your customer value commitments.

1. How is your performance on the three value principles? Is it real? Can you win the business with your customer value commitments? Is it profitable to do so?

2. Does your current performance justify changing what you're doing for new opportunities in any way?

3. Are you the dominant value creators for customers in your target customer value segment?

4. Has your relationship within the current customer value segments become the customer franchise that you want to maintain and can grow with?

5. Would pursuing a new opportunity dilute current effort enough or change your cost and capital expenditures enough to cause you not to reach the dominant Value Creator position in your targeted customer value segment(s)?

Communicate Internally and Externally

Customer value commitments need to be communicated to the target customer value segment once the KIPs have been defined. In the traditional marketing mix, this is the function of the fourth P, *promotion*, which includes sales, advertising, public relations, trade shows, and E-commerce, among others, where much attention is spent selecting communication channels, creating messages, and establishing budgets.

In the world of Pentadigm, each target customer value segment has unique value needs and expectations, which means that there cannot be a "one size fits all" promotional message. Communicating your customer value commitments is dependent on the information needs and expectations of the targeted customer value segment. What information about the customer value commitments is needed to make a value-based purchasing decision? How and when and in what format does the customer want that information conveyed? Why demand that a customer spend time meeting with your national account team when all it wants is access to your website to gain an understanding of your customer value commitments and a means to place an order electronically?

Creating customer value commitments does little if your company can't close a transaction with potential buyers. Painting with a very broad brush, the role of the sales function traditionally has been to create a transaction. To its detractors, successful sales means selling to customers products and services they don't need and can't afford. Selling refrigerators to Eskimos. Oil to Arabs. Bibles to atheists. Barbecue to vegetarians. A professional salesperson is great at getting the appointment, expert in the company's product or service features, knows how to probe to uncover customer objections, has the ability to turn the objections into benefits, and is an expert on closing.

But being technically good at closing a transaction does less and less for the customer. Sales forces are finding it more difficult to close on the sale and customers are finding the sales calls less valuable and aren't willing to invest as much time with the salesperson as they used to.

As Paul Goldner noted in his book, *Red-Hot Cold Call Selling*, the goal of a salesperson should be to find the customers "who are most likely to make major purchases. Although it might seem as though you are limiting your opportunities by excluding some buyers from your target market, you are not. What you are doing is setting priorities so that you work first with the buyers in your market offering the greatest potential for sales. . . . By defining your target market in a quantitative manner, there is no doubt whether a prospect is in or out (of your account list)."[3]

There is inherent dissonance between transaction-based sales objectives and purchasing objectives based on obtaining the maximum value—the best ratio of Desired Benefits over Relative Costs. Selling has to change and focus on the customer's value expectations, and evolve into value selling.

The last time we typed "value selling" into google.com, 2.01 million hits popped up. Hundreds of companies offer training programs in value-selling processes, techniques, systems, and software. Without reinventing all of these wheels, it's important to understand that value selling is essential to achieving bottom-line success through value-based marketing. Again, creating customer value commitments does little if your company can't close a transaction with potential buyers.

The essence of value selling is long-term relationship and profitability rather than short-term transaction and revenue. It's bottom-line rather than top-line. It's a slow dime versus a fast nickel. There are innumerable clichés that could be used. The objective is that value selling is long-term Customer Lifetime Value (CLV) and customer loyalty.

Customer loyalty is different from inertia, which some salespeople and marketers confuse. Remember high school physics? Inertia—an object at rest tends to stay at rest unless force is applied. Buyer inertia means that the buyer will make repurchase decisions given the absence of a reason to change. Your company hasn't missed a delivery date the past five years. The last two months you missed three.

The customer is sourcing other suppliers, not only because of the recency effect—looking at short-term supplier behavior rather than the historical track record—but because force has been applied. Late delivery is justification for a change. Loyalty means that the customer will continue to work within the relationship even when there might be a reason to leave. Customer loyalty is a conscious decision of preference for your customer value commitments, your brand. The historical track record is more important than the short-term problems that can be resolved because a mutually beneficial partnership has been established based on the exchange of value. The supplier has become the value supplier of choice.

The traditional stereotype of the seller having the "gift of gab" needs to be replaced with the realization that the value seller needs to have the gift of listening. Active listening skills are required to keep the attention on the customer and not fall into the trap of traditional product feature monologue. A basic rule should be that the product or service and its features shouldn't be presented by the salesperson in a value-selling activity in the first sales call. The objective is to gather information and understand.

Value selling means understanding the customer's world and what the customer perceives as value. This requires presales investigation and analysis to uncover the customer's value needs and expectations in order to develop appropriate customer value commitments. During the sales call, additional probing to validate the customer's value drivers is required. If you want your sellers to sell the value, you have to train them to be penetratingly inquisitive, to look for signals and information that point to unfulfilled customer needs and benefits.

Five questions provide a useful framework for all customer interactions. These are especially relevant in a sales situation but can be used in any touch point with customers.

1. *How does the customer do business today?* Define the customer's business activity. How does it make money? How does it measure success? What impacts that success? Where does our offering fit into the customer's equation? How critical is our customer value commitments to the customer's success?

2. *What does it cost?* Define the customer's cost model. Where and to what extent does the cost of our offering fit into this model? What proportion of the customer's costs does our offering represent? Does our offering impact other costs in the customer's equation?

3. *What's wrong?* Define the challenges and issues the customer faces in its business, both big picture and day-to-day. What challenges and issues does the customer face in using our offering, both big picture and day-to-day?

4. *To the customer, what's the monetary value of improvement?* Quantify the answer.

5. *What will change in the customer's environment and how will it impact the customer over the next one to three to five years?* Identify changes that will likely occur in the overall marketplace, in the value chain, in the competitive environment, technology, society, legislation, etc.

Equipped with the knowledge derived from these investigations, either pre-call or during a presentation, you can better define how your customer value commitments address the customer's specific needs and value expectations. If you're not addressing unmet, poorly met, or determinant customer needs—those needs that drive the choice or preference of supplier—you're *not* selling the value.

These questions not only provide insight into the customer's business and customer value segment, but help establish credibility.

Value selling also means being alert to all opportunities to sell to a customer any offerings within the company portfolio. This is a major dilemma for many larger companies which are organized on a product line or divisional basis and have multiple sellers calling on the same accounts to sell different offerings. Many customers would benefit from a single point of contact, where the supplier's sales organization and structure are transparent. The difficulty is accountability for the sale. In Pentadigm, the point is moot. If a broad portfolio offering is meeting the customer's value expectations, then the credit for the Customer Lifetime Value is shared.

Some companies have created a Solutions Group or Customer Account Manager (CAM) whose responsibility is to service customers who buy multiple products or services from the organization. The role of the Solutions Group or the CAM is to gain a holistic view of the multitude of opportunities for your organization at the account and to mobilize at a supradivisional level whatever forces are needed to exploit the entire opportunity. This group or individual becomes the eyes and ears of the organization within the customer and also the trusted solution provider for the customer within your organization.

This doesn't mean that other contacts with customers are minimized. In fact, what happens is usually the reverse. Managed properly and effectively, this transparent holistic approach to value delivery can lead to greater multi-level and multifunctional contacts cementing, deepening, and strengthening the relationships between the organizations and erecting greater barriers to competitive entry. The benefits of customer account management can be seen also in increased sales value, mutually beneficial cost-reducing efficiencies, improved overall account profitability, and longevity of business tenure.

In short, Pentadigm value selling means being able to

- understand the real needs of the customer and how much the customer is prepared to pay to have those needs fulfilled
- present the customer value commitments that match the customer's value needs and expectations proficiently and profitably
- demonstrate and differentiate the superiority of the customer value commitments in the mind of the customer
- enable the buyer to systematically rule out the competition
- motivate customers to take action

Value selling also has a value for the sales organization, including the ability to sell at the decision-making level in their customer's organization, shortened sales cycles, and an increased share of the customer's purchasing expenditures.

A customer once paid one of the authors the greatest compliments he'd ever received as a salesperson. "We don't consider you to be our sales rep," was the comment. "We think of you as a part-time, unpaid employee of our company, working with us and for us." This is the essence of value selling.

External communications—typically advertising and public relations and websites under the promotion component of the traditional marketing mix—should communicate to your targeted customer value segments that (1) you understand their respective value expectations, (2) you have chosen to meet or exceed those value expectations, and (3) they will acquire more value from your company's customer value commitments than from any other supplier. This external communication should be managed as part of an integrated marketing communication strategy that results in seamless communications with the customer value segment consistently exposed to the same relevant value message.

The biggest communication trap is emphasizing your product or product features, because the belief inside the organization is that this is what generates your sales revenues. It's easy to fall into this pattern because you typically know more about your products and services than you know about the customer's needs and expectations. When you promote product features, the customer has to make the effort to translate your features into benefits that fulfill their needs and value expectations and then make the assessment of how your customer value commitments match up against competition. Even communicating to customers just about their needs still requires them to make a judgment of what value your product offering has. You can build it and sell it and they won't come.

In the end, what really matters to the customer is a better value. Customers don't buy products or features; they buy value. That's what triggers buyer response. Customers want information about your customer value commitments on which a purchase decision can be based. As Exhibit 4-4 reflects, a value-centric communications style satisfies this expectation better than the product-centric style.

Value-centric communications satisfy the customer value segment's information needs. Having developed an understanding of the customer value segment's

---

EXHIBIT 4-4

Comparison of Product- and Value-Centric Promotional Campaigns

PRODUCT-CENTRIC COMMUNICATIONS		VALUE-CENTRIC COMMUNICATIONS
Focuses on your product, its features and benefits.	**Strategy**	Communicates the customer value commitment.
Convince customers you have the best product or service relative to the competition.	**Objective**	Convince targeted customer value segments that your customer value commitment best fulfills their value needs and expectations.
Positioning and differentiation of product/service features and benefits relative to competition. Attract as many and the biggest customers to drive demand.	**Tactics**	Positioning the customer value commitment to communicate its relevance, meaning, and impact for each targeted value segment.
Better understanding of your product may trigger sales, or customers trigger new demands because they want a variation to meet their needs.	**Customer Impact**	Customer value commitment generates a quicker, more cost-efficient decision for the customer value segment because the value ratio is evident.
Potential for sales increases can be offset, but overspending is needed to generate sales from a broad, diverse customer base with a one-size-fits-all offer. This costs more and takes longer, since each customer doesn't quite hear what and why your offer is best for them.	**Impact on the Business**	Focused promotions for each target customer value segment generates more bang for the buck.

value needs and expectations, it moves beyond features and needs to explain and quantify how the customer will obtain more of the value it seeks from your customer value commitments than it will from the competition. A business with truly strong customer value commitments that can effectively communicate them to targeted customer value segments also has the best chance of overpowering competition, because it has removed all customer doubt about the superior value of its offering. The customer's purchase or repurchase decision is automatic.

Many industrial customers have gone through considerable supplier rationalization in the past years with the goal of reducing the number of suppliers in order to reduce costs. For buyers of undifferentiated products, the price component of relative cost tends to be the differentiator, unless you can establish another value in the buyer's mind, like security of supply.

What you say in your promotions, how you say it, and to whom your value message is directed must be focused and aligned specifically with the value expectations of the respective customer value segment. It must convey that your customer value commitments are meaningful, relevant, and superior. The customer value commitments should never be implicit in your communications; they should be explicit. The target shouldn't have to decipher or interpret the value message; it should be prominent and predominant in your message—and it should be in a clear and simple language that the customer understands.

In the mid-1990s, Frito-Lay realized that consumer eating habits were changing and developed BAKED LAY'S brand Potato Crisps. Traditional potato chips have ten grams of fat per ounce. BAKED LAY'S have 1.5 grams of fat. Test marketing on the new chip seemed to validate that it would be a hit with consumers, and several new and expensive production plants were built. Frito-Lay brought the chip into several markets in the summer of 1995. Sales were not what was expected and the company wondered whether it might have seriously missed the target customer segment's expectations.

The national launch for the BAKED LAY'S brand Potato Crisps was concentrated on New Year's Day, 1996. Frito-Lay aired commercials featuring supermodels Vendela, Kathy Ireland, Naomi Campbell, and The Muppets' Miss Piggy munching on the new chip. The campaign theme—"You can eat like one of the guys and still look like one of the girls."

The Frito-Lay supermodel campaign wasn't cheap; estimates are that the company spent around $20 million. But sales exceeded the company's most ambitious projections. There was so much demand for the new chip that people reportedly followed company delivery trucks to grocery stores to make sure they were able to buy some. BAKED LAY'S became the company's most successful Frito-Lay new-product launch to date.[4]

The BAKED LAY'S story isn't as much of an advertising campaign story as it is a story about a supplier who failed to communicate the customer value commitments to the target customer value segment. The prenational launch promotional campaign focused on the traditional messages of lower fat and calories with good taste features, but it didn't help chip eaters live the experience. When the target customer value segment saw what it could experience with Potato Crisps in the supermodel campaign—eat a bunch of great-tasting chips without feeling guilty about unhealthy eating habits—the message became more meaningful. The real value of the BAKED LAY'S product was conveyed.

Since communicating value isn't about "one message fits all," communicating different value messages to different customer value segments requires management, imagination, and budgeting committed to a multiple communications strategy. This doesn't necessarily mean a big marketing communications budget. Ultimately, the size of the budget doesn't correlate highly with effectiveness, as any study of Super Bowl advertising indicates. But when value communication is focused and specific to each customer value segment, communication spending tends to become more productive and less costly because the message is effective and generates the desired response.

The difficulty for many organizations is that they view communication costs as an expense that can be sacrificed when business performance is weaker than management expects and budget cuts are announced. Sales are slowing, competition is more fierce, and yet the messages to targeted customer value segments are curtailed. The result is almost a self-fulfilling prophecy. Customers lose sight of your customer value commitments and don't respond, which leads to more budget cuts and a downward business spiral.

Granted, this is an oversimplified analysis, but it's intended to suggest that communication of the customer value commitments you've taken time to construct and deliver needs to continue. It's important to reiterate the point that you can have the world's greatest product or service, provide the best customer value commitments, meet or exceed the customer's expectations, and still not generate revenue or profit because your message doesn't reach the target customer value segment.

It's axiomatic that the companies which maintain or even increase the communications budget when costs are being tightened are in a better position to validate the customer value commitments than those that cut communications budgets. Also, companies which continue communications are always in a better position in the mind of the customer when recovery occurs.

Finally, the value message must be delivered at the appropriate time and in the appropriate medium or media, such as mass or trade media, electronic, face-to-face, or word-of-mouth. "Appropriate" time and medium or media must be defined by the targeted audience's needs and expectations.[5]

KEY INSIGHTS

1. Customer value segment strategies need to be considered at a macro level to ensure a balance among growth, maintenance, and harvest. Objectives and strategies will change over time as the customer value set and market dynamics evolve.

2. Pentadigm customer value commitments compel the customer because they offer relevant value better than the competition and win because they embody unique elements that competitors cannot or will not offer. Pentadigm customer value commitments are written in the language of the customer.

3. In Pentadigm, you may need several customer value commitments, each targeted at a different value chain member, in order to successfully exploit a market opportunity. Form follows value.

4. Pentadigm customer value commitments are well communicated to and clearly understood by customers and internal audiences and are reinforced by strong branding strategies.

5. KPIs need to reflect the customer's scorecard, not your internal metrics.

CHECKLIST

For each target segment

❑ Have you defined and quantified your segment strategy based on selecting the value commitment on which you've chosen to compete?

❑ Have you developed superior customer value commitments for the targeted value segments?

❑ Have you created the right organization to deliver your customer value commitments?

❑ Have you enabled the clear commitment to fulfill customer value needs and expectations by creating standards of service, business rules, and exceptions. Have you communicated these to the customer value segments and internally within your own company?

❑ Have you defined the relevant Key Performance Indicators (KPIs) to track and the appropriate performance measures, benchmarks?

STEP 3: CREATE —
CREATE CUSTOMER
VALUE

If the same set of activities were best to produce all varieties, meet all needs, and access all customers, companies could easily shift among them and operational effectiveness would determine performance.

—Michael E. Porter[1]

There's an anecdote we heard from a microwave oven manufacturer in 2002 about the turntables that are inside the appliance. In the early days of microwave technology, the turntable performed a real function by turning the food so that it was cooked evenly. As technology improved, the turning function wasn't necessary and the turntable was removed. Microwave oven sales dropped, even when features were added and the price was lowered.

It took a while to discover that the declining sales had to do with the consumer perception that a microwave without a turntable wasn't cooking the food evenly and that the food might not be safely prepared. Turntables were put back into the microwave oven to perform no function other than to assuage the market's fear that food that doesn't revolve in the microwave process isn't safe. Sales improved when the microwave OEMs created the value customers expected.

Any business, big or small, succeeds initially because it brings a product or service to the market for which a number of people in the market are willing to pay. Either by instinct or deliberate planning or chance or a combination of all three, the business offering has value for a group of customers interested in what was being offered.

After the initial introduction, when the newness of the product or service is no longer a basis of value and the innovator buyers have gone away, the real work of creating new value differentiation begins. Offerings now have to promise a new value for customers, value that is superior to the customer value commitment offered by competitors; and you must continually create and deliver the value promised. This is the basis of bottom-line success through value-based marketing, which we call Pentadigm.

Five Actions in Pentadigm Step 3: Create

There's nothing more damaging to a customer relationship than having the sales organization sign a deal with a national account to install 600 document reproduction systems nationwide. Then, after the contract has been signed, the company finds that it can't produce and deliver the equipment, there aren't sufficient technicians to install the equipment, and accounting doesn't have the hardware or the personnel to add the new accounts for billing purposes. Understanding and committing to the customer have little relevance if you're not able to create the value the customer needs and expects to receive.

Create includes five major actions:

1. *Develop customer value commitment culture.* The customer value commitment has to be more than a slogan; it has to be expected, normative behavior throughout the organization, a commitment that the workforce is empowered to implement. Every customer touch point is an opportunity to create or destroy value.

2. *Plan customer value processes.* This requires identifying and defining all the processes, subprocesses, and individual activities that must be in place to deliver customer value. These processes and activities include understanding the customer, creating customer commitment, converting that customer commitment into an implemented customer value, and assessing the customers' levels of satisfaction with your customer commitment. Continuously improving your commitment in line with changing customer values keeps you ahead of your competition in delivering the desired value to the customer.

3. *Populate customer value processes.* The people skills and competencies necessary for a customer value commitment have to be defined and acquired. Your people resources have to be deployed, trained, and developed, and value delivery has to be measured and compensated.

4. *Invest in appropriate infrastructure.* To deliver customer value you have to invest in the infrastructure. This may be infrastructure to create and support the physical, service, and intangible elements of your customer value commitments. It may be to select and manage appropriate value channels that deliver the value to the customer. It may include the knowledge management systems to support your customer value creation.

5. *Implement customer value cost-effectively and efficiently.* Having understood, designed, and created your customer value commitment, you have achieved nothing until it is implemented effectively. Implementation actions have to be clearly defined, planned, prioritized, communicated, and agreed to.

Develop Customer Value Commitment Culture

An odd thing happens to most businesses as they grow and evolve—management tends to become less concerned about value being delivered to customers and more concerned with maximizing business operations. Business becomes more competitive, customers seem more recalcitrant, margins are squeezed, and reorganization becomes the rule rather than the exception. The company selling document repro systems mentioned in the beginning of this section was operationally excellent, but it hadn't done due diligence in determining whether or not the value proposition could be supported.

Every customer value segment has specific elements of its value set that, if fulfilled, will attract a non price-sensitive response. The key is to identify these elements. Once the value expectations of customer value segments are understood, the company must create internal alignment to deliver the expected value.

Everything your company does says something explicitly or implicitly about your company, and employees say it the loudest, by word and by action. If your employees aren't knowledgeable about your customers' value expectations or the value your company brings to the marketplace, they can't deliver that value. How often do you form an unfavorable attitude about a company because someone you talk to in that company doesn't understand your needs and expectations? What effect does a product manager, installer, or customer service or technical service representative have when he or she does not understand your customers' value drivers and your company's willingness or unwillingness to meet those expectations? Once the value expectations of customer value segments are understood, the company must create internal alignment to deliver the expected value.

All parts of the organization must understand their contribution to customer value. The workforce must be empowered to create and deliver customer value, to which everyone's compensation must be linked. Skills and competencies must be in place to create and deliver customer value, and customer feedback and KPIs (Key Performance Indicators) must be communicated to all parts of the organization regularly. But first and foremost the customer culture *must* be led from the top. The danger is a loss of more than revenue; it's a loss of the relationship and Customer Lifetime Value (CLV).

A company's communications strategy is all too often focused solely on external communications. Pentadigm marketers must develop a parallel marketing communications strategy directed at internal audiences. It's essential to communicate your company's customer value segmentation strategy internally, the customer needs on which it's based, and what strategic and operational decisions have been implemented to meet or exceed those value expectations.

Everyone in the organization must understand what the customers' value expectations are and how the organization intends to deliver the expected value better than the competition. Each individual in the organization needs to know how his or her role is important to making the customer value commitment a reality. The profit implications of customer satisfaction and CLV need to be communicated, since they will be inevitably tied to measurement and compensation issues. The order fulfillment function needs to know that you're trying to manage disruptive rush orders from a group of clients by working with them to be better forecasters and understand that being 100 percent responsive to orders from these customers may be counterproductive to that effort.

In addition, and perhaps most importantly, all employees need to understand what part of customer relationships they own, no matter how small. If 5 percent of customer satisfaction is based on the timeliness and accuracy of billing, then the billing department should know how it's performing.

The best way that we know for achieving this ownership is to ensure that customer focus, customer value, and customer commitment are written into everyone's job description. This ensures a real and regular awareness of customer-related issues, as they are discussed every time the jobholder and his or her manager discuss performance and related topics (including career development, skills and competency development, and remuneration). The authors have witnessed this firsthand in organizations where they have worked; they have seen the impact of a company actually taking the initiative to write an item called "customer focus" into every single job description in a major multi-national corporation operating in business-to-business markets.

Another well-documented example is the Ritz-Carlton hotel chain, which pioneered a problem ownership value model and became the first service organization to win the Malcolm Baldrige Award. When a Ritz-Carlton guest has a problem to be resolved, there's an expectation that the problem will be solved quickly, efficiently, and as transparently as possible. Problem ownership means that the employee who is made aware of the guest's problem owns it until it's resolved. The problem isn't passed off to someone else.

For example, if you're a Ritz-Carlton guest, need some additional towels, and ask a maintenance person walking down the hallway for assistance, problem ownership means that the maintenance worker doesn't tell you to call the front desk or housekeeping or guest services or notify housekeeping himself or herself. It means that the maintenance person gets the towels and asks if there's anything else the guest needs. When the maintenance person goes to the housekeeping area, she or he isn't challenged and the problem appropriated by housekeeping. It's understood that the maintenance individual has problem ownership.

All employees should not only share ownership of customer need fulfillment, they should share in the benefits of profitable customer relationships. Manage, measure, and compensate all employees for contributing to the customer value commitment. If people aren't compensated for the profitability of customer value segments, they won't focus on profitability.

There are myriad ways to make sure that the company's value messages are communicated internally. There needs to be a carefully crafted, clearly articulated, company mission statement that focuses on the customers' needs and value expectations and the company's commitment to meeting or exceeding these. This mission statement needs to be not only widely disseminated, but assimilated into the culture. The long-standing mission of a Nordstrom's floor sales representative meets all of these criteria: "Do whatever it takes to satisfy the customer." This mission must then be reflected throughout the organization in a consistent set of clearly communicated goals and objectives.

One of our clients had invested in developing value-selling skills in its sales function, stressing that a slow dime is more desirable than a fast nickel from a customer relationship. The problem was that both the external and internal salespeople were measured on and compensated for quarterly revenues. Management's message was, "We don't care whether the product satisfies the customer's expectations; show us the revenues." Quarterly revenues are an important business measure. But the revenues from Q3 should have been "seeded" in the previous year. When a revenue target is sagging, sales or any business function is likely to focus on short-term transactions to the detriment of long-term profitability.

We've conducted a number of role plays with clients to afford people from a number of different functions the opportunity to interact in nonthreatening practice situations with customers, played by other employees. It's a rich way of hearing what the customers' concerns and expectations are and how the company is willing and able to respond.

Periodic surveys of employee awareness of and attitudes toward the company's customer value commitments and customer value segments conducted with human resources assistance can be invaluable. Start with an analysis of a benchmark survey to assess existing levels of understanding, then update the data at least twice per year. Internal newsletters focusing on your customer value commitments, changes in customer expectations, success stories, and failures are functional for sharing information and enfranchising employees to participate in value delivery. As new promotional campaigns emerge, make an employee presentation about the campaign, its objectives, its creative rationale, and the customer value segments to which it's targeted. Post the ads as visual reminders of the value delivery mission.

With sales and other functional or departmental management, develop an incentive program for all employees to find new customers, to expand business within existing customer value segments, or to report back customer information. A driver making a delivery could learn about a customer's expansion plans or complaints that may not have made it onto the formal customer service radar screen. Make it worth everyone's effort to bring in a possible lead.

Use E-mail or voice-mail to reinforce the customer value commitment consistently and provide special messages about basic company facts, new customer value commitments, and relationship stories. Hold monthly or quarterly meetings to keep employees current about the mission and to take their questions, even if this is only done departmentally. If management isn't always accessible, a short video from the CEO or COO or CMO responding to employee questions can be made available for on-demand viewing through several technologies.

Many large companies produce an annual report to employees. Separate from the annual stockholder report, it summarizes the year for employees while briefing them on the operations of remote divisions or subsidiaries. Such a report is especially helpful for organizations that have been affected by mergers and acquisitions. Remember that *repetition* builds *fact*.

A simple rating checklist like the Pentadigm customer value commitment checklist in Exhibit 5-1 can help evaluate the customer focus culture within your company.

Plan Customer Value Processes

Organizational alignment to support Pentadigm is crucial to long-term sustainable profit. A company's organizational form, including management, people, resources, measurement, and compensation structures needs to support the Pentadigm model. The plan for all of these starts with the identification and definition of the customer value processes.

You've probably been exposed to many creative organizational frameworks that claim to make a business flatter, leaner, and with empowered workers who are better in touch with customers. As we discussed in the previous chapter, the concept of "form follows value" advocates something more—concentrating every resource in every function where it can be directly connected to what your target customers most value in your offer, from planning and finance to product development and marketing, from manufacturing to human resources.

For example, if a large manufacturer has technical expertise that directly links to creating value for customers, it might decide to keep this expertise in its business. Whatever the day-to-day operational needs of the technical function are, they're secondary if technical expertise doesn't provide customer value and drive the manufacturer's profitability. Once your business understands that the most critical value-creating activities are based on customer priorities, you can decide how to manage other less directly connected resources to run the business.

Extend the example of the large manufacturer to its payroll-processing department. While the manufacturer's employees want to get paid, the critical ques-

EXHIBIT 5-1

Customer Value Commitment Checklist

Scale: 1 is Disagree Strongly, 2 is Disagree, 3 is Neither Agree nor Disagree, 4 is Agree, and 5 is Strongly Agree.

QUESTIONS	SCORE	NEEDS IMPROVEMENT
We have detailed information on our customers.		
We know what our competitors offer.		
We can define which customer segments are the most profitable.		
We know the cost to acquire, keep, and serve our customers.		
Our employees have the responsibility and authority to solve customer problems.		
We regularly assess how well we meet customers' needs.		
We analyze why we lose orders and customers.		
We resolve our customers' issues and complaints effectively and to their satisfaction.		
We learn from customer queries and complaints and change what we do.		
We understand what makes our most valuable customers loyal.		

tion is whether payroll efficiency makes a direct contribution to the customer value commitments. Is the manufacturer's payroll function something that responds to customer value expectations? If not, perhaps outsourcing or contracting for such services would allow the manufacturer to allocate more resources to functions that do provide value.

A classic example of value-driven resource management that created value for its customers, because its organizational form concentrated resources and people around the processes most critical to its target customers, is Nike. These are contributors, but Nike's profitability was due to exceptional alignment of resources to what customers valued. Nike wasn't profitable due to its low labor cost or because its marketing was exceptional at convincing people to spend a lot of money for its shoes. Interestingly, Nike has manufactured almost nothing in its history except air bladders. Nike shoes are manufactured through alliances with other companies.

The traditional business mantra is that manufacturing is absolutely critical and brings great value to the customer, and that without manufacturing there would be no Nike shoes to sell in the marketplace. Absolutely true. But Nike formed its organization around the customer values that have the *most* impact on customers. Even though manufacturing is a vital function, Nike realized that there were ways to manage this function, thereby both maintaining its focus on the critical customer value areas and saving cost.

Nike's target buyers were interested in the latest innovative performance products. You might argue that Nike's products don't perform better than its competitors' products. But Nike's marketing identified a segment of the global population who thinks the image, technology, and design of Nike's products has the edge they need to live their life at a higher level of performance. This customer value segment was willing to pay for this value and, as a result, consistently bought the latest and greatest Nike products.

To meet these target customers' expectations, Nike had three critical value-creating resources: (1) design/R&D for new products, (2) marketing to drive the demand, and (3) distribution to make certain the latest most innovative products are available to customers quickly. These drove the growth, not Nike's manufacturing expertise or breadth of product. In general, Nike did an outstanding job of achieving maximum profitable growth, high productivity, low cost, and the flexibility to respond to fast-changing consumer tastes.

Marketing by Nike in fact did convince many people to use its products, but the customers also had the option to buy a different brand. Faced with fierce competition, Nike allocated scarce talent and money for marketing rather than for manufacturing. Achieving a Six Sigma level of quality also added little value for the buyers because Nike consumers were consistently buying the latest products. Nike recognized this trend, which minimized the need for long-lasting high-quality designs and investments. Nike created an organization that had the ability to innovate. Those parts of the organization that hindered innovation were better accomplished through partnership with suppliers. In addition, Nike never had to worry about being locked into old manufacturing technology.

If you're running a business where the customers value the latest high-performance innovation, in what capabilities will you invest? Why is manufacturing often a hindrance to a business supplying customers who crave the latest innovations? If you work for a manufacturer, you need to appreciate how your capital investments work for or against being innovative.

The structure of your company's functions, resources, assets, and people is determined once you figure out the winning customer value commitment for your target customer value segments—form follows value. Avoid the temptation to debate whether you ought to outsource manufacturing, R&D, or any function to make the business more profitable before you've done the customer value commitment background. Otherwise, you're starting in the wrong place.

Populate Customer Value Processes

There is one capital asset your organization has that no competitor can duplicate— your people. Delivering value requires people who have specific skills and competencies for all customer value processes. This means having assessed what skills and competencies are required at all functional levels, identified the gaps, and quantified the human resource needs for each process. Since creating value typically represents major organizational and cultural changes, you have to have an effective people training and development system in place. Most importantly, you must measure and reward performance linked to customer value creation and delivery.

This is one of the most difficult cultural and organizational transitions for a company to make when shifting from a product-centric strategy to a customer value commitment culture. As we've said repeatedly, "form follows value" and the form of management, measurement, and compensation must follow value. This enables your business to concentrate training and rewards on the key people critical to customer value, rather than spread across many people and functions with variable links to value.

There is a major disconnect when a sales manager says, "I know we're talking about value and solutions and CLV, but then I get called every month and am asked what my revenues are. It's hard to think about the future when you're being driven by the present." There's a major disconnect when customer service representatives are evaluated based on how many calls they can turn each hour and therefore don't believe that or understand how their function can legitimately impact customer relationships and profitability.

If organizational performance—from sales and marketing to operations, customer service, and other support functions—is managed, measured, and compensated on the basis of revenues (transactions), the organizational focus will be on transactions and revenue rather than long-term relationships and CLV. It's a matter of acquiring a fast nickel or a slow dime.

All of this reinforces why a customer value culture *must* be led and driven from the top of an organization. When the organization is managed, measured on, and compensated for CLV, the focus becomes the customers' value expectations and relationship maintenance. The emphasis is on the long-term $100,000 profit to be gained from the customer relationship rather than the short-term $5,000 of revenue. Quarterly revenues are relevant. But the revenues from the current quarter should have been "seeded" a year or two or three years ago.

Managing a value-driven organization means that CLV must be measured and compensated for. One company's approach is to provide a bonus pool from which everyone has the chance to draw. Sales reps aren't on commission; they're paid a relatively good salary and then earn bonuses based on the value of their customer relationships. The value of these relationships can be calculated in a number of ways, including on an actual or average value basis. Some customer relationships are very difficult to acquire but easy to maintain once acquired. Others are very easy to acquire but difficult to maintain over time. Fifty percent of each year's bonus is drawn and 50 percent is added to the sales reps' bonus bank. As the value of the managed relationships increases, so do the bonus and the bonus bank value. The sales reps now have incentive to focus on long-term customer profitability. A major by-product is that the sales force experiences more stability and less churn, which benefits the customer by having someone who can proactively anticipate the customer's changing value expectations and then manage those changes. The result is more business, increasing CLV from the customer relationship, and more profit.

But sales isn't the only function responsible for customer relationships and CLV, so each business unit and employee needs to know the quantified extent to which it has an impact on the customer relationship. This compensates value-driven behavior and allows everyone to participate in the bonus. Measurement of value performance is based on a combination of the customers' Preferred Vendor Ratings, Customer Satisfaction Data, and CLV. If on-time delivery (OTD) is 25 percent of a customer's value expectation, then every function which has responsibility for OTD would share 25 percent of the bonus according to its percentage of responsibility. If billing accuracy and timeliness is 5 percent of the customer's satisfaction, then all shifts in the billing department share 5 percent of the annual bonus. If technical service response time is 15 percent of the customer's value, the technical service function is eligible for 15 percent of the bonus pool.

One hundred percent of the bonus is awarded if the metrics are between 100–95 percent; 95 percent of the bonus is awarded for ratings from 95–90 percent; 90 percent of the bonus for ratings from 90–85 percent; 85 percent of the bonus is given for ratings from 85–80 percent, and there is no bonus for anything below 80 percent.

Invest in Appropriate Infrastructure

When Southwest Airlines took off on its maiden flight in 1971, it joined an industry with a legacy composed of small regional airlines that had succeeded and grown because they had focused on customer value commitments. Success was an albatross for most regionals as they decided that bigger was better, that passengers wanted to travel farther than point-to-point. They adapted their business resources, processes, and even their aircraft fleets to become like the "big boys." Painting with a very broad brush, airlines in the hub-and-spoke world try to be all things to all passengers. This proves costly. Reducing cost ultimately reduces the value for every passenger. Processes falter and airline employees lose their customer focus. Many competitors were lost to bankruptcies or acquisition transitioning from successful regionals to national carriers.

Southwest Airlines took a different approach from its inception, resisting the siren song that had grounded other carriers like PeopleExpress. The seventh largest airline in the United States in 2001, Southwest remains extremely profitable despite expanding its regional airline strategy nationwide. In 2001, the airline generated $5.55 billion in sales and was the number one airline performer in North America in profits, profits as a percentage of assets, profits as a percentage of revenue, and earnings share growth from 1990 to 2001.

From 1996 to 2001, Southwest generated total return to investor of 33.7 percent, beating the first most-admired company GE, who returned 21.2 percent from 1996 to 2001. Additionally, industry peers ranked Southwest Airlines number one in Innovation, Employee Talent, Quality of Management, Social Responsibility, Financial Performance, Use of Assets, and Investment Value. For eleven consecutive years, Southwest ranked number one in fewest customer complaints, according to the U.S. Department of Transportation's Air Travel Consumer Report. The airline began the first profit-sharing plan in the U.S. airline industry in 1974. Through this plan, employees own about 10 percent of the company's stock. And the airline is approximately 81 percent unionized.

In 2002, despite the falloff in business following the September 11, 2001, terrorist attacks in the United States, Southwest Airlines continued to prosper, while everyone around them floundered. In the second quarter of 2002, Southwest reported a $102.3 million profit, with bigger rivals reporting heavy losses for the same period. In 2002, Southwest ranked as the fourth largest U.S. airline in terms of domestic customers carried and carried 90 percent of all discount air travel in America.

Southwest is one of the most admired companies in America according to the March 4, 2002, issue of *Fortune*. Southwest ranked second among companies across all industry groups and first in the airline industry in the magazine's 2002 America's Most Admired Companies list. Among airlines, Southwest came out on top as the most admired airline in the world for 1997, 1998, 1999, and 2000.

In an industry where competitor behavior reflects a belief that the only way to operate is to control airports and routes and maximize hubs, Southwest Airlines defines what it means to be an airline from a customer value point of view, a company where form follows value. This is reflected in the business decisions it makes, the employees it hires, the planes it buys and flies, and the decision not to provide food service.

Southwest's primary target customer is a short-haul business traveler. Everything the airline does aligns with the customer's three key value drivers: (1) fast, efficient transportation from Point A to B, (2) more economical than any other form of transportation, and (3) an enjoyable experience. While casual and vacation flyers may choose Southwest, these travelers aren't the airlines' primary target customers. Southwest hasn't altered its customer value commitments to satisfy the expectations of these travelers while sacrificing the value drivers of its core target customer value segments. A message from Southwest President and Chief Operating Officer Colleen Barrett on the company's website in mid-2002 reinforced this position. "I can promise that we are doing everything possible to minimize your inconvenience (due to long lines and a boarding process impacted by federal security directives). Air travel needs to be not only secure, but also convenient, and we are pledged to be both secure and convenient." The key point is that Southwest first considers the needs of its target customers and then develops an appropriate infrastructure.

Infrastructure can be developed internally or can involve other channel members and third parties. For many customer value segments, you may choose not to or be unable to provide all of the value expected to your customers directly. Success can depend on the effectiveness of your strategy and management of the channel members. Numerous channel options are available, from direct sales to E-commerce and from supplier delivery to distribution, wholesalers, or specialized channels. A single channel strategy may be able to meet a customer value segment's needs completely or could miss opportunities to fulfill customer value expectations. A multiple-channel strategy might be necessary to fulfill customer needs and expectations, but then you have the challenges of managing branding, positioning, and cross-channel pricing. A targeted channel strategy needs to be based on clear understanding of customer value segment needs and analysis of your competitive position and ability.

The function of a channel partner is to provide some form of customer value. The function could be to

- supply products to the end user
- improve the efficiency of the supply process
- improve the range of products/services available to the end user
- balance economies of scale—the need for large-scale production and small-scale usage
- provide a local efficient service to local customers
- fulfill the different needs of different customer value segments
- provide new and better solutions for customers by fulfilling unmet needs

It's critical to establish what that value is and how relevant it is to the target customer value segment.

This value provided by the channel can be multi-faceted, and may involve one or more aspects of the order-to-payment process as well as aspects of the marketing and sales process. The key question to be answered is "How can this channel meet or exceed the customers' needs and value expectations and be mutually profitable?" The channel must also provide value to the supplier.

The generic Pentadigm classification model includes Standard, Mass-Customized, or Value-Commitment channels as described in Exhibit 5-2. Standard channel means the same base customer value commitments for each customer value segment. Mass-customized channel means customer value commitments are created and managed by the customer value segments for which they're provided. Value-commitment channel means that the customer value segments themselves dictate how the channel participates in delivering the customer value commitments.

EXHIBIT 5-2

Pentadigm Generic Channel Options Matrix

	OWNED	PARTNERSHIP	PROCURED
STANDARD CHANNEL	Sales and marketing, company website, order taking	Purchasing cooperative	Outsourced purchasing
MASS-CUSTOMIZED CHANNEL	Customer and technical services	Company credit cards	Delivery services, billing, and collection
VALUE-COMMITMENT CHANNEL	Key account management	Account database	Contract negotiating service

Channel options can be defined as *owned*, which means it's the supplier's function; *partnership*, which means that the supplier has created an affiliation with a channel member to deliver the value; or *procured*, which means that the value delivery responsibility is outsourced. Putting these channel options together into a matrix and plotting each element of the offering helps optimize the channel selection, its management, and the customer value commitments to respective customer value segments.

The channel options matrix helps you easily define which elements of the offering will be provided solely from within the company, which will be provided through some form of partnership between supplier and channel, and which will be outsourced. This analysis ensures clarity of role definition for each channel member, assures that each party in the channel understands the value delivery for which it is solely or jointly responsible, avoids duplication of value, and enables appropriate sharing of value created. A fundamental basis for any channel decision is a clear segmentation of the ultimate customer, and a detailed understanding of the needs and buying behavior of those customers. This is the theme of Pentadigm Step 1, Understand the Customer, discussed in Chapter 3.

To assist in channel selection, a simple question should be asked of the customer value segment: "What are the five key offerings of your preferred or ideal supplier source for products or services listed in order of importance?" This information can be organized quickly into a Customer Value Expectations Priority Matrix like the one described in Exhibit 5-3. This knowledge can help you select the appropriate channel to serve the target customer value segment.

Once you're convinced of the ability of one or more channels to fulfill the customers' needs, you must also ensure that the channel can fulfill your requirements. A scoring method for evaluating the ability of each channel to provide the

EXHIBIT 5-3

Customer Value Expectations Priority Matrix for One Customer Value Segment

How well does the channel fulfill customer needs?

CUSTOMER NEEDS: IMPORTANCE

	1	2	3	4	5
1			Expert advice		
2				Fast delivery	
3		Prompt service			
4	Wide choice				Additional services
5					

CHANNEL CAPABILITY TO FULFILL CUSTOMER NEED

EXHIBIT 5-4

Scoring Channel Performance for One Customer Value Segment

CHANNEL SELECTION CRITERIA	WEIGHT	CHANNEL 1	CHANNEL 2	CHANNEL 3	CHANNEL 4
Additional Services	30%	80	40	100	40
Fast Delivery	25%	40	20	80	20
Expert Advice	20%	10	10	20	20
Responsiveness	15%	60	20	40	20
Portfolio Depth	10%	80	10	60	80
	100%	**53**	**23**	**66**	**32**

expected customer value is demonstrated in Exhibit 5-4. The importance of each of the key offerings to a customer value segment is weighted on a 100-point basis. Each customer value segment, by definition, would have a different set of criteria. Each of the channels is then scored on each of the customer value commitments by utilizing satisfaction estimates or quantitative research data. By multiplying each of the score attributes by the weighted value and then totaling the results, the channels can be compared on the basis of how well each delivers the expected value. In this example, the third channel is best at delivering the value the customer value segment expects.

Only when you have identified a channel that can fulfill both the customers' needs and the requirements of your business/marketing strategy should you finalize your channel strategy. There may not be an optimum choice, in which case, you must trade off the customer needs and those of the business/marketing strategy and assign the greatest weight and importance to the fulfillment of customer needs. Consideration should also be given to both current and future need fulfillment and capabilities.

The selection of a channel partner or partners is a critical contributor to the success of Pentadigm, yet is often surprisingly underestimated and neglected. Once the roles of the individual channel members have been defined, individual channel partners can be selected. Within a selected channel, the key questions to be answered are (1) How well does the partner fulfill customer needs? and (2) How well does the partner perform against our company-partner selection criteria?

Examples of potentially relevant selection criteria for channel partners are listed in Exhibit 5-5. This isn't intended to be a formulaic blueprint or all-inclusive list. The selection criteria for your channel partners should be based on what value expectations you would expect a channel partner to provide that you can't.

Scoring is accomplished using the same approach described previously for assessing channel performance by customer value segment. The importance of each of the selection criteria is weighted on a 100-point basis. Each of the potential channel partners is then rated, as shown in Exhibit 5-6 on page 93. By multiplying each of the partner's ratings by the weighted value and then adding the results, the partners can be compared on the basis of how well each satisfies the selection criteria. In this example, the third channel partner is rated as best at being able to deliver the value you expect from a channel partner serving this customer value segment.

Another crucial aspect of infrastructure, not to be underestimated or to be taken lightly, is that of information and communications technology and systems. We're not experts in these technologies, but we would urge a systematic and pragmatic approach to their design and selection in order to avoid the mistakes of many who have invested vast sums of money in supposed "state-of-the-art" technologies without first figuring out what they needed. The Gartner Group has estimated and reported that hundreds of billions of dollars were invested in information technology (IT) in the 1990s for customer relationship management and E-business without returning a single dollar of profit to those investors.

Since "form follows value," you must first figure out what your customers value and design the processes to deliver that value, and then define the information and communications technology and systems that will deliver that value most cost-effectively. In today's global environment, successful value commitment com-

EXHIBIT 5-5

Example of Channel Partner Selection Criteria

PARTNER SELECTION CRITERIA	CHARACTERISTICS
Financial strength	Revenue, profit and loss, balance sheet
Sales strength	Number and competence
Product lines	Competing, compatible, complementary
Reputation	Leadership, position in business/market, expertise
Market coverage	Geographic, industry, segment, intensity
Sales performance	General growth, account penetration, success reaching target markets, after-sales
Management strength	Planning, employee relations, marketing orientation, strategic direction
Communications program	Integrated marcom based on customer value commitment
Training programs	Self-delivered, supplier participation
Sales compensation	Based on contribution margin or other profitability measure
Plant, equipment, facilities	Transport and delivery methods and record, inventory levels and management, warehousing
Order and payment processes	Credit references
Installation and repair services	After-sales, warranty service
Quality of demonstrators	Experience of staff
Willingness to commit to individual brands	Demonstrated history of behavior
Willingness to cooperate in joint programs	Demonstrated history of behavior
Willingness to share data: market, customers, sales force, inventory, delivery	Demonstrated history of behavior

panies have consistent technology platforms enterprise-wide, enabling a free, easy, and rapid exchange and sharing of knowledge, with accessibility around the world from corporate and remote locations.

In a world of increasingly rapid change, knowledge affords enormous customer competitive advantages. The winning companies will be those who have the fastest access to knowledge about customers, markets, the competition, and so on, and those companies who excel at sharing such knowledge within their organization and with their marketing partners and using such knowledge to impact business results.

EXHIBIT 5-6

Example Assessment of Potential Channel Partners

PARTNER SELECTION CRITERIA	WEIGHT	PARTNER 1	PARTNER 2	PARTNER 3	PARTNER 4
Financial strength	10%	80	75	90	100
Sales strength	15%	85	75	100	85
Reputation	10%	100	80	95	90
Market coverage	25%	90	90	95	80
Sales performance	15%	90	90	100	90
Management strength	10%	85	100	90	90
Willingness to commit to individual brands	5%	90	100	75	75
Willingness to cooperate in joint programs	5%	90	100	75	75
Willingness to share data	5%	70	65	50	40
	100%	**87.75**	**86.00**	**91.25**	**83.75**

Implement Customer Value

Implementation of a value-based customer focus is a key challenge for many companies. The challenge is exacerbated by the constant demands of the bean counters to reduce costs by reducing headcount and outsourcing "non-core" activities. These initiatives put increased pressure on the staff and infrastructure that survive such programs. However, the staff are often given little or no help to enable them to work more effectively or more efficiently. There are already myriad texts on this subject and we cannot do full justice to it in just a few paragraphs. Nevertheless, we would like to encourage our readers to adopt some simple practices that we have found useful in oiling the wheels of implementation.

First, implementation can only succeed if you have identified and clearly defined all the actions that need to happen in order for your customer value commitments to be delivered to your chosen target customer value segments. In order to be sure that you don't overlook something, we recommend taking each line of your customer value commitment and breaking it down into all the constituent elements of the marketing mix that are needed to create that customer value commitment. For the purposes of an example, assume that one of your customer value commitments is to be first to the innovator customer value segment with innovative, leading-edge products. One of the commitment elements that will help you create and deliver the value is to be the first to expose your customers to innovations from your R&D labs. A simple customer value commitment matrix like the one in Exhibit 5-7 can be linked to the Pentadigm Action Plan.

Next, complete the Pentadigm Action Plan template, described in Exhibit 5-8, following these guidelines.

EXHIBIT 5-7

Simple Customer Value Commitment Template

CUSTOMER VALUE	COMMITMENT ELEMENT
1. To be first to the Innovator customer value segment with innovative, leading-edge products	1. To be the first to expose our customers to innovations from our R&D labs
	2. To develop a meaningful feedback mechanism from these meetings for the R&D function

1. All actions should be defined specifically in a complete sentence with subject, verb, and object—shorthand statements are too ambiguous and ambiguity breeds uncertainty, which leads to lack of action.

2. All actions must be owned by an individual. Even if that individual recruits others to help complete the action, the named individual takes ultimate ownership and responsibility for the action being completed accurately within the agreed upon time line.

3. Timings must be specific dates. "Q1, 2003" means January 1 to some and 31 March to others—so always use a specific date, month, and year. For those of you working in global companies, we recommend writing the month in words so that there can be no confusion: "02/12/2003" means February 12, 2003, to an American and 2 December 2003 to a European.

4. Time needed is a realistic estimate of the time needed to complete the task. This is important for two reasons. First, it enables you to calculate the full amount of resources needed for implementation. Second, it enables each individual to be fully aware of his or her commitments and to set them against available time. One of the greatest mistakes made in implementation is over-committing time. Many old clichés are the truth and the reality in this step, for example, "If a job's worth doing, it's worth doing well," "You can't fit a quart into a pint pot." Or for the metric-minded, "You can't contain a liter in a half-liter jug."

5. Desired outcome should clearly describe what is the final outcome or result of the action. Once again, we recommend a full description and not shorthand. As simple as this may be, we've never seen such a simple and practical linkage between the customer value commitment and an action plan in any business text.

We recommend two simple matrices in setting the priorities for cost-effective, efficient implementation of your customer value commitment.

In Matrix 1 in Exhibit 5-9, each individual action is plotted on the matrix based on their delivery of customer value and their ease of implementation. The "Winners" actions should receive the highest priority, indicated by the *A*. Winners' actions are those which most readily enable you to deliver superior customer value.

EXHIBIT 5-8

Customer Value Commitment Action Plan Template

CUSTOMER COMMITMENT ACTION PLAN

CUSTOMER COMMITMENT DETAIL		ENHANCED ACTION PLAN				
Customer Value	Commitment Element	Action Detail	By Whom	By When	Time Needed	Desired Outcome
1. To be first to the Innovator customer value segment with innovative, leading-edge products	1. To be the first to expose your customers to innovations from your R&D labs	1. Define a monthly R&D outputs review with key customer value segments	Marcom Director	31 November 2002	2 person days	A one-year schedule arranged with customers in the target customer value segment for monthly R&D reviews
		2. Commit one-half day each month to sharing your latest capabilities and technologies with the customer value segment	R&D Director	15 November 2002	0.5 person days each month	Ensure that customers will be able to quickly benefit from our latest ideas and technology
	2. To develop a meaningful feedback mechanism from these meetings for the R&D function	Etc.				
2. Etc.						
3.						

The "Strive for Improvement" actions, indicated by the *B*, should be your second priority. These are the actions that enable you to deliver superior customer value that you are not currently proficient in providing. For those actions in the "Wasted Energy" sector, focus on reexamining the actions against the value drivers of your target customer value segments to identify your capabilities that add no value. Either take away the value-added things you do at a cost to you that have no value for the

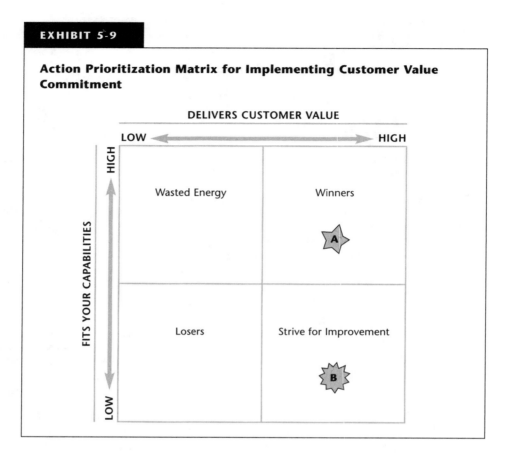

EXHIBIT 5-9

Action Prioritization Matrix for Implementing Customer Value Commitment

customer or shift these actions to "Winners." "Loser" actions receive the lowest or no priority and probably should be removed from your action list.

The classification in Matrix 2 in Exhibit 5-10 is based on Ease of Implementation of the customer value commitment and the Impact on customer value or your business results. Focus on the "Must-Do/Quick Hits" actions, the *A* in the "High/High" sector of the Matrix. The second priority is *B*, "Strategic Wins," where the impact is high despite the difficulty with implementation. The actions in the high ease of implementation—indicated by the *C* in the "Low Impact" sector—may be infrastructure items which still need to be undertaken.

The rule is that you need to prioritize all actions required to implement customer value in the customer value segments, define and design the organization required to create and deliver customer value, and deploy resources appropriately for the customer.

EXHIBIT 5-10

Impact Prioritization Matrix for Implementing Customer Value Commitment

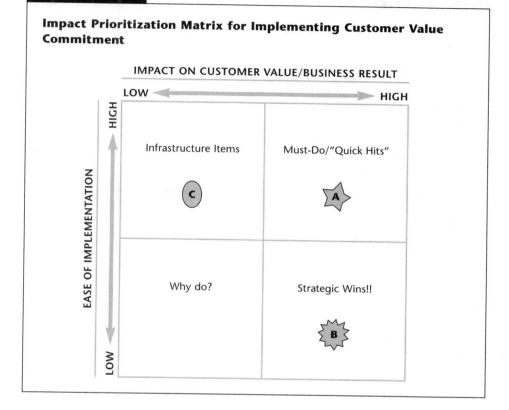

KEY INSIGHTS

1. Customer value processes must be identified, defined, and implemented. This goes against the concept of focusing on core competencies and insists that the company's activities be aligned to excellence in the processes necessary to deliver superior value to the customer.

2. Link staff motivation to customer value delivery through training and development programs, scorecards, and compensation systems.

3. Plan customer value processes before defining, designing, and investing in infrastructure.

4. Lead all customer value creation from the top.

5. Link all actions to the elements of the customer value commitment—if they don't add customer value, don't do them. And prioritize all actions based on customer value creation, business impact, and ease and capability of implementation.

CHECKLIST

❑ Have you developed a customer culture throughout the organization and empowered the workforce to implement it? Is it led from the top?

❑ Have you planned the key customer value processes?

❑ Have you populated your customer value processes by defining the requisite people skills and competencies, deploying people resources, training and developing the staff, and measuring and compensating for value performance?

❑ Have you invested in an infrastructure to deliver customer value by building knowledge management systems, defining a channel strategy, and selecting channel partners and using E-commerce where appropriate?

❑ Have you implemented a customer value orientation by planning and prioritizing your actions, defining and implementing organizational structure to support customer value, and deploying resources accordingly?

CHAPTER 6

STEP 4: ASSESS— OBTAIN CUSTOMER FEEDBACK

Get the facts, or the facts will get you. And when you get them, get them right or they will get you wrong.

—Thomas Fuller, preacher and author (1608–1661)

It's been calculated many times that the cost of winning a new customer is somewhere between 5 and 100 times greater than retaining a current customer, depending upon the nature of your business.[1] But most companies don't know exactly why business was won or lost; overlooked is a detailed and rigorous examination of wonlost business. The more undifferentiated or "commoditized" a business is or the more a business is being driven toward competitive tendering, the more critical it is to track and monitor business and the reasons for success and/or failure.

For example, in the concrete products business in the United Kingdom, a significant proportion of sales are derived from annual tenders to local authorities for their road construction and street maintenance projects. The tenders are issued once per year, typically around December, and as a rule, bidders are given three months to submit their tenders. For some concrete suppliers that means submitting tenders to as many as 64 different UK local authorities. Clearly, this is a huge work burden, especially if starting from scratch each year.

One successful supplier, for whom one of us used to work, had on staff an individual who had managed these local authority tenders for many years as a fulltime job. Three months each year were spent writing and submitting the tenders and nine months were spent investigating why the company won and lost business. Questions asked included the following:

- Who were the competitors in the bidding?
- Against which ones were we successful or unsuccessful and why?

- What did the competitors' customer value commitments look like compared to ours, that is, what were the similarities and the differences?
- What were the value drivers for supplier choice for the respective local authorities?
- What were the successful and unsuccessful price levels and the differentials in pricing? This was relevant to make sure that apples were compared with apples.

The company's track record in winning tenders was very good, but that was due to the rigor with which one individual tracked every single tender. A key to being successful is knowing what to bid by knowing what contributed to success or failure. Pay particular attention to the time frames involved. This individual spent three months creating and submitting tenders and nine months—three times as long—investigating the whys and wherefores of the tender successes and failures.

Often this type of won-lost analysis can only be achieved by assigning someone to pursue it who hasn't been directly involved in the customer relationships in order to ensure an objective and unbiased breakdown.

At another company we know, the Managing Director assumes the specific role of following up on all lost business. The recommendation is, at a minimum, to have someone track won-lost business and, in the best-case scenario, to appoint a Lost and Won Business Manager. The value derived will be gains in customer retention and bottom-line success.

Five Actions in Pentadigm Step 4: Assess

Did you ever ask your spouse or significant other, "Why me?" Why is the answer to that question relevant to you? Haven't you made the sale, acquired the relationship? And what's this have to do with business?

A number of our clients can't answer the question, "How did you get the business?" or "Why did you lose the business?" They're so focused on the next sale, the next transaction, that the reason business was won or lost is moot. It just "is."

The fourth Pentadigm step is required to make sure that Steps 1, 2, and 3 have value for the customer and are profitable for you. Step 4 is all about assessment, obtaining customer feedback in several forms and from several sources. This enables you to validate that (1) the value being delivered to the customers in a customer value segment is in line with or, preferably, exceeds their expectations and (2) you are proactively identifying the shifts, changes, and evolution of your customers' value expectations.

Step 4 in the Pentadigm model has to be integrated with the other four steps—each of which is important to bottom-line success through value-based marketing. The five-step combination is important. Feedback may come at any step. Step 4 is a formal step to catch something that has been done very well or something that has been missed. It may be something you didn't pick up from your tracking of Pentadigm Steps 1 or 2 or 3. Be open to as full as possible feedback on the customer's response to your customer value commitment from all possible points in Pentadigm.

Assess includes five major actions:

1. *Track won and lost business.* The reasons for won and lost business must be rigorously examined systematically and regularly, ideally by an objective won-lost business manager.

2. *Proactively seek customer feedback.* All customer interfaces should be identified and integrated into appropriate feedback systems that track meaningful measures.

3. *Resolve customer complaints.* Analysis isn't beneficial without implementing corrective actions.

4. *Assess performance against customer expectations.* In addition to regular direct contact with customers, we also recommend obtaining feedback via independent third parties. A key is to communicate the results internally and to your customers so that the customer value commitment is understood.

5. *Combine analyses to improve.* Regular analysis helps to identify what you are doing well so that you can reinforce and repeat, and to identify the gaps in your value performance against customer expectations, thus permitting appropriate corrective actions.

Track Won and Lost Business

Tracking is looking at customer value segments after the fact to understand why you won or lost the business. It's evaluating where you've been and it's anticipating where you're going. As businesses become more customer-oriented, satisfaction and loyalty measures are becoming the norm.

The assumption has traditionally been that if customers are continuing to buy from you that they must be satisfied and loyal and that you are therefore a value-oriented organization. This assumption is false; there are any number of legitimate reasons for repeat buying behavior that have nothing to do with your customer value commitment. What you measure and how you measure the actual value delivered to customers is an acid test of how product- or value-oriented your business really is. Equally important is how you interpret the findings of your measures. There is research evidence to show that even customers who give a 75 percent rating of satisfaction are indifferent to the supplier and could easily be won to a more attractive competitive offering.

The Pentadigm Value Ratio chain is $V^A \geq V^P \geq V^E$. The Actual Value delivered (V^A) should be greater than or equal to the Promised Value (V^P). The key measurement is whether or not you met or exceeded the customer value commitment that was promised if the customer made the purchase decision. This is what needs to be measured and communicated to customers. Being able to state that "We delivered $3.75 million in savings to customers with the average customer receiving $295" is more powerful than "We offer you value."

This helps explain why many studies on loyalty and satisfaction effectiveness often report that it's the highly satisfied or loyal customers who defect. The company just didn't realize it was one benefit more or less away from losing its customers.

A simple checklist is all that is needed for you to start tracking won-lost business:

- Customer details
- Customer history
- Business under investigation
- Business won or lost
- Reason for business won or lost [verbatim from the buying decision maker(s)]
- For lost business: How can the business be regained?
- For won business: How can the business be retained in the future?

A *caveat*: it is extremely important that these questions are asked and investigated by someone not involved in the sale.

As one of our clients reported in 2001, "I have always marveled at the lost and won business reports submitted by our salespeople. When we win business, the favorite reason quoted is 'The excellent relationship that the salesperson has with the customer.' When we lose business, the favorite reason quoted is 'The price was not competitive' and never the excellent relationship that the competitor's salesperson has with the customer."

There are four simple mechanisms that are extremely useful in gathering relevant customer feedback to supplement a won-lost business analysis:

1. *Customer-Initiated Feedback*—questions and complaints generated by customers.

2. *Regular Surveys*—customer fulfillment assessments before becoming a customer and after ordering.

3. *Defector Research*—surveys with lost customers to identify root causes and to take corrective actions.

4. *Customer Groups*—ongoing assessments of performance and gaps.

Proactively Seek Customer Feedback

We've alluded to the high cost of discovering and developing new customers versus the wisdom of retaining existing customers. Customer retention demands a high attention to customer loyalty, which is built on fulfilling customer needs and managing the total customer relationship. Most companies don't use the natural interfaces with their customers to obtain knowledge about those customers.

In managing the customer interface you must first identify all the possible interfaces with the customer, many of which either are overlooked totally or are given scant regard. These would include, but are not limited to, initial awareness of your company, inquiries made to your company, placing an order, making payment, interaction with corporate and business management, marketing, sales, supply chain, R&D, manufacturing, customer service and technical support, and intermediate channels—arguably every person or function in the organization that touches a customer either directly or indirectly.

You also shouldn't overlook the post-sale contacts, such as after-sales service, invoicing, complaints handling, and satisfaction research, as well as recycling and packaging returns. Everyone in your company should be primed to seek and be rewarded for sharing customer feedback through the natural day-to-day, week-to-week, month-to-month interactions with the customer.

The marketing director for a bottled water company told us a story about customer interface not realizing how enlightened her solution was. Katie realized shortly after taking over her position that the delivery and customer service functions frequently worked against the company's customer-focused value position and even against one another. Drivers would fail to deliver the water or coffee break supplies to the right location in the client company or fail to deliver the invoice to the proper individual. Customer service identified so strongly with the customers that the fault for delivery miscues were accepted out of hand as being a driver problem.

If a customer has a complaint, that's feedback in its simplest form. But complaints also threaten relationships. You must deal with a customer complaint quickly, efficiently, and to the customer's satisfaction. A by-product of this response is to reinforce your commitment to customer value.

Katie proposed an idea which management approved with a few reservations. Each of the drivers worked for a week in customer service, fielding calls with a customer service representative (CSR) partner. They began to realize what the response was when they parked the delivery truck in the wrong location or trundled the bottles across the main lobby instead of using the freight elevator.

Katie then required each of the CSRs to ride the truck with their driver partner for a week; she took the initial ride. CSRs learned what it was like to have to maneuver a truck to a far part of the delivery area, dolly the bottles up the freight elevator in the back of the building for delivery to the employee break room in the front of the building on the fourth floor, and then stop in a second-floor corner office to hand an invoice to a person who might or might not be at his or her desk. The resulting empathy by both the drivers and the CSRs for each other's position resulted in a commitment to partner more closely in assuring that the customers' expectations were met, avoiding a number of customer complaints.

Perhaps a more important by-product of the exchange was the realization that both the drivers and the CSRs knew a lot about the customers' expectations and satisfaction levels, in many cases more than was known by management and marketing. Katie developed a short field intelligence report to be submitted to her that could be filled out by anyone having contact with a customer.

For example, a driver delivering to a customer hears that the company is opening another office in a different state. The water company can proactively call to establish service at the new location when it opens rather than have to wait to be contacted by the customer, perhaps delaying the initiation of the additional service. Or a driver reporting that the desks are empty and people are sitting around reading or talking or playing video games at one of the accounts could have identified a credit risk. These intelligence reports have both monetary and other rewards for the people whose insights result in improved delivery of customer value or increased profitability.

One of our clients had a weekly sales force meeting to share and discuss "the word on the street." The sales manager gave a $100 prize to the salesperson who shared a customer objection that she or he wasn't able to overcome. Success stories were also shared, but it was important for the people to be able to admit a loss and to share what happened so that the group could learn how to anticipate and deal with the objection and to develop the "best case" responses.

In Chapter 4, we presented five questions that also provide a framework for obtaining customer feedback. This brief list can be easily remembered by everyone in your company who has a customer interface. These questions should be top of mind and used as a framework for feedback dialog every time there is an opportunity to do so. These questions shouldn't simply be asked directly and bluntly. But they could be asked in a number of different ways in a variety of sequences using different wording to obtain the relevant information. The basic questions are:

1. What does the customer's world look like today?

2. Where do the costs of your offering figure in your customer's total cost picture?

3. What keeps the customer awake at night wondering how the business could be improved?

4. What's the value to the customer of such improvement?

5. What will change in the customer's world in the next three years?

Your customers possess rich data that should also be mined. Many will conduct their own satisfaction surveys to assess supplier performance. Many will have implemented formal Preferred Supplier Lists (PSLs). In either case, the items that are being measured represent the customer's value expectations, its desired benefits, and relative costs. They may also benchmark your performance against suppliers from completely different industry sectors, which may be important for you to understand in terms of the standards they are expecting based on their experience with those other suppliers.

The basic objective of a PSL is to reduce the cost and risk in the purchasing process through a constant process of evaluating and prequalifying suppliers. The criteria are carefully developed to reflect what's critical in a supplier's performance and have a tendency to be more objective and quantified than satisfaction assessments.

Criteria could include tracking on-time delivery, quality, price or delta price, inventory management, responsiveness, and flexibility. A specific measurement or formula is derived for each item, which is then weighted and combined with the other criteria to typically create a 100-point rating.

As a simple example, Wal-Mart cooperated with P&G to develop a best-in-class order and supply process for P&G products to Wal-Mart outlets. This resulted in a significant reduction in Wal-Mart's costs. Wal-Mart then applied this benchmark to suppliers of other products reasoning that if P&G could offer that level of service at low cost, Wal-Mart shouldn't pay for the inefficiencies of other suppliers' ordering and supply systems.

The data derived from the PSL have a tendency to be more objective than subjective, and can be a very sound benchmark from which to build a needs- and behavior-based customer value segmentation. Your own company may have a PSL. Talk to the people in purchasing and find out:

- What are the evaluation criteria?
- How are these criteria measured?
- How do the top three suppliers perform in relationship to all the others?
- What relevance does this information have for your company's purchasing process?

A sales manager we knew once called a customer and asked, "Do you have a Preferred Supplier List and, if you do, would you share the criteria with us so that we can make sure that we're focusing on the proper value expectations?" The response was, "Yes, we have a Preferred Supplier List, but the criteria are proprietary and secret." The sales manager was flabbergasted. One of the primary functions of PSL criteria is to let suppliers know up front what they will have to deliver to be able to sell to the customer. This was a dumb purchaser playing his cards so closely to the chest that it made itself a risky, if not unprofitable, customer. The sales manager knew not to ask the second question, which would have been, "How are we performing in relationship to your other suppliers?"

Even more troubling, however, is that for every sales manager who asks this question regularly of its customers, there are nine who don't think about or don't ask this question. By discovering, understanding, and focusing on these drivers, from whatever source is available, you have a stronger segmentation basis upon which to build a meaningful strategy and compelling offering to your customer.

A couple of final lessons. Understand that any time you solicit customer feedback you are raising the customers' expectations that you will be doing something as a result of the data you obtain. You can't go through the motions of gathering data without the customers understanding what has happened or will happen as a result. When you don't do anything, it's just as important to explain to the customer why you won't be doing what they suggest. This follow-up discussion still builds your relationship because you acknowledge the customer's views, and it gives another chance for the customers to give further insight or potentially correct any misconception you may have come away with.

It's also relevant to understand that customers are surveyed to death. The question that has to be answered is, "What's the value added for a customer if it participates in your feedback mechanism?" An obvious response is that a summary of the feedback will be shared. This has several implications for you and the customer. One, it helps you to demonstrate to the customer the value which you are providing or, if there are gaps, a chance to state what you're doing to improve the customer value commitment. It can also afford you the opportunity to demonstrate your company's performance in relationship to that of competitors. Your feedback could be value-added for a customer that doesn't have the inclination or the wherewithal to do its own research.

Finally, data that aren't shared data have no value. You must ensure that in all customer interfaces and contacts, customer and primary research data are recorded and shared in a system where it's easy to enter and access information. There are several providers of such systems in the market. The key is that these data are invaluable to understanding and managing your value relationships.

Resolve Customer Complaints

The majority of companies spend 95 percent of their customer service time fixing problems and only 5 percent analyzing why they had a problem in the first place. If your customer complaints were segmented into three generic categories, you'd find a general pattern in terms of how customer retention is affected.

Category 1 customers, for example, are those whose complaints weren't recognized and, as a result, weren't resolved. A typical retention rate among these customers is less than 10 percent. Category 2 customers are those whose complaint was registered but wasn't resolved to the customers' satisfaction. A typical retention rate among these customers is around 20 percent. Category 3 customers are those whose complaints are recognized and solved. The typical retention rate for this group is 54 percent.

Customer complaints must be managed, which means you must be empathetic and responsive. Your customer complaint process should satisfy these expectations.

1. It should be easy for customers to complain.

2. Customer complaints should be acknowledged.

3. Promise a response within a specific time frame and stick to that commitment.

4. Propose a solution.

5. Check that the customer is satisfied or more than satisfied with the proposed solution.

6. Those handling complaints must be empowered to resolve them.

7. Log all complaints in detail and then analyze them to understand the causes.

8. Complaints should be handled by a human being, not a phone system or computer. If you use an automated system, make it easy for customers to find a person to speak with; don't just circle them back to the options menu of automated responses.

Assess Performance Against Customer Expectations

It's always interested us how a simple resolution of a customer problem results exponentially in retention and increased business, which directly impacts the customer lifetime value (CLV). If you assess your performance against your customer expectations, you'll add value to your offerings.

There's a story in customer service folklore about the man who walked into a Spokane, Washington, bank and asked to have his parking ticket validated. The teller looked at the senior citizen dressed in worn, faded blue jeans, plaid shirt with a torn pocket, well-worn dirty boots, and a stained Resistol cowboy hat and asked if he had conducted business in the bank. "No," the man replied. "I just came in to get my parking validated." The teller informed him that the validation was only for customers conducting transactions. Did the man have an account with the bank? He did. "Then you should know the rules," the teller advised him.

The customer asked to see the manager. "Gone to a meeting," he was told. What about the assistant manager? "At the same meeting," was the reply. "I'll wait," the man said and he sat down in one of the lobby's chairs. Thirty minutes later the manager returned and seeing the man sitting there, walked over and greeted him. "Good morning, Mr. Miller. What can we do for you today?" The customer's response was that he wanted all of his accounts closed and the money transferred to a rival bank. As the story goes, the accounts represented more than $4 million and almost 10 percent of the bank's total customer deposits. Mr. Miller was one of the largest ranchers in the area. For a one dollar parking ticket validation, the bank lost millions in deposits.

Should the bank teller have bent the rules? After all, rules are rules. The teller was correct. The bank's policy was parking validation only for customers conducting transactions. The customer's expectation was unreasonable, given that rule.

Should the bank have had a different set of rules for customers based on the sizes of their accounts? Would the teller have bent the rules had he or she recognized the customer for who he was? Or should all customers be treated equally? Should the bank have made the rules clearer so the customer wouldn't have had an unrealistic expectation? Or should the bank be more flexible to meet customers' unspoken expectations? What's your answer?

If employees truly understand your business—which means your value commitment, customers, and operations—they need to be able to make judgments in cases that may seem outside the strict interpretation of the business rules. Given that *caveat* in this case, the teller would have recognized the poorly worded business rule and made the judgment to validate the parking ticket. It makes one wonder whether the bank trained its employees to use judgment.

We might also argue that, if the bank truly knew its customers, it would know that they were using the parking lot on occasion for other than bank business. Perhaps the bank should encourage its customers to park in its lot free of charge as a convenience while shopping in the neighborhood. This would also benefit other area merchants.

Whatever your answers to these questions, the bank should have had a better understanding of its customers' expectations, and its customer value commitment should have been designed accordingly.

It can be beneficial at times to invest in primary research to gather data in addition to that provided from internal or customer sources. The function of this research is to gather data where none exist, to supplement the data you have, or to validate the current data.

Historically, marketing managers and marketing researchers haven't made good bedfellows. The marketing managers unrealistically expect the research to provide answers, and they often don't understand the time line, complexities, and nuances of valid, reliable research. The key to obtaining relevant data that can help validate your success in delivering customer value is to manage and be involved with the marketing research process rather than handing it over to a researcher to provide the "absolute" answers.

The first step in managing customer and market research is to decide what business decisions can be improved meaningfully by the results of market/customer research. This will identify when such research is needed to discover relevant information about whether or not customer value expectations have been understood and met.

Also, customer and market research can be useful in terms of validating the informal data. This requires a clear understanding of how the data will be used in your decision making, so that you and the researcher can define the scope of the research project. Customer and market research can help if a company wants to understand the needs and satisfaction levels of potential customers (with whom it does not currently trade) or to obtain an objective benchmark of performance relative to competition.

The second step is to collect and analyze secondary data; this is information that has been gleaned from existing sources outside your company. Secondary data include obvious sources from the customers' industry like trade publications, industry association data, industry analyses, and customer press releases about won business, especially if you weren't the supplier selected. In some cases, these data will answer your questions. More often than not, the secondary findings provide additional questions that need to be answered and/or validate the research design.

Once the research objective has been formulated and the secondary data scanned, identify knowledge gaps relative to the business decisions to be made and write the specific research questions that need to be answered. You should share responsibility with the market researcher for developing and approving the research method, whether it's in-depth interviews, surveys, or customer focus groups, for example, or a combination of data-gathering methods. Understanding the design and its intent makes it easier for you to understand the data and apply them in the decision-making process.

Whatever you do, don't prevent the customers from expressing their real views and opinions. Many customer research programs utilize closed questions and checklists, often internally developed, for misguided reasons of expediency, cost limitation, and ease of analysis. The result is usually a misinformed supplier and a frustrated customer. Your customer survey should include open-ended questions to allow customers to identify what they see as the key priorities and areas of unsatisfactory performance.

Be prepared to support the research with a financial commitment. The budget should not be established on the basis of cost justification, that is, the question to the researcher shouldn't be "What kind of research can we do for $10,000?" The question should be "What do we have to spend to learn what we need to know?" If it takes $10,000, but the resulting profitability from the customer value segment increases by $100,000 annually, that's a good return on investment. If it takes $50,000, but the resulting profitability from the customer value segment increases by $100,000 annually, it's still a good ROI.

The next step in a customer and market research process is selecting the sample. The research objectives and project design could require an investigation of all of the customers in the customer value segment or simply a representative sample of customers.

With the sample identified, the data can be collected. An important hint for this stage of the research is to not send the researcher away with a mandate to do his or her "voodoo." Stay informed about the data collection, obtain reports of preliminary findings, and be involved actively in ensuring the research is achieving your objectives. In addition to funding involvement, it makes sense whenever possible to participate in the data collection. In this way research findings will come alive to the management team as they have heard and seen firsthand responses from customers. It's also a great way to build relationships directly with customers.

Once the data are collected, the researcher analyzes and interprets the data. Again, that doesn't mean the researcher is going to provide answers to the research questions. It means that the researcher will help organize the data points and look for relevant indicators. Make sure that you understand what the data indicate and their relevance to your decision-making needs. Be able to explain some of the more technical nuances of data collection or data reduction and analysis.

The last step in managing the research process is to integrate the data into what is already known about customers' reactions to the value you believe you have been delivering. Never forget that decisions are made based not only on data, but also on intuition and experience.

Combine Analyses to Improve

The following data reflect something we all know through experience, if not intuitively. Depending on your data source, as many as 91 percent of your unhappy customers—nine out of ten—will never purchase from you again. The average business doesn't hear from 96 percent of its unhappy customers, which means you never have an opportunity to correct the situation. Each of these customers will tell the story about the value that wasn't delivered to somewhere between 10 and 16 other people or companies. The 4 percent who bring a problem to your attention have the expectation that you'll correct it. A prompt effort to resolve a dissatisfied customer's issue will result in roughly 85 percent of them repeating as customers. You can obtain customer satisfaction data from your industry association or by doing a google.com search for "customer satisfaction."

A CEO we know had a negative experience with a computer manufacturer when the computer company was in its infancy and the executive was beginning her career. Her purchasing department has a mandate to never buy any hardware or software from the computer company, even if that company would pay the client's company to take the equipment. Institutional memory usually focuses on the most recent and negative behavior rather than the long-term track record and the positive value that has been delivered.

Most of our clients still have archaic planning processes and procedures which are driven by an annual reporting system that is driven, in turn, by the bean counters. There's an old cliché that the accountants know the cost of everything and the value of nothing. You need to establish a dynamic strategy and planning process that reflects the nature of your marketplace, your business, and the speed of change. Establish flexible time frames within which you will review and correct strategy and tactics, rather than the dogmatic time frames associated with the traditional corporate planning approach.

For companies whose fiscal year is the calendar year, planning begins in July with the strategic course for the following year set by the beginning of the fourth quarter (Q4) in October. The problem is that if there's a major change in your customers' needs happening in Q1 of the next year and your strategic plan for that year won't be approved until Q4 of this year, you could be too late to react.

Rather than planning January to December, business and marketing plans should be dynamic, constructed on a *rolling* basis to reflect the last 12 months of business and to project three years ahead—that is, an annual detailed plan and three-year forecast, updated at least quarterly if not monthly.

The objective of a rolling planning process based on dynamic tracking doesn't necessitate a U-turn in the customer value commitment or supporting business processes from one month to the next. That would have horrendous profitability implications. A rolling, dynamic planning process means that you're always checking, which helps you keep ahead of the customers' needs and expectations, to update your understanding of the customer, your commitment to the customer, and your ability to create, deliver, and capture customer value.

It's also important to encourage multi-level, multi-functional contacts with customers, as we've mentioned several times. But it is equally important to appoint an account responsible person—an *account manager*—for all sizes, types, and classes of customers. The person chosen will depend upon the nature of the account and may also be driven by the key relationship with the account. For instance, if there is a large amount of development work, you might select a research person as the account manager; if the account is more dependent upon customer service, the account manager should be appointed from the customer service organization.

The key is to ensure that someone in your organization feels responsible for that customer and feels empowered to represent the customer within your organization, and that the customer knows someone is representing their interests within your company. The more important the customer, the more senior the account manager should be. In some companies, there may be a case for a cadre of senior corporate account managers, handling very large accounts with multiple business unit and functional interfaces.

The customer account managers should be responsible for providing feedback for each stage of Pentadigm. No customer is so unimportant as to not warrant an account manager, meaning that *every* customer is important enough to warrant an account manager.

It's also extremely important to make sure that all data gathered about won-lost business, customer satisfaction and loyalty, and your company's responses intended to improve your customer value commitment are communicated internally and shared with customers. This has multiple effects. It reminds everyone in your organization about what value drivers are important to the customer value segments and it indicates how well you are performing against not only the competition, but against the customers' expectations. It validates for customers your commitment to providing value and gives them tangible, quantifiable assessments of how the value you deliver is equal to or greater than the value that was proposed prior to the purchase decision. Customers buy value, not products or services. This is another way of reinforcing that behavior.

KEY INSIGHTS

1. Appoint someone to own and be responsible for tracking and researching won-lost business and give them the authority and teeth to do something with their findings.

2. Five simple questions should frame all conversations with customers:

   a. What does the customer's world look like today?

   b. Where do the costs of your offering figure in the total cost picture?

   c. What keeps the customer awake at night?

   d. What's the value to the customer of such improvement?

   e. What will change in the customer's world in the next three years?

3. Data not shared are useless and of no value.

4. Ensure that customers have the freedom of expression to identify to you their priority issues and where you are not meeting their expectations.

5. Reinforce the positives; improve the areas of dissatisfaction and underperformance.

6. All accounts—whatever size—deserve an account manager.

CHECKLIST

❑ Are you tracking and analyzing won-lost business?

❑ Are you proactively seeking customer feedback by identifying all customer interfaces and developing appropriate feedback systems and tracking measures?

❑ Are you prepared to manage and efficiently resolve customer queries and complaints and to implement corrective actions?

❑ Are you assessing customer satisfaction regularly through external research, and communicating the results internally and to your customers?

❑ Are you analyzing all customer feedback, identifying the gaps in performance against customer expectations, and implementing appropriate corrective actions?

STEP 5: IMPROVE — MEASURE AND IMPROVE VALUE

Even if you're on the right track, you'll get run over if you just sit there.
—Will Rogers

Value-based marketing for bottom-line success is dynamic and continuous, driven by the fact that customers' needs and value expectations are dynamic and continuous, not static. The value ratio changes with time—as Desired Benefits and Relative Costs are satisfied, new value expectations appear.

Remember Ziroli's Italian Ristorante from Chapter 2, the one you frequent, passing other Italian restaurants between your house and its location because it gives you more value? The first time you went there your value expectations were relatively simple. Your Desired Benefits included a broad selection of good-tasting food in appropriate portions, responsive service, and a pleasant ambience. Your Relative Costs concern was how much time it would take to drive to the restaurant, the amount of time it would take to be seated and served, the risk of food poisoning, and the price.

After six months of regular patronage, most of the Desired Benefits have now become an expected given. Relative Costs are also a constant; the restaurant has not changed its approach to business. But your expectations have now changed. In addition to expecting to be greeted by name and be escorted to your favorite table between the front window and the salad bar, you also expect them to know your favorite aperitif, your predilection for certain types of food, and other likes and dislikes relating to your eating experience. Your needs have changed and your expectations are higher—you have raised the bar for the restaurant just to stay at the same level in your order of satisfaction.

In itself, this is a challenge for the restaurant. But what if its world has also changed? The restaurant owners, their focus shifted to churning tables every 45 instead of every 60 minutes, change the seating process. The hostess is now simply a scheduler, a coordinator who passes patrons off to the first available waiter or wait-ress or busboy for seating, giving the guide an impersonal number that makes you feel like a shift worker. For efficiency, the drink, appetizer, and entrée orders are all taken at once. The salad is delivered before you're halfway through the appetizer, the entrée before the salad is done, and the inquiry about whether or not you'd care for dessert this evening is delivered with the check. Parking is now by valet only.

The restaurant has abandoned understanding, much less satisfying, your value expectations. Even the "How was everything tonight, Mr. Debalski?" is a now rote recitation. So, the next time a friend or colleague or spouse asks, "Where would you like to have dinner?" Ziroli's isn't even on the radar screen.

Planning to provide the same value for your customer value segments next year that you did this year by definition reduces the value you provide and they will derive. You were originally selected as a supplier because you provided cost effi-ciencies. But your customers are in a competitive battle to remain in front of the competition in their industry. Next year they need innovation from you.

Five Actions in Pentadigm Step 5: Improve

To maintain bottom-line success through value-based marketing, questions need to be asked and answered in order for you to enhance your customer value com-mitments. You must formally update your understanding of your customers' needs and expectations and choose to make the necessary improvements where there are gaps. The feedback obtained in Pentadigm Step 4 may require you to go back to Step 1 and ask, "What don't I understand about the customer today?" It may require a recommitment to value or improvement in the way you create value. It may require you to change the feedback mechanisms in Step 4. You may have to say, "We're not understanding the unmet needs of the customer. We're not asking the right questions."

Coca-Cola's disastrous launch of its new formula has been analyzed to death. At the simplest level, the research failed to ask focus group participants enough questions, the right questions, or understand their buying behavior. When asked if the new Coke formula tasted better than the old, focus group members said *yes*. After the public outcry against the change, it became apparent that the unasked question was the crucial one. "Does the new Coke taste significantly better, enough to get you to switch from the traditional formula?" The answer was overwhelm-ingly *no*.

Hindsight is 20/20, but Coke needed to test the behavior of Coke drinkers when given a choice. Coke relaunched the original formula as Classic Coke, which was a huge marketing success, and the rest, tritely phrased, "is history."

Measure and improve means auditing and evaluating customer value segments for their marketing impact and their ability to provide profitability. It means that anticipating customers' changing needs and expectations by identifying future trends is also required to maintain a position as a value leader. Finally, you must update and enrich your customer value commitments by refining your customer value processes, the population of them, and the infrastructure to support them.

Improve includes five major actions which follow effective measuring.

1. *Spot gaps and "quick-hits."* These are items arising from an analysis of regular and systematic measures that need to be in place to track results and performance on customer value.

2. *Challenge customer understanding.* Customer value needs and expectations are dynamic, not static.

3. *Redefine customer value commitments.* Changing customer value expectations requires a redefinition of your customer value commitment.

4. *Improve customer value.* As value needs are fulfilled, the value ratio changes.

5. *Anticipate change.* Your customer value commitments result in a better understanding of future customer value needs and expectations. Your ability to anticipate these changes enhances the value of both your customer commitment and customer relationships.

Spot Gaps and "Quick Hits"

The intent of business measurement is to achieve two main objectives. One, measurement provides information that potentially enables improvement or correction to the goal achievement. These data should indicate where you are delivering value that is important to your customers and where you are failing to do so. It's important to reinforce the former, but where gaps exist, it's necessary to reexamine your basic segmentation strategy or redefine your customer commiment. Remember that Pentadigm is intended to be mutually beneficial, that is, delivering expected value to customers while being profitable for you.

Two, business measurement provides a relative position assessment on how well something is being accomplished at a certain point in time relative to a goal. Consider your customer commitments balanced against your cost to serve your target customer value segments and their profitability. You may be forced to make choices. In either case, create an action plan for improving customer satisfaction with measurable goals and a timetable, and then constantly monitor the plan and adjust it when necessary. Mine the data and results for any immediate issues or problems that need resolving or whose resolution would provide an immediate benefit or "quick hit." These are the short-term motivators to pursue the longer-term gains.

While the intent of measurement is often right, what typically plays out in business is somewhere in the spectrum of either measuring everything or a claim that some things just cannot be measured—a leap of faith is required.

Marketing is a function that traditionally requires such a leap of faith. Often, marketing spending and results seem to be only vaguely linked. In cases where a business has a history of marketing initiatives that parallel successful growth, it's not uncommon to find faith guiding decisions more than a marketing discipline. Even companies considered marketing masters, such as Toyota, Coke, Procter & Gamble, and Apple can shake one's faith in marketing after seeing their best efforts fail in the marketplace despite their use of hard data. Does the Toyota T-100 pick-up truck ring a bell?

Value-based marketing and measurements of outcomes need to be connected, but not always in terms of marketing cause and effect. The delivery of customer value commitments requires more than just marketing. For example, aggressive marketing for cellular phone services often generated a high response, but the inability of the service providers to actually provide the services desired meant that response rate didn't correlate with revenues or profitability.

Value-based marketing is an integral process. Any measurement of results must assess how the business is interacting with customers at all of its touch points and how it's running all business processes to provide its value commitments effectively.

A business frequently misses meeting goals, not because it's not measuring, but because it's

- measuring things in the wrong order
- measuring the wrong things about customers
- measuring a consolidated view of the market and customers
- measuring what matters to business efficiency, not customers
- measuring its product against competition
- measuring too much

Measuring in the Wrong Order

The business may be measuring important things in the wrong order of when they should be measured, such as measuring and improving its product quality or supply chain or manufacturing efficiency before it knows whether the specific improvements really make a difference to customers. In an organization with diverse capabilities, this can be particularly acute. Every function and team member acknowledges and acts upon the company's goal to improve.

The flurry of plans, actions, and results gets measured every time the dust settles, and every report describes improved performance, except maybe with the customers. The measurements do tell how much faster the product is getting to customers and how good this is for the business's inventory management; but it's not measuring the impact on the customer's operation. More demoralizing occurs when the customer has noticed your improvement and has also noticed the competition made a similar improvement effort. So it's back to working harder and faster, to only get tougher negotiation with customers with each improvement.

The Performance Measurement Matrix in Exhibit 7-1 describes the Pentadigm approach to prioritizing measurement. This performance measurement matrix is developed around customer value based logic. It starts with measuring what value matters to customers and ends with the measurement of how much money a business made. Profits are a result of providing superior value to customers.

First, determine what value factors are critical to customers. CTVs (critical to value) are those value drivers identified for each customer segment that the business has determined form the basis of a superior customer value commitment for each of the respective segments. For example, the goal of Cutting Edge, in Chapter 1, was to provide better innovation value to the automotive industry. "Better innovation" is vague and hard to measure. So Cutting Edge needed to measure the financial impact of the innovation for the automotive company for each design submitted. Cutting Edge also needed to measure and track each innovative design's cumulative contribution to the automotive company's business performance. Without the type of CTV information for the opportunities that Cutting Edge pursued, the best a business can ever hope for is to improve its transactional and product performance. If it competes in an industry of aggressive competitors, such as the automotive industry, this performance is a hard road of short-term wins.

In transforming a business into a value-based marketer, CTV factors should be the most important focal point of measurement because CTVs are what matter most to the customers' purchasing decisions and process. Finding the winning value with customers is the starting point for everything else happening in the business. Realistically, many traditional measurements may stay in place in the near-term to improve transaction and product performance while the business discovers the value most meaningful to customers.

However, the business team needs to have the courage to lead the transition to replace current metrics with CTV metrics as the first measurement priority when running the business. Otherwise, the business will be seduced into believing that the current improvement measures (for example, lowering sales channel costs) are indicators of how well the business is being run. Value-based marketers, though, won't know if the lower sales channel costs are a good thing until they can assess the sales channel's performance relative to the customer value commitments and how the costs that impact particular customer segments are being lowered.

Once a business has clear CTVs to focus on, the second step is to measure whether changing processes, systems, resources, suppliers, and/or people can deliver on the value commitments to customers. Value-based marketing shouldn't be confused with the marketing technique of simply changing the customers' perception of a product through clever promotional campaigns. Value-based marketing is about

EXHIBIT 7-1

Value-Based Marketer's Measurement Priorities Matrix

MEASUREMENT PRIORITY	KNOWLEDGE GOAL	WHAT NEEDS TO BE ASSESSED	KEY FACTORS	WHAT TO MEASURE	WHEN TO MEASURE	HOW TO MEASURE
1. MEASURES WHAT REALLY MATTERS TO CUSTOMERS?	**Determine Customer Value** Do you really have value that will be important to customers?	**Real Value?** • Value segments • Value commitment • Historical and current customer performance • Value gaps	• CTV (Critical to Value) factors • CTV's results within segment	• Gaps within CTV factors • CTV's results in segments	Ongoing activity to gather insight and information with semiannual assessment	Six Sigma Methodology
2. MEASURES HOW WELL YOUR BUSINESS IS TRANSFORMING ITSELF?	**Form Follows Value** Are you aligning people, process, systems, budgets, metrics?	**Processes, plans, systems, suppliers** • Networks, channels • Partnerships • Alliances	Process, systems, and enterprise response to CTV factors	• Organizational changes • People alignment • Process improvement	Quarterly	Six Sigma Methodology
3. MEASURES HOW CUSTOMERS RESPOND TO YOUR VALUE?	**Customer Insight** What are customer's actions and responses?	**Superior Value?** Assess the customer's behavior and value expectations	• Who makes decisions • Basis of buying decisions • Why customers make decisions	• Sales cycle time • Customer turnover • Price response	Every time customer wants to do business	Six Sigma Methodology
4. MEASURES CUSTOMER IMPROVEMENTS FROM VALUE RECEIVED?	**Customer Results** How has the customer's life and business been improved?	**Superior Value?** Is the customer better off?	Customer's recognition of value and their ability to measure your impact to them	Effects on: • Costs • Sales • Profits • Value impact	Semiannually	Six Sigma Methodology
5. MEASURES YOUR BUSINESS RESULTS AND PERFORMANCE?	**Your Results** What have you achieved, changed, and improved?	**Profitable Value?** Is the business succeeding at what it's doing?	• New Business • Retention • Revenue • Costs, margins • Economic profit	Effects on our: • Costs • Sales • Profits Economic profit	Quarterly Annually	Six Sigma Methodology

Source: SYNECTION, LLC, 2002.

creating both better values for customers and a better-run operation that can consistently and profitably deliver the value. Without the right alignment of resources, sustainability is unlikely.

The third priority is to measure how the customer is responding to the value offered. This occurs after measuring the operational changes that are starting to take place. The business can then assess both the customer value it's providing, and its ability to run the operations and market channels through which the value is being delivered. Assessing customer response to value without the operations and channel assessment can give a false read on the market. It could tell that you have a great new customer value but then encourage the operation to be run in the old ways. This only undermines the great new value discovered, as with what has happened to so many cellular phone providers.

The fourth priority and the one ignored by most companies is to measure how the customer is better off with the new value being offered. If the customer isn't better off, it won't be long before the customer discovers alternative value options or just beats upon price terms. Interestingly, with all that has been written about Jack Welch and his successor, Jeff Immelt, in 2002, this point has emerged as perhaps the only difference in their business approaches and what Immelt could build his legacy upon. "Immelt is determined to reshape GE for the next generation . . . making the front-line workers obsessed with helping customers. That's right—obsessed. He will measure managers by how much they improve their customers' bottom lines—something Welch never did—and how much time they spend in front of their customers."[1]

Finally, measure how well you are doing. This is the *result* gained from doing the first four measurement priorities correctly. Ironically, the point of business is to satisfy someone else's needs, yet most of the measurement attention is focused on how the business is doing without knowing how the business makes a difference to its customers. It makes one think sometimes as if all the measurement is just for better pitches to Wall Street. Pentadigm value-based marketers know there will only be a bottom line to measure if their products and services are in high demand from their target customers and they determine first what their specific value link is with customers.

The Wrong Customer Perspective

Businesses often measure the wrong things about customers because the business has created the wrong perspective on its customer, such as believing a better product is better for customers, when in some cases a better price with the existing product is what the customer really values.

This is the time to be brutally honest and ask, "If I were my customer, how would I do what they are trying to do?" Forget about having the best, most wonderful product. The focus needs to be on what the customer is trying to achieve, why they're trying to achieve it, and how it could be better achieved.

The Six Sigma movement, with the Voice of the Customer (VOC) tool, is also prone to helping develop the wrong perspective on the customer. The VOC exercise assumes, often wrongly, that customers are able to describe their most pressing needs. It assumes that customers have enough insight about what they are buying to describe improvements or issues or that changes with customers are substantiated with clear supporting statistical data. Six Sigma also has a hard time with handling the early warning signals that may come from things around a customer, but it can lack clear data.

Consolidated Customer Viewpoints

Many companies, in becoming more customer focused, develop extensive market research surveys that ultimately become part of a consolidated view of customers rather than develop a customer value segmentation approach that recognizes the different value drivers between customer groups. Many customer satisfaction surveys roll up all customers into one database and then analyze the most dominant data points. When the data are consolidated, the top issues, needs, and customer products and services are analyzed to determine where to focus efforts and resources. What the business doesn't learn is that the top-rated needs and issues are not the same for all customers; it just looks that way from the analysis done.

As Exhibit 7-2 shows, without using customer value segments, the business can measure and make decisions based upon a sum total composite of many different customer inputs. The best of the best doesn't emerge. Rather, the best middle-of-the-road answer comes out that doesn't really matter to any one group of customers. The longer a business uses this approach, the more mediocre its results become and the more frustrated it becomes since it can't explain why all its work studying customers has not made a difference.

Measuring What Matters to You

Measuring as though it really matters, but not to the customer, is another common misguided use of measurement. The business has developed measures that it believes are important to its own success and makes assumptions about what the customer's needs are. These assumptions about the customer form the basis of what a business thinks it must do to meet its own success criteria. It focuses totally on execution, measuring frantically against its internal goals and perhaps getting fairly creative along the way to explain what actually happens in the marketplace relative to its goals.

Exhibit 7-3 shows the typical metrics of a company running its business by what's important to it. Usually the product or service forms the core identity for the business, so measurement is centered on the product or service.

Exhibit 7-4 shows how measurements change when using a value-based marketing approach to running a business. The central focal point becomes the cus-

EXHIBIT 7-2

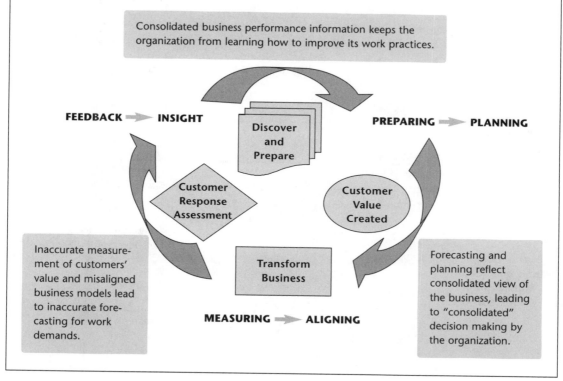

Without Customer Value Segments

Business performance suffers without an aligned organization. Most performance systems tend to reinforce consolidated business priorities.

Consolidated business performance information keeps the organization from learning how to improve its work practices.

FEEDBACK ➡ INSIGHT   PREPARING ➡ PLANNING

Discover and Prepare

Customer Response Assessment

Customer Value Created

Inaccurate measurement of customers' value and misaligned business models lead to inaccurate forecasting for work demands.

Transform Business

Forecasting and planning reflect consolidated view of the business, leading to "consolidated" decision making by the organization.

MEASURING ➡ ALIGNING

tomer value segments and how the business is aligning its costs and resources to provide its customer value commitments.

Measuring Products Against Competition

Measuring the product/service and business performance relative to the competition is based on the fallacy that the business believes the better product, service, or business wins the customer's business. In a world of similar customer options, this works until one competitor wakes up and says "enough" and changes the game based upon new value, technology, product, or service. Great value creators all share the ability to discover new value, even in mature markets. This usually doesn't happen by studying the competition, but by studying the world of the customer.

EXHIBIT 7-3

Typical Product-Focused Metrics

Enterprise Management System

LEADERSHIP/BUSINESS LEVEL

Strategic Enterprise Focus
Making the business numbers
Delivering consistent numbers
Managing assets and organization costs

Common Metrics
- Revenue, volume
- Prices, margins
- Productivity
- ROS, ROA, net income
- Corporate soft targets

Functional and Individual Management System

MANAGEMENT LEVEL

Strategic Focus
Meeting functional or department budgets
Momentum in function/department

Tactical Focus
Juggling conflicting organization and functional demands

Common Metrics
- Costs by functions
- Sales revenue by area
- Volume by products
- Functional variances
- Functional soft targets

INDIVIDUAL LEVEL

Tactical Implementation Focus
Make their individual numbers
Keep customers in the function happy
Resolve conflict between customer requirements, functions, and business

Common Metrics
- Sales revenue by individuals
- Individual budgets
- Soft targets, e.g., new products
- Little influence or connection to customer value
- Personal soft targets

Measuring Too Much

Having more data isn't inherently better. More data can mean a diminishing return in understanding and applying it. Eventually there is so much data that no one remembers what the question was. Or the company suffers from "paralysis by analysis."

Some businesses become so convinced that the latest globally connected customer relationship management (CRM) system will save the day in answering any

EXHIBIT 7-4

Value-Based Marketer's Business Metrics

Enterprise Management System

Functional and Individual Management System

LEADERSHIP/BUSINESS LEVEL

Strategic Enterprise Focus
Making the business numbers
Improving lives and/or businesses of customers
Aligning assets and organization costs to customer segments and DTC/DTS

Common Metrics
- Customer value, capital use
- Numbers: economic profit, margins
- Resource alignment/costs to customer segments
- Implementing value for chosen segment(s) and DTC/DTS

MANAGEMENT LEVEL

Strategic Focus
Meeting the segment customer value plan
Improving customer's performance with their customers
Developing DTS/DTC

Tactical Focus
Implementing chosen segment and customer offers

Common Metrics
- Revenue/profit by segment/customer
- Productivity of resources to deliver value commitments
- Value contribution to each customer segment

INDIVIDUAL LEVEL

Tactical Implementation Focus
Make their numbers by segment
Make a difference each day to customers in customer value segment
Feedback deficiency in value commitments

Common Metrics
- Sales/profit by accounts
- Alignment of offers to segments
- Deviations for value commitments
- Costs per segment/customer

question or targeting customer needs that they lose sight of the two-legged computers they employ who have more data than the Central Intelligence Agency.

The issue isn't more data, but tapping the right data, in the right place, at the right time. Though this is the promise of CRM systems, only a human brain has the processing capability to glean real insight from mounds of data. Otherwise it remains a mound of wabashi. In short, the essence of measurement from a value-based marketer's approach is to make the case within the business that great business performance comes from delivering something of value to customers. The discovery of value can only come from discovering what really will make a difference to the customers' life or business. Measure what will impact customers long before counting how much money the business will make.

Challenge Customer Understanding

Anyone who has teenagers will understand the clothing industry's constant scramble to predict and be on the leading edge of the target customers' expectations. One such company we know has a three-segment strategy view of the world: 18–24, 24–30, and Old People. Understanding these customers is like trying to capture snowflakes to prove that no two are ever identical.

Customers' perceptions are their reality, and perceptions constantly shift. This means that your understanding must also shift. Given the data, are your customer value segments correctly defined? Have new customer value segments appeared and, if so, are they viable, profitable target customer value segments?

One of our chemical company clients conducted a comprehensive study of its end-user customers and identified four needs- and behavior-based customer value segments: Committed, Switchers, Strugglers, and Complacent. For each customer value segment the company had developed a clear customer value commitment and was implementing a well-defined strategy in each customer value segment, shown in Exhibit 7-5A. The new strategies were working well, and the business was being transformed into a much more focused and more profitable enterprise. But after two or three years, it became apparent that the least successful part of the client's customer value commitment strategy was "Stop the Switchers."

This discovery caused the company to reassess its segmentation and identify a new customer value segment that needed to be addressed—the Goners. These were former Switcher customers the client had failed to stop from switching. Based on this insight, a new customer value commitment was created called "Win back the Goners," as shown in Exhibit 7-5B on page 128.

When you're meeting the value expectations for one customer value segment but not another, challenge yourself. Why are you stronger in one and weaker in another? What do you understand about the former and don't understand about the latter? Are your commitments different to the two customer value segments? Why? What about your ability to create value? What does the difference in satisfaction indicate? Do you have enough or the right resources to support the weaker segment?

Redefine Customer Value Commitments

As a result of challenging your customer understanding, your customer value commitments will have to be redefined. Changing customer needs and customer lifetime value means that last year's customer value commitments are already outdated. Organization alignment may have shifted, which could hinder the ability to provide customer value. The competition might have changed its customer value commitments.

The lesson is that satisfaction, for example, may not be the appropriate customer value commitment for a customer value segment where the product has matured into a cash cow with high margins. The customer value commitment may need to be realigned to an exit strategy.

Dow Chemical's Epoxy Products business examined its customer value commitments a number of years ago and recognized that none addressed the needs of a certain customer value segment. This group of customers regularly sought to buy standard epoxy products in bulk quantities in a no-nonsense way at a competitive price. Dow redefined its customer value commitments and created a brand-new cus-

EXHIBIT 7-5A

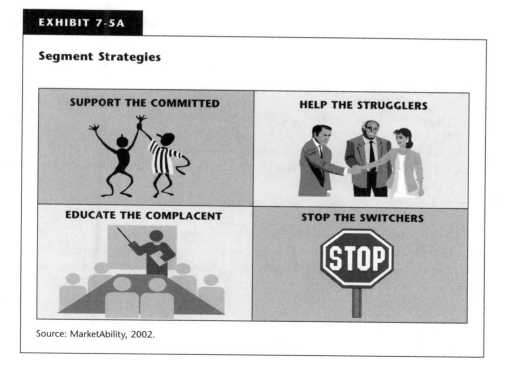

Segment Strategies

SUPPORT THE COMMITTED

HELP THE STRUGGLERS

EDUCATE THE COMPLACENT

STOP THE SWITCHERS

Source: MarketAbility, 2002.

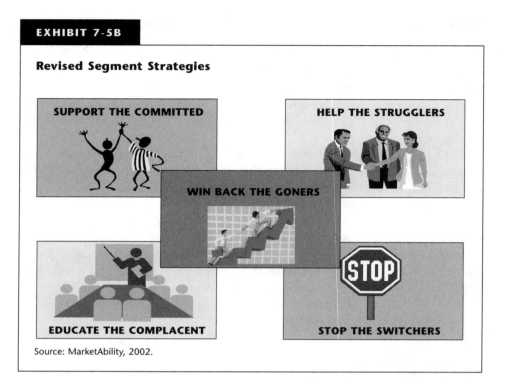

EXHIBIT 7-5B

Revised Segment Strategies

SUPPORT THE COMMITTED

HELP THE STRUGGLERS

WIN BACK THE GONERS

EDUCATE THE COMPLACENT

STOP THE SWITCHERS

Source: MarketAbility, 2002.

tomer value commitment based on a new E-business solution: e-epoxy.com which offers the following:

- *Customer Value Segment:* purchasers of bulk and full truckloads of epoxy
- *Customer Value:* convenient and easy to purchase; transparent pricing
- *Superior Value:* lowest price; easiest to do business with
- *Profitable for Dow:* low cost to serve, adherence to clear business rules, no confusion
- *Banner Headline:* fastest and cheapest bulk epoxy; no-nonsense

According to John Everett, Global Leader of e-epoxy.com, "Our success is clear to see in the number of new accounts we have generated, representing 70 percent of our sales in the first year. Also we have achieved EBITDA breakeven within twelve months of launch."

Improve Customer Value

The next step is to address all the organizational, people, and infrastructure issues based on the changes in customer understanding and customer value commitments.

The root cause of each change needs to be identified, as well as any barriers that could hinder your making the improvement. Following are some techniques we have found helpful.

- Set up a multi-function workshop that involves everyone who could influence the customer satisfaction. Have the participants review, understand, and analyze the data. If they do, they will take ownership for what the data reflect.
- Even better, set up a multi-function workshop with representatives from your own company and the customer company, then review, understand, and analyze the data.
- Separate the changes into short-term (need resolution tomorrow), medium-term (need resolution by next month), and long-term (need resolution before the end of the quarter).
- Brainstorm the gaps or changes and the possible solutions for each category. Brainstorming is a non-evaluative process—no idea is too out-of-the-box or too "not doable."
- Rank the solutions for each from most likely to succeed to least likely to succeed or from easy hanging fruit, low resource no-brainers to those that are more difficult.
- Set measurable target objectives for each solution.
- Assign responsibility for implementation of specific solutions; ownership is assigned in the workshop. There also needs to be someone to chase the solution owners.
- Assign timetables, milestone targets, and review sessions.

Again, don't get caught in the trap of focusing so much on the changes that you forget to reinforce what's operating well. Where your data have indicated that you are doing well in delivering value, you should be looking for ways to enhance the current value delivery and anticipate change.

Take a lesson from Internet failures. Many Internet businesses enjoyed millions of hits on their websites. Unfortunately, many dot-coms rejoiced a little early. Internet use changed.

One of our clients was confronted with a customer who threatened to switch its three-year contract to an alternate supplier. At our suggestion, the client arranged a joint meeting at the customer's location; even the chief purchaser flew in just for the meeting. There were nine representatives from each company at the meeting who represented each aspect of the supplier/customer interface—from sales and purchasing to technical and manufacturing to supply chain and marketing.

The opening negotiation position of the customer's chief purchaser was to tell the client that, without a minimum 20 percent price reduction in the upcoming contract negotiations, it would be ruled out as a supplier for the next three years.

Fortunately, both parties were able to move beyond that gambit and develop some serious discussions.

The major outcome of the day was the identification of 10 key initiatives to address sources of unmet or poorly met customer value needs. Someone from each company was assigned to tackle and jointly resolve each of the 10 key initiatives. Seven of the ten initiatives were successfully achieved prior to the completion of contract negotiations and progress had been made on the other three. Our client won the contract at a 5 percent price revenue increase.

Anticipate Change

As we've mentioned several times, Pentadigm marketers operate in a world of constant and often rapid change. The dynamics of societies, economies, markets, companies, customers, potential customers, and competitors impact the success or failure of the Pentadigm marketer's strategies, commitments, and plans. Pentadigm marketers need to have highly efficient change radar in place to be able to anticipate and respond to these changes.

This means having regular, interactive dialogs with customers and asking pertinent questions about their futures. This means conducting regular economic and market research to anticipate changes in the macro picture. This means monitoring competitor activities closely and regularly reviewing and assessing competitor strategies. All of these activities should be an integral part of your Pentadigm value planning model.

We've all seen planning processes and systems fail because they became a "fill-in-the-blanks" exercise. Planning is a serious process, demanding a high level of analysis and dynamic creativity in the interpretation of data and the development of scenarios; it's not about forgetting the development of your own strategies in the glow of the scenarios.

A number of tools we've discussed can help with this activity. No single tool is a panacea. The better approach is to use each tool and its analysis to shed light on the value issue you're analyzing or the market for which you're creating a value commitment. When the data collectively present a clear picture, make your decisions. Judge the quality of your knowledge and set it against the risks associated with the decisions you have to make, as described in Exhibit 7-6.

There are five important actions that will affect your ability to anticipate and plan for the future.

1. Define the market opportunity or customer value segment based on the customer value sought.

2. Use the PMLC Value Cycle to "predict" where the value is headed in your markets and customer value segments.

3. Use the value planning tool described in Chapter 2 to drive the future, rather than hope you'll be ready when it happens.

4. Have sufficient people in the organization looking at the future to balance those following the day-to-day business.

5. Align your metrics to drive the future of your customer value commitment.

Describing the customer value segment or market opportunity in terms of the value sought by the customer is the first and most fundamental step in changing the mind-set of you and your organization into a Pentadigm customer-value driven mind-set. It is not easy, because it does not come naturally to most of us brought up in a product-driven culture. So it takes practice. Think about these scenarios:

- There is no market for buttons, but there is customer value in closing gaps on clothing to protect decency, to keep warm, or to keep cool and ventilated.

EXHIBIT 7-6

Quality of Knowledge and Business-Decision Risk

	DON'T KNOW	INTERNAL OPINION	INTERNAL FACT	EXTERNAL OPINION	EXTERNAL FACT
VERY HIGH RISK					
HIGH RISK					
MEDIUM RISK					
LOW RISK					
VERY LOW RISK					
	No knowledge	Knowledge based on opinions of own staff	Knowledge grounded in facts derived from own staff	Knowledge based on opinions of customers	Knowledge grounded in facts derived from customers

Source: MarketAbility, 2002.

- There is no market for insulation, but there is customer value in Warm and Comfortable Building Occupants, long-term well-preserved produce, minimized risk of food poisoning, etc.
- There is no market for (your product or service), but there is customer value in the benefit it delivers to your customers. It's your turn to put your own offerings into this simple mind-set change model.

The PMLC value cycle and its four generic Pentadigm customer value segments—Innovator, Optimizer, Operationalizer, and Economizer—can be used to plot current and anticipate future value expectations by examining well-established behavior that exists in all markets. The most important variable is the time between a new introduction and when the product or service no longer matters to customers. To make this tool work for you, you can't rely on your current product orientation, which tends to focus on the changes in the technology, competitors, and products in the market. The key is to focus on the nature of customer value in your markets and customer behavioral characteristics within the four Pentadigm customer value segments or the customer value segments you've defined.

For example, Innovator customers will predominately be interested in the unique advantage of a new technology that enables them to do something better than they can do it today. A new blockbuster drug may be most meaningful today as a unique cure. But the Operationalizer and Economizer customer value segments may not believe in its curing powers or have the capability to affordably access the drug. These customers can and will influence the value in the marketplace for the drug over time. Your firm can determine and anticipate the implication of these value expectations and proactively plan your response.

Customer behavior of three of the four Pentadigm customer value segments on the value cycle for electrical component buyers is shown on the top of Exhibit 7-7. The critical strategy considerations for suppliers and manufacturers of components to these customers are shown in each of the three segments in the value cycle. Whether customers actually exist in these customer value segments already is not as important as accepting that they will exist at some point and that you can anticipate what values will be important to them based upon understanding the four Pentadigm generic customer value segments. If the four customer value segments already exist, then you can anticipate movement up the value curve knowing that, in time, a new Innovator customer value commitment will be developed. This new value commitment will allow Innovator customers to do something else that they can't do today. You can either guess at what that might be, or you can drive the market using the value planning tool.

Strategic value planning, depicted in Exhibit 7-8, is a means by which your company can both influence customer value and create an ongoing laboratory with your customers to develop the next new innovation. In Strategy 1, you describe what you're currently doing and what is possible today. Determining Strategies 2 and 3 requires that you identify what would be the next meaningful value expecta-

EXHIBIT 7-7

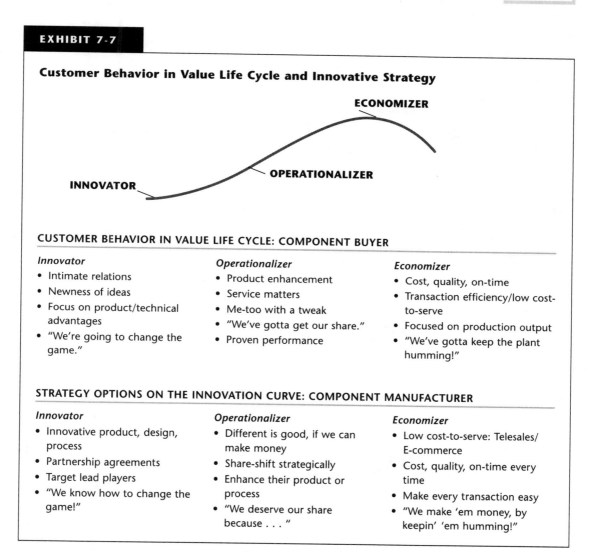

Customer Behavior in Value Life Cycle and Innovative Strategy

ECONOMIZER

OPERATIONALIZER

INNOVATOR

CUSTOMER BEHAVIOR IN VALUE LIFE CYCLE: COMPONENT BUYER

Innovator
- Intimate relations
- Newness of ideas
- Focus on product/technical advantages
- "We're going to change the game."

Operationalizer
- Product enhancement
- Service matters
- Me-too with a tweak
- "We've gotta get our share."
- Proven performance

Economizer
- Cost, quality, on-time
- Transaction efficiency/low cost-to-serve
- Focused on production output
- "We've gotta keep the plant humming!"

STRATEGY OPTIONS ON THE INNOVATION CURVE: COMPONENT MANUFACTURER

Innovator
- Innovative product, design, process
- Partnership agreements
- Target lead players
- "We know how to change the game!"

Operationalizer
- Different is good, if we can make money
- Share-shift strategically
- Enhance their product or process
- "We deserve our share because . . . "

Economizer
- Low cost-to-serve: Telesales/ E-commerce
- Cost, quality, on-time every time
- Make every transaction easy
- "We make 'em money, by keepin' 'em humming!"

tion for customers. Accuracy isn't as critical as creating prototype concepts you can share with customers either by hypothesis or from direct customer input. These value prototypes will help your customers understand better the implications of what you can do for them by seeing what you're talking about. This creates opportunities for customers then to provide far more useful feedback to you, which you can use to refine Strategies 2 and 3.

The fourth item you need to consider is your people. This means having the right people and using the right discipline to anticipate the future. William Bridges points out in *The Character of Organizations* that organizations ". . . differ in character. A play-it-safe, old-line manufacturing company has a very different charac-

EXHIBIT 7-8

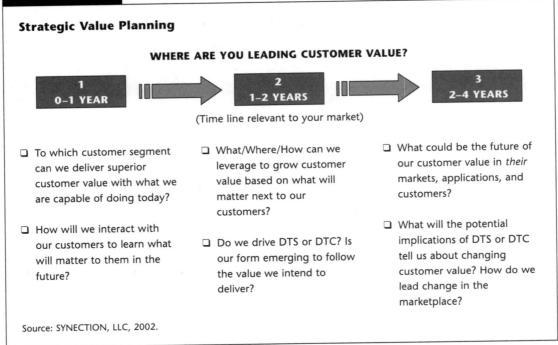

Strategic Value Planning

WHERE ARE YOU LEADING CUSTOMER VALUE?

| 1 0–1 YEAR | → | 2 1–2 YEARS | → | 3 2–4 YEARS |

(Time line relevant to your market)

❑ To which customer segment can we deliver superior customer value with what we are capable of doing today?

❑ How will we interact with our customers to learn what will matter to them in the future?

❑ What/Where/How can we leverage to grow customer value based on what will matter next to our customers?

❑ Do we drive DTS or DTC? Is our form emerging to follow the value we intend to deliver?

❑ What could be the future of our customer value in *their* markets, applications, and customers?

❑ What will the potential implications of DTS or DTC tell us about changing customer value? How do we lead change in the marketplace?

Source: SYNECTION, LLC, 2002.

ter from a new start-up software company. They differ in the same way that two individuals do. And the character of both the manufacturing company and the software company differ from those of a state university, a community hospital, or an architectural firm."[2]

His more relevant insight focuses on how businesses typically evolve from being innovative to being better at running an operation efficiently. This phenomenon is critical to growth, but it affects the people who have been driving the customer value commitment.

As a company focuses more on efficiency, it tends to be less friendly to innovative people. The forward thinkers leave and are replaced by efficiency-oriented people. If your customer value commitments have also evolved to efficiency as the primary value, this may be OK. Odds are, though, that you are trying to manage a mix of customer value segments, including innovators and economizers. The company is evolving to one customer value expectation, but it is still attempting to respond to all the competing needs. Strategy becomes hostage to debates about what customers want.

People focusing on capturing available growth have replaced the people who understood and designed the company's customer value commitments and customer value segments. This results in a myopic perspective, which in turn results in a lack of understanding and an inability to anticipate the changes in customers' value needs and expectations. The company becomes less and less disciplined in its customer value planning, and form is less and less likely to follow value in the future.

You need to be aware of what's happening not only to your cost structure, but also to the way your organization works, to the way it makes decisions, and to changes in the type of people who are making or influencing decisions. Developing Pentadigm as a dynamic model in your organization improves how you see, develop, and capture opportunities, plus it embeds those organizational traits and personalities that are essential for sustainable performance into your business culture.

We've used the Myers-Briggs Type Indicator (MBTI) quite successfully as a personality assessment tool to analyze the people who make up an organization. It can also be very useful in identifying people within an organization who are better suited to anticipate future trends and "predict" how things will change.

The fifth way to anticipate how customer value expectations and your customer value commitments will change in the future is to measure the impact your customer value commitments have on your customer value segments and their businesses. This is the most critical leading indicator of performance and yet often the least measured item. Measuring the impact of your current customer value commitments provides insight into your customers' current decisions and future intent and value needs.

Establishing your future customer value commitments to deepen your customer relationships is something you can plan for and control, as described in Exhibit 7-9. This tool challenges your company to transform its relationship with its customer value segments proactively from selling them products to becoming an integral partner of your customers' businesses.

KEY INSIGHTS

1. The value-based marketing environment is dynamic and constantly changing, and the Pentadigm marketer needs to anticipate those changes to stay ahead.

2. Constantly update, review, and challenge your customer understanding, customer value commitments, customer value creation, and customer feedback.

3. Use tools appropriately and sparingly to improve your decision making. Avoid "box filling," shooting from the hip, and paralysis by analysis.

4. Judge the quality of your knowledge and balance the level of quality against the risk of the decisions.

5. "Good results without good planning come from good luck, not good management." —David Jaquith, President of Vega Industries, Inc.[3]

EXHIBIT 7-9

Connecting Your Customer Value Commitments to Customer Expectations

What's in the mind of the customer at different levels of doing business with you?

NOTE: Levels are not to scale. During transformation and while increasing proficiency between levels, it gets harder as you become more important to the customer.

PROFICIENCY LEVELS OF AFFECTING AND IMPACTING THE CUSTOMER'S SUCCESS AND LIFE

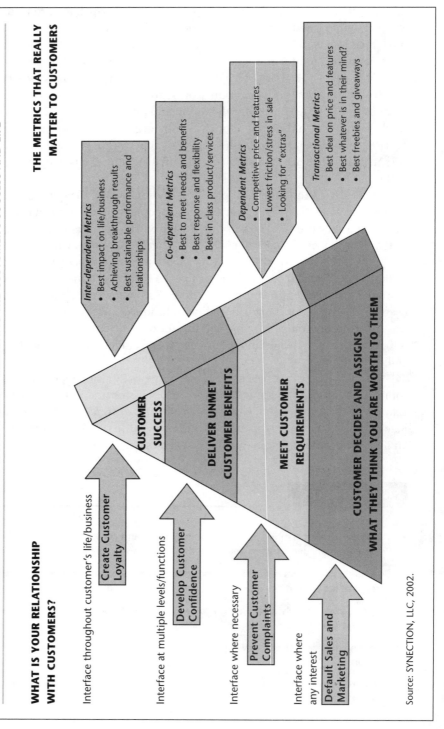

THE METRICS THAT REALLY MATTER TO CUSTOMERS

Inter-dependent Metrics
- Best impact on life/business
- Achieving breakthrough results
- Best sustainable performance and relationships

Co-dependent Metrics
- Best to meet needs and benefits
- Best response and flexibility
- Best in class product/services

Dependent Metrics
- Competitive price and features
- Lowest friction/stress in sale
- Looking for "extras"

Transactional Metrics
- Best deal on price and features
- Best whatever is in their mind?
- Best freebies and giveaways

CUSTOMER SUCCESS

DELIVER UNMET CUSTOMER BENEFITS

MEET CUSTOMER REQUIREMENTS

CUSTOMER DECIDES AND ASSIGNS WHAT THEY THINK YOU ARE WORTH TO THEM

WHAT IS YOUR RELATIONSHIP WITH CUSTOMERS?

Interface throughout customer's life/business

Create Customer Loyalty

Interface at multiple levels/functions

Develop Customer Confidence

Interface where necessary

Prevent Customer Complaints

Interface where any interest

Default Sales and Marketing

Source: SYNECTION, LLC, 2002.

CHECKLIST

❑ Are you measuring and reporting the KPIs, identifying the performance gaps, and defining the necessary improvements?

❑ Are you challenging your understanding of the customer with customer research that improves your customer knowledge, sharing customer data, and critically reviewing your market segmentation?

❑ Do you regularly redefine your commitment to customers by updating and enriching your customer value commitments, service standards, and KPIs in line with changing customer value needs and expectations?

❑ Are you consistently working to improve your customer-focused culture by refining your customer value processes, their population, and the infrastructure to support them?

❑ Do you anticipate change by working to identify future trends and changes, creating and analyzing business scenarios, developing contingency plans, and managing change effectively?

MANAGING
PENTADIGM

One never knows what will happen if things are suddenly changed. But do we know what will happen if they are not changed?

—Elias Canetti, *Die Provinz des Menschen,*
Aufzeichnungen 1942–1972 (1973)

It may seem that the only constant in business today is change. Just when you've begun to see the success of your last business initiative, it's outdated or rejected by the customer or annihilated by the competition.

Business has become increasingly complex. Global economies are inextricably connected, yet each has specific, unique local needs, business and cultural customs, and regulatory environments. Customers have acquired more power and are demanding that suppliers be more responsive to their needs. Competitors aren't always rational. Some employee relationships have been reduced to a grudge match over who will be the first to flinch during the next cost-cutting initiative. It takes a combination of knowledge, insight, intuition, and action to survive the onslaught of competition, market pressures, and customer demands.

The new economy, much like the old economy, has been captivated by a number of myths of business. These myths are ideas, paradigms, norms, and popular truisms that shape the business economy. Ideally, all these ideas are supposed to be for business's well-being and, therefore, for the well-being of everyone in business as well.

Unfortunately, most businesses's grand ideas are unsupportable by facts. Proponents of the big ideas tell us we don't get it and we need to believe. The older we get the less we believe the hype. Given all of this, you may still be wondering if value-based marketing for bottom-line success is relevant in this brave new economy.

Jim Collins cited the explanation of Internet competition by the CEO of a hot Internet company: "It's a big land rush, (the CEO) explained. It's all about being first to build critical mass and create a brand name. His whole strategy hinged on being there fast, be there first and you win." When Collins asked the CEO what would protect his company from the assault by huge companies with deep pockets, the response was, "Inertia! Our competitive advantage is their inertia! By the time they wake up, the game is over and we will have won."[1]

A pattern of trailing entrants prevailing over the innovators is a consistent theme in the history of technological and economic change, according to Collins. He cites as examples the fact that IBM was a Remington-Rand "me too." De Havilland pioneered building commercial jets, not Boeing. Diners Club predated American Express. "Starbucks didn't pioneer high-end coffee, GE didn't pioneer AC electric systems, Wal-Mart didn't pioneer discount retailing, and Excel didn't pioneer the spreadsheet. HP didn't pioneer, but entered late in PCs. JVC didn't pioneer home video. Palm Pilot didn't pioneer electronic organizers."[2]

Pentadigm and Innovation

Business history is rife with companies like Lucent, EMC, Oracle, Qualcomm, Sun, MCI Worldcom, Coke, and Enron that were seemingly unstoppable in their growth and profit machine, but which then faded or failed. Myriad explanations for this phenomenon of business prosperity followed by a painful decline have been written, ranging from loss of focus, loss of leadership, spending too much, lost sight of customers, competitive response, weakening market forces, lack of process, bad systems, wrong employees, employee shortages, arrogance, complacency, and on *ad infinitum*. Before there were accounting scandals, many companies had come to the realization that every quarter it was becoming less possible to meet Wall Street expectations with the way they ran their businesses.

While all of these are relevant factors, the catalyst for decline has a simpler explanation for most businesses. As a business grows, it often loses sight of the value expectations of its customer value segments and its customer value commitments and focuses on growth. In fact, growth becomes the only acceptable goal: growth in revenues and growth in shareholder value—no mention of growth in customer value. It fails to consider whether or not the new customers represent distinctive new customer value segments with significantly different value expectations. Pentadigm demands that the business strategy be driven by customer value and that new customer value segments shouldn't be targeted unless the company can meet or exceed the new value expectations and do so profitably. Once any successful organization, whether a business, sports team, educational institution, or even a religious institution, loses sight of what it's really about and for whom, the organization's decline is inevitable.

This can be acute, particularly for a market innovator. Given a window of opportunity, the company directs as much money, resources, and people as it can afford into selling its innovative product or service ahead of the competition. The supplier slowly begins to believe that all customers are equal, except for the amount they can purchase. Allocation of resources reverts to the familiar pyramid structure designed to gain maximum production capability, often losing sight of the value expectations on which the business was built.

Sales opportunities don't necessarily mean that the business can equally profit from them. The critical issue is what happens to cost structure. The new form of the company follows cost reduction, not value.

Grouping customers into meaningful customer value segments and determining relevant resource costs for each customer value segment is a hard discipline to follow anytime. But it's especially difficult when a business is prospering and the focus needs to be on business development and sales revenue or when the business is floundering and the focus needs to be on cost reduction. The result is a shifting cost structure designed to serve a variety of different customers, not one allocated according to customer values. What happens is that each customer value segment pays for some of the business costs that bring no value to it. Once the business realizes it needs to cut costs to improve performance, each customer value segment loses valuable resources. Costs that are cut during the restructuring can't be assigned to any specific customer value segment. As a result, all customer value segments suffer.

It's also difficult to stick to the original customer value commitments as the market grows and attracts competitors. Competitors enter the market with similar customer value commitments to attract and win business. An insightful, creative competitor selects a customer value segment not well served by the innovator. This niche has its own distinctive value expectations. If the innovator decided to let the niche player have the customer value segment uncontested and the niche player was content with the segment, both could coexist in the market. But that's not the competitive model.

As customers respond to the competitive offers, their value expectations change. The balance between Desired Benefits and Relative Costs may shift, requiring companies to modify their customer value commitments. One customer value segment wants free service calls, another expects marketing incentives, while the value driver for a third customer value segment is next-day delivery on custom orders. Competitors respond by trying to fulfill all three. The reality of the world is some combination of (1) orderly segmentation of markets, (2) follow-the-leader markets, (3) mature, intensely competitive markets, or (4) markets where utter chaos reigns. The zero sum game is accelerated. The more productive, effective, and higher performing the competitors become, the faster everyone gets to make no profit. The best-case scenario is break even for everyone. The worst case is everyone competing on price.

The result is that a company loses value focus—less focus on the customer value segments in which it initially chose to compete and more focus to get people to buy the product or service. The broader, more diverse its customer base becomes in terms of the number of customer value segments it's trying to satisfy, the more diverse the typical organization has become with a matching complex and ambiguous cost structure. Growth has been achieved at the expense of little attention and forethought to the implications of what new costs are hitting the business. Tired of slugging it out on price, someone offers a new and better product or service targeted at a customer value segment. Form again starts to follow value.

Despite being successful in the short term, when a company loses sight of its targeted customers, it

- becomes convinced that every buyer wants the same thing; after all, if customers are buying, they must like what we have
- changes the way it conducts business
- doesn't care because life is good

One of the key causes of this breakdown is that the development of the business strategy hasn't been grounded in a model such as the Pentadigm model we have described to you in this book. Without that grounding, when the chips are down, the strategies being pursued are easy to challenge and abandon because those who developed and are trying to implement the strategies don't have a model in which they have faith and to which they can turn to defend their stance.

Pentadigm demands a certain discipline:

- A discipline to understand customers and the value set of those customers that drives their needs, buying decisions, and buying behavior.
- A discipline to build a customer value commitment in direct response to that value set that drives customer buying decisions and behavior.
- A discipline to design and develop your organization, your people, resources, and other infrastructure based on your customer value commitments to ensure the relevance of these elements to the creation of customer value.
- A discipline to obtain feedback regularly and rigorously from your customers about your customer value commitments and customer value creation.
- A discipline to measure your performance using the customer's scorecard rather than your own.
- A discipline to never rest on your laurels, to always be looking for ways to improve your understanding of the customer value segments' needs and expectations, and to improve your customer value commitments.
- A discipline to plan rigorously around the changing needs and values of customers and to manage and transform your business, business model,

and your organization based on the changing needs and values of your chosen target customers. In addition, Pentadigm demands a mind-set focused on the understanding of customers and the creative application to developing differentiated customer value commitments to create value for chosen customers.

Pentadigm marketers have been to the optician, have had their customer value specs fitted, and use them daily to help them receive signals from customers. Pentadigm marketers use a combination of models and tools to understand their customers and their customers' value sets. Pentadigm marketers name customer value segments according to the values sought by customers in that segment. Pentadigm marketers describe customer value commitments in the language of the customer. Pentadigm marketers dialog regularly with their customers to understand what is important to those customers and what is changing in their value set. Pentadigm marketers lead change in their market offerings; they don't wait for change to overtake them.

Pentadigm and Marketing Dynamics

Much of the traditional marketing perspective tends to break down the subject into one-dimensional perspectives and encourages marketers to look at the customers, markets, and competitors through a particular model or tool. The Pentadigm model and mind-set highlight and stress the complexity and the dynamics of marketing and the market environments, demanding a multi-dimensional approach to customer, market, and competitor analysis and understanding.

The Pentadigm mind-set encourages you to derive all of your strategic business thinking from the customer value set but also demands that you take into account market and competitor dynamics. While the traditional tools and models of marketing can help you in this, the dynamics provide the greatest insight if you use them in a nontraditional way—in the Pentadigm way. A few examples will help demonstrate what that means.

The truism of the product-market life cycle curve represents one of the oldest marketing realities, as shown in Exhibit 8-1. The definition of marketing opportunities using the Ansoff Matrix—slightly enhanced and refined—is also well known. (See Exhibit 8-2.) But when you examine a customer or market or competitive situation using the two together, you can gain new insights into the nature of the market opportunities and how to exploit them. See Exhibit 8-3.

Understand that the needs of customers falling into any of the Ansoff cells will change over time as their market evolves through the life cycle. You can even try to predict how and when this might occur so as to gain a competitive edge by anticipating these changes as you redefine your customer value commitments to reflect those anticipated changes. Staying with the enhanced Ansoff Matrix, let's

EXHIBIT 8-1

The Traditional Product-Market Life Cycle Curve

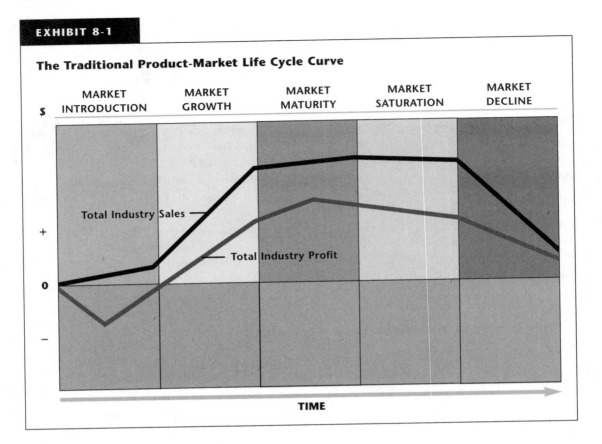

EXHIBIT 8-2

Enhanced Ansoff Matrix

		OFFERING		
		Current	*Extended*	*New*
CUSTOMERS	*Current*	Market Penetration	Offering Expansion	New Offering Development
	Extended	Customer-Base Expansion	Market Expansion	Offering Discovery
	New	Market Development	Market Discovery	Diversification

EXHIBIT 8-3

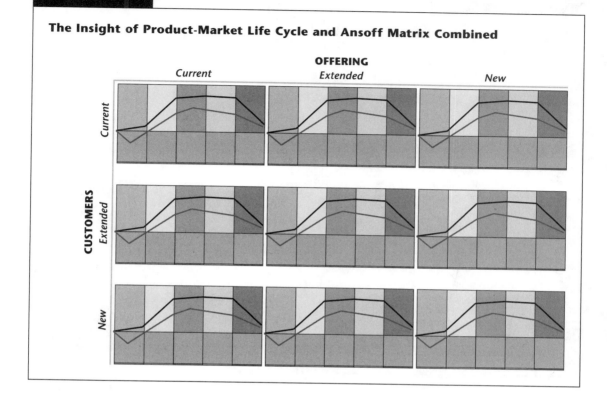

The Insight of Product-Market Life Cycle and Ansoff Matrix Combined

examine the impact of a combination with Everett Rogers's Diffusion of Innovations Curve, sometimes referred to as the *Adoption Curve*, as shown in Exhibit 8-4.[3]

Adapting Rogers's model to target markets, Innovators represent roughly 2.5 percent of your market, Early Adopters 13.5 percent, Early and Late Majority 34.0 percent each, and Laggards roughly 16 percent. When you combine this model with the enhanced Ansoff Matrix, as in Exhibit 8-5, you gain further insights about possible subsegmentation of customers within each of the cells and how you may need to target one or more of these subsegments and—depending upon your strategy in that market—how you must adjust your customer value commitments accordingly. For instance, if you want to penetrate the "New Customers, Current Offering" cell, you should target the Early Adopters in that market, in order to be successful at getting an entry, before moving on to target the Early Majority in order to build your position.

Greater insights abound when you carry this integrated model approach further, combining the enhanced Ansoff Matrix with other models and tools, such as the Target Segment Tracer (see Appendix 2) or Porter's Five Forces model. Other tools and models which could be combined to provide additional market insights

EXHIBIT 8-4

Rogers's Diffusion of Innovation (Adoption) Curve

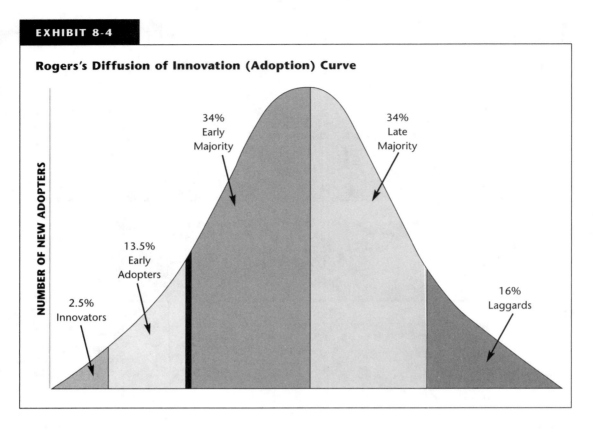

include Target Segment Tracer and Diffusion of Innovation; Target Segment Tracer and Product-Market and Value Life Cycle (which also includes DTS and DTC analysis). From the combination of some of these tried-and-tested marketing models, tools, and concepts, you can develop your own ideas and insights within your Pentadigm approach to business success. As our detailed case study illustrates, this can be highly productive and profitable.

Pentadigm Applied: The Dow Corning Story

The Pentadigm value-based marketing approach has been put to the test in many different companies and customer situations over the years. For our case study, we could have picked a company that had every bit of luck, market trends, and technology advancement stacked in its favor. But we have seen plenty of companies that have everything going for them, and often it's hard to tell if it's the business approach or the wind at the companies' backs that made the difference.

Keeping true to the belief that our approach to bottom-line value-based marketing can make a real difference to any company, we felt a company that faced some formidable wind in its face seemed like a better story. And most people would agree

EXHIBIT 8-5

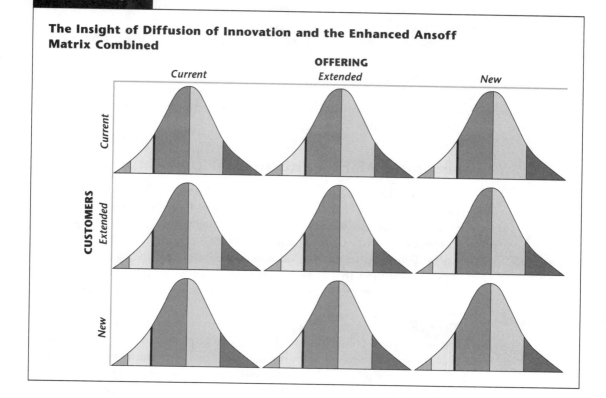

The Insight of Diffusion of Innovation and the Enhanced Ansoff Matrix Combined

that Dow Corning Corporation has had its face in some gale force winds in the past years.

Background—Dow Corning Corporation

In 1930, Corning Glass Works began the development of a new material made from sand that combined some of the best properties of glass and plastics. Over the next decade, Corning scientists worked with the scientists at The Mellon Institute of Research in Pittsburgh to develop the promising innovation. Dow Corning was formed in 1943 as a start-up 50/50 joint venture between Corning Glass and The Dow Chemical Company to explore and develop the commercial potential of the new technology. Over the coming decades, Dow Corning grew to be one of the most successful business joint ventures of all time with $2.5 billion in sales and 7,500 employees worldwide.

Throughout its history, Dow Corning pioneered the development of silicon technology innovations to be used in applications as diverse as sealants and gasketing, waxes and polishes, textiles and water repellent treatments, pulp and paper processing, and skin care and antiperspirants. Today, Dow Corning is the largest global producer of silicon-based materials, offering more than 7,000 different silicon-based products and services. It competes against some tremendous competitors, including GE and Bayer.

Historically, its strategy was focused on innovation and new customer applications. In Pentadigm terms, it focused and organized to dominate the segment (DTS) for customer innovation. Dow Corning grew through discovering and delivering the most advanced technology for demanding customer applications, achieving 4,800 active patents worldwide. As such, the company was customer-focused before it was fashionable to be so.

Change in the Market Situation for Dow Corning

As we have consistently pointed out throughout the book, all market innovations inevitably mature. For a market innovator like Dow Corning, growth resulted in two businesses within one business model. In addition to business growth it achieved through innovation, Dow Corning also grew from maturing innovations that were becoming widely used in the marketplace. The latter matured to become Dow Corning's core business that loaded its sales statements and manufacturing facilities. It also attracted competition that ultimately exerted pressure on its pricing and cost position.

More insidious were the market forces that created a gap between what its maturing innovations could command in the marketplace and what had become a widespread belief in the Dow Corning culture—their commitment to customers and being "innovative" should always command a higher price. Over time, Dow Corning's business model, systems, processes, and organizational management and rewards further evolved to strengthen its innovation focus with its customers and DTS.

While Dow Corning continued to grow and innovate new products and applications with customers, the reality was that it was creating an ever larger collection of mature businesses. Paralleling its own success were customers who were innovating and growing their businesses using Dow Corning materials. Both Dow Corning and its 25,000 customers worldwide prospered together, but over time—as the customers' business grew and their markets matured—the customers' value ratio or relationship changed with Dow Corning. Many customers in these maturing markets needed Dow Corning not just to innovate new product technology, but to help them create new value through lower costs in their mature product lines to stay competitive in their markets. The need to Dominate the Cycle (DTC) of value was emerging.

For a company with a history of success through innovation, this change in customer value and needs represented a contradictory message for Dow Corning's business model. It had built a "form follows value" business model to effectively serve customer innovation, but the model did not serve the changing customer values that were emerging in the market. Additionally, it was becoming ever more clear that some competitors who didn't invest in innovating with customers were willing to buy the customers' business with a lower price.

How Did Dow Corning Tackle This Challenge?

In the spring of 2000, Dow Corning Corporation's Electronics Industry and Advanced Engineering Materials Business Unit began to explore resegmenting its market with the intent of developing a more customer-focused strategy.

"We just knew from our customer research and from direct customer feedback that we were missing the point somewhere," recalls Ian Thackwray, the unit's general manager. "We were doing the right things in terms of getting the customer feedback and we had a mountain of knowledge in the organization, but we were struggling to know what to do with it."

The business leadership team went through an extensive strategy review, during which it realized a need to involve more people who had direct customer interface. "Our attitude had been that we didn't require needs-based segmentation in order to develop a strategy. How wrong we were," says Thackwray. "That strategy review meeting was a milestone in changing our thinking to the realization that customer needs and a true, full, and deep understanding of customer needs is fundamental to developing a meaningful and profitable business strategy."

A second meeting was convened in September 2000 with 36 people from the business team, technical, marketing, sales, supply chain, and new business groups. The objective was to reevaluate implications of customer value segmentation as a basis for reviewing the business's strategy using the 5-step Pentadigm model.

"The really exciting thing was that no one had a preconceived idea of what the outcome would be and everyone went in with an open mind," remembers Babette Pettersen, then responsible for Marketing and New Business Development in the Electronics Industry Sector. "The idea was to stimulate an open-minded reappraisal of our customer value segmentation, formulating our intimate customer knowledge alongside frameworks and segmentation approaches from both theoretical models and practical examples." The resulting set of customer value commitments was simple, but Dow Corning's Electronics Business had never developed its strategy from this customer needs-based perspective before.

"We defined and profiled each segment and we assigned customer applications into each segment, enabling us to quantify and evaluate each segment in terms of attractiveness and our ability to compete as a basis for targeting," Thackwray explains.

Based on the success of applying the value-based marketing principles in the Electronics Industry Business, similar sessions were conducted by each of the global business units. "This is where the *real* insight came," relates Scott Fuson, Global Executive Director Marketing and Sales. "After applying the customer needs-based segmentation methodology, we began to realize that there was a significant amount of existing customers who buy for very different reasons. This led us to develop an enterprise-wide look at our customers, then creating distinct and compelling value propositions and business models for each of the customer needs-based segments we identified.

"We were particularly excited about how this also better took advantage of our market-based structure and operations," continues Fuson. "These new business models resulted from converting the needs-based segmentation into customer-focused value that better aligned our resources and structure to improve business model performance with our customers." Dow Corning recognized that there was other real value that their customers sought.

"A critical outcome of the reevaluation is that it forced us to reappraise our entire market positioning and brand presence," Fuson explains. This included the essence, attributes, and hierarchy for the Dow Corning brand itself and the creation of an entirely new business model for customers that required a price-reliable supply. This new brand positioning became the company's XIAMETER brand.

Value-Based Marketing at Dow Corning

Application of Pentadigm Step 1: Discover—Understand the Customer

As a company built on developing customer innovation, Dow Corning had a substantial amount of customer information from numerous sources:

- Purchased studies of their customer base
- Regular customer satisfaction studies conducted by an outside research firm
- Regular customer feedback through its Customer Relationship Management process

All of this contributed to a full and deep understanding of their customers' needs and value expectations. Yet it was when Dow Corning started to look at its information both from a segmentation and customer value perspective that the information started to tell them new things. For example, three broad customer value segments were identified: (1) customers who innovate into new markets, (2) customers who were in fast-growing markets, and (3) customers looking to reduce costs and improve productivity in large, highly competitive markets.[4]

Innovation-focused customers are defined as those committed to being first to the market with new technologies and state-of-the-art products, and who seek advanced innovation and creation of unique technical or market positions. Dow Corning's customer value commitment for this group of customers is both innovative solutions based on cutting-edge technologies and services and expertise in assisting customers to get their products to market faster with better value differentiators for the customers' customers.

For example, Dow Corning helped Reliance Industries reformulate its fiber-optic cable conduit inner lining to improve the lining's slipperiness. The superior slipperiness allowed fiber optics to go into conduit faster and at longer lengths. This enabled Reliance Industries' customers to install fiber-optic cables significantly faster and for 30 to 50 percent lower cost. In another instance, Dow Corning helped a consumer products company get the new household cleaner to market faster by taking on the manufacturing of the cleaner in their own facilities.

Customers in fast-growing markets are defined as those looking for easy, drop-in solutions that give them speed, efficiency, convenience, and reliability to meet growth demands. Their value drivers are lower cost offerings with proven performance and demonstrated use. For them, Dow Corning's customer value commitment offers proven performance in technology, manufacturing, and supply chain management.

Dow Corning helped its customer's global sealants and adhesives business by working with its larger customers to convert to bulk delivery systems. The change from 55-gallon drums to a new 8,000-gallon storage facility reduced handling and labor costs, dropped waste 7 percent, and freed up 10,000 square feet of space in the customer's operation.

Customers in large, highly competitive markets, typically with products in the mature stage of the product life cycle, form the third segment. These customers expect improved process efficiency and effectiveness in manufacturing to help them achieve maximum profit by reducing costs. They are looking for such things as ideas from suppliers, outsourcing capabilities, inventory control and supply chain services, and disposal assistance. Dow Corning's cost-effective solutions that drive overall costs down is the customer value commitment for this customer value segment.

One tool Dow Corning developed for these customers was software that could more precisely pinpoint lubrication for critical plant equipment. The Integrated Oil Analysis software enabled plant operations to perform a complete oil and lubrication analysis on vital equipment to optimize maintenance programs rather than follow routine scheduled maintenance.

As Thackwray makes clear, "We could define and profile each segment and we could identify customers in each segment, enabling us to quantify and evaluate each segment in terms of attractiveness and our ability to deliver a superior value to these customers." Building upon the three broad segment groupings, the electronics business identified seven new customer value segments based on the needs and values of their customers.

The key was to take all the various inputs about customers from multiple sources and to integrate them in an interactive and creative thinking process to deliver an insightful output that helped the business better understand what really mattered to its customers' success. Dow Corning developed a summary matrix of customer value for its business. Exhibit 8-6 is a generic matrix that you can use to develop a summary matrix within your business.

EXHIBIT 8-6

Generic Industry Customer Value Segment Matrix

	SEGMENT 1 INNOVATORS	SEGMENT 2 OPTIMIZERS	SEGMENT 3 OPERATIONALIZERS	SEGMENT 4 ECONOMIZERS
BEHAVIOR OF CUSTOMERS IN SEGMENTS	• First to market, risk takers • Reputation for the latest ideas	• Fast followers • Let someone else prove, then exploit market	• Best at optimizing total acquisition and use costs	• Focused on best pricing • Trade-offs to drive cost out
VALUE NEED IN SEGMENT	Leading ideas or technology to create edge	Fast and responsive support to make transitions	Supply chain optimization support	Continually drive costs out of business
TYPICAL CUSTOMER COST DRIVERS	• R&D • Marketing • Engineering	• Marketing • Production • Purchasing	• Supply Chain • Production	• Productions • Logistics
CUSTOMER'S PROFIT MODEL	Profit generated through a stream of innovation	Profit generated by quickly capitalizing on opportunities	Efficiency of operations drives profits	Selling as much stuff as cheaply as possible drives profit
WHAT DO THESE CUSTOMERS MEASURE?	• Time to market • Market response • Develop costs	• Market share and its growth • Price/costs variances	• Share protection • Purchasing costs • Supply chain costs	• Purchasing costs • Market share • Operation costs
CUSTOMER'S MARKET DRIVER'S/ SITUATION	• Unique ideas are valued in market • Few competitors can match	• Customer sees opportunity and battles over growth in market	• Market is mature, need to win the race to run efficiently	• Market declining but these customers hang on
LEADING COMPETITIVE OFFERING/ SITUATION	Competitor wants to play one-upmanship	Variable offerings with high differentiation to attract customers	Unbundling of offerings and a la carte purchasing	Suppliers are exiting, but some will streamline operations to serve
YOUR STRATEGIC VALUE COMMITMENT	Centered on driving innovation in ideas, products, and solutions	Centered on helping customers capture growth opportunities	Centered on streamlining supply chain, ease of doing business	Centered on driving every possible cost out

According to Dow Corning, there are two key lessons of Pentadigm Step 1.

1. It's crucial to have the correct data.

2. Use Pentadigm to bring out the context and meanings for customers about what they value most.

Application of Pentadigm Step 2: Commit—Commit to the Customer

Once Dow Corning's business units had identified the key customer value segments it wanted to target, it was a relatively straightforward process for them to proceed with defining the customer value commitments for its respective target customer value segments. Each customer value commitment represented a change in the way Dow Corning approached these customers. It was the first time the company moved from assuming all customers equally valued Dow Corning's innovation to figuring out what was relevant to and valued by specific customers in each customer value segment. The company learned more clearly what were the real and superior value points with its customers.

An important additional insight from the work conducted was the realization that one or more of the needs-based customer value segments cut across the traditional industry sector structure around which Dow Corning had been organizing its business and the corporation.

The value propositions—called customer value commitments in the Pentadigm model—were derived from the individual customer value segment profiles. The biggest challenge in most cases was to identify a truly unique, superior element in the offering, initially because of the strong product innovation-focus in the group. Once Dow Corning minds opened to value differentiators beyond product features and benefits, the ideas started to flow.

"We have spent the past five years transforming Dow Corning into a customer-directed organization," comments Dow Corning Executive Vice President Stephanie Burns. "The result has been our ability to commit better and deliver historic change to the marketplace by offering silicon-based solutions tailored to specific customer needs. The introduction of the new XIAMETER brand reflects a key element of our revitalized and precision-focused company."[5]

The specific value propositions for each of the specific customer value segments, according to Dow Corning, "became linked to what really mattered most to our customers' success in each segment through a more focused understanding of each segment's different needs and value drivers." Equally important was recognizing that innovating not just the product, but the way business was conducted with customers, could develop a successful business and deeper relationships with customers. Additionally, the company's core customer value commitments remained true to providing a "full range of services and innovative technology expertise for customers who want to leverage them to give their products a competitive edge. Value-added services are also available with the purchase and use of Dow Corning's other product lines, and include technical innovation, product application, and development support."

According to Dow Corning, there are two key lessons of Pentadigm Step 2.

1. There is a need to be open-minded to completely rethink what the customer considers as superior value commitments and ultimately organizing (form follows value) around the value needs and expectations of the customer value segments.

2. Long-entrenched structures and perspectives need to be critically examined and challenged.

Application of Pentadigm Step 3: Create — Create Customer Value

Having created clear segmentation based on customer need and differentiated value propositions for each customer value segment, making Dow Corning's customer value commitments real to its customers was a relatively easy next step. This involved their need to create resourcing and infrastructure aligned to the target customer value commitments. Dow Corning defined clear customer value commitments to deliver the desired value to its customer value segments and this enabled management to define the needed resources in terms of people, infrastructure, and financing. Its new emerging *form* would now *follow* and be aligned to the distinctive *value* it identified in each customer segment, with the ability to manage the changing customer value (DTC) occurring in the marketplace.

Also, one new segment was identified in which the customers valued a low price, ease of doing business, and the guarantee of on-time shipments. Dow Corning also backed up the shipment guarantee with a 3 percent financial reimbursement to the customer if it missed a shipment commitment time. These customers tended to value less research and technical support. It was also recognized that customers in this segment tended to make large purchases, but not necessarily of a wide variety of products. This customer value segment became the basis for establishing a new business model and channel to market, which was launched in March of 2002.

To serve this new segment the business model and channel needed to be streamlined, tied to Dow Corning global manufacturing and supply chain capability, and simplified for both customers and Dow Corning. Internally, this meant focusing operations to supply the most popular customer products, favoring a Web-based channel, and leveraging the SAP systems to manage order entry and inventory commitments with customers. The changes for customers led to more clearly defined and transparent business practices on such things as pricing, delivery, and order quantity; the best way for the customer to order; and communications practices. This helped guide customers to a better way for them to conduct business with Dow Corning based upon the way those customers might want to conduct business rather than on how Dow Corning wants to conduct business with them.

"What's really amazing," Services and Customer Processes Director Tom Cook remembers, "is that with this level of clarity and simplicity it was easy to explain similarities and—more importantly—differences in what we should be offering to different customers to best meet their needs. For the first time it was also easy to explain WHY! And, more importantly, customers could understand how they could more easily meet their needs with us."

A bonus benefit was the widespread level of understanding and commitment derived by involving people from many of the implementation functions in the original development work. "Involving people from a complete cross-section of our global business paid real dividends when it came to rolling out the results," states Bob Schroeder of Dow Corning's Construction Industry. "We had our own group of apostles to go out and tell the story to their own colleagues and peers in their own language. The adoption of our new customer value commitment has been immediate and the skepticism is more along the 'show me' line of thinking versus 'have you lost your mind?'"

These new insights led Dow Corning to redesign its organization from being focused on business sectors to aligning with the newly identified customer value segments. This included the appointment of a Customer Value Segment Manager with a specific focus on the newly defined customer value segments and the responsibility for delivering the newly defined customer value commitments. It launched a new Dow Corning for each customer value segment identified as being present across all the industry sectors it serves.

According to Dow Corning, there are two key lessons of Pentadigm Step 3.

1. You can only define your organization and your infrastructure when you know what you want to deliver to whom.

2. Involving a broad cross-section of the organization builds stronger commitment and buy-in to the end results and speeds implementation.

Application of Pentadigm Step 4: Assess—Obtain Customer Feedback

After a long history of succeeding with customers primarily through product innovation, Dow Corning now more than ever needs to assess feedback from its customers on many new dimensions important to them. The new segmentation also establishes a business rationale for changes and can help sort out voices from the customer into specific segment groups.

Dow Corning's review of its customer value commitments was instigated by the feedback from customer research from an outside, independent research firm and from specific situations documented through its Customer Relationship Management (CRM) process. Dow Corning also encourages all staff with customer interface to pose questions about customer satisfaction and obtain direct feedback from the customer using its Customer Relationship Management Process.

"Using our Customer Relationship Management Process, Service Level Management provided our customer interface people with a methodology to capture specific customer needs and issues in a one-on-one situation," explains Jamie Moore, CRM Business Process Manager. "We can capture and address with each specific customer their insights and then later aggregate these inputs for analysis in order to act upon them across the entire customer base."

An important insight from Dow Corning's experience is that it's difficult for the company to become complacent with the responses to these feedback data. It continues to assess by conducting research on a regular basis and is looking constantly for pointers to the next needed change in its customer value commitments. As Moore describes it, "Dow Corning's commitment to satisfying customer requirements resulted in the use of needs-based segmentation methods to deepen our understanding of what mattered most to their success. The use of these methods has enabled the proactive segmentation of customers to create unique value propositions, improved behaviors in our business units in how we treat customers, and better aligned resource development options in anticipation of customers' changing needs.

"For instance," continues Moore, "using customer needs analysis in a structured manner with our CRM process, we specifically know where and how we can provide improved service to customers. This approach to CRM also provides the ability to aggregate information, identify trends with customers and markets, and make better-focused decisions and actions. This is because we have a factual and quantified mechanism for communicating customer needs throughout the organization and use this as the basis for responses."

According to Dow Corning, there are three key lessons of Pentadigm Step 4.

1. Customer feedback must be obtained from a variety of sources, but at least one must be independent and objective.

2. The sum total of the customer feedback may be greater than the individual feedback when creatively and critically reviewed, integrated, and analyzed.

3. Never be complacent—always look for the next change in what value will be affecting customers.

Application of Pentadigm Step 5: Improve—Measure and Improve Value

Preliminary results of the Dow Corning customer value commitment have been very positive and encouraging. But it's a story in development, in transition.

"While we do believe that some of our latest customer value commitments put us ahead of our competition," Fuson affirms, "we recognize that delivering superior value to our customers is not about beating our competition. Focusing on the competition as the basis of improving our business with customers could and would prevent us from truly understanding our customers and discovering unique insights about how we can help them succeed better. Also, focusing on the competition would trap us in a common shared point of view about customers and our markets rather than developing the breakthrough ideas."

Fuson also points out that "if we measured ourselves primarily against competitors, then it would lead most likely to a marketplace of similar offerings for customers, which in the long run would mean poorer responsiveness to changing customer value. So our establishment of regular and rigorous reviews of our customer interfaces and feedback programs fosters the continued development of our customer value commitments, maintaining the best value for our chosen target customers. The final realization is that providing superior value for customers is profitable for customers and also profitable for us."

The other interesting aspect of the new Dow Corning is how Dow Corning is leveraging its existing capabilities better and developing new customer capabilities that utilize the Web. But its focus wasn't to get on the Web *per se*. Having gone through the segmentation work first, Dow Corning better understood the value drivers of its customers and, in some value segments, realized that the Web was a better way to provide this value to customers than traditional channels.

A number of Internet-based business start-ups sought to service the same customer segments that Dow Corning focused on as well. While the Internet businesses may have recognized this customer segment, they have failed to succeed in this market space since they lacked the necessary infrastructure and supply chain investments. Dow Corning already had in place and operating a $100 million investment in a SAP system, the world's largest manufacturing and distribution system for silicon-based products with 40 locations worldwide, and a great deal of information about buying habits and behavior of customers. So it knew it had a global back-office operation that could support the global front-office operations their customers interacted with. Dow Corning practiced "form follows value." In contrast, most Web-based companies trying to serve the same customers focused on getting customers to their nice virtual front-office websites, but had few capabilities in place to deliver their value propositions.

Dow Corning's challenge was to see value from the customer perspective, not just product innovation value, then sort out its customer information to create the business processes and then build channel strategies, including customer touch points like the Web.

According to Dow Corning, there are two key lessons of Pentadigm Step 5.

1. Rigorous and regular strategy and customer performance reviews are essential to maintaining a leadership position with customers.

2. Customer value is not just telling the customer you bring them value, but first making the commitment, resource changes, and leadership choices that enable a business to deliver what it says it can do for its customers.

Final Observations

Pentadigm is based on our experience and belief that the most important aspect to long-term profitability is providing superior customer value. We draw in part from an extensive chemical industry background. The chemical industry is a $1.7 trillion, fiercely competitive industry with the most pervasive and ubiquitous value chain of any industry in the world. Look around. No matter where you are right now—your house, your office, your car, a plane, or a boat—or what you're wearing, eating, or using, the chemical industry has made it possible or better to a greater or lesser extent. This connection to the world's value chain gives us unique insight into customer value.

One of the challenges we also faced in writing this book was sorting through and selecting relevant examples of Pentadigm applications, knowing that readers would want to learn about how someone else did or does it. This presented a number of issues.

First, customer value-focused and value-aligned businesses are rare breeds among publicly traded companies, although there are some rich data in the public domain. For example, we talk about companies like Southwest Airlines, Nike, Dell, and Nucor whose success and enduring leadership in their respective markets seem to validate the Pentadigm model. Second, in cases where we've been intimately involved with helping an organization learn to apply Pentadigm, these clients are works-in-progress. A number are understandably reluctant to share their insights with possible competitors in the marketplace. Third, your own industry, market position, and organizational character influence how you interpret an example. It's more important to consider the implications for your business of any of our examples than to speculate about which company it's from.

Taking a page from Jack Webb's "Dragnet," our approach in writing was to change or genericize the names of some of the companies at times to protect proprietary or sensitive information. In some cases, the company example may be a composite. Sometimes we use a company for examples illustrating a specific Pentadigm step, but that doesn't necessarily mean that the company is effective or efficient in the other Pentadigm steps.

In truth, even if we had 1,000 examples that unequivocally proved Pentadigm, you would still have to assess your own situation in terms of where you are today and where you want to be. We might wish we were scratch golfers, but from a handicap of 25, there's more work to get there than for someone with a 10 handicap.

Once you have honestly assessed your own business handicap, Pentadigm offers a framework to focus and organize your transformation around its five core themes.

Your shareholders aren't paying you to imitate someone else. They're paying you to be profitable. Pentadigm provides a model for developing the customer value commitments that result in profitability. Within the very roots of your business was likely a great success story that just happened to lose its way.

And, frankly, if there were 1,000 examples, you'd be in a whole lot more trouble than you even think you are today. That would mean that Pentadigm had become the competitive business standard.

KEY INSIGHTS

1. Pentadigm demands that the business strategy be driven by customer value and that new customer value segments shouldn't be targeted unless the company can meet or exceed the new value expectations and do so profitably.

2. In addition, Pentadigm demands a mind-set focused on the understanding of customers and the creative application of developing differentiated customer value commitments to create value for chosen customers.

3. Pentadigm marketers have been to the optician, they have had their customer value specs fitted, and they use them daily to help them receive signals from customers.

4. Pentadigm marketers use a combination of models and tools to understand their customers and their customers' value set.

5. Pentadigm marketers name customer value segments according to the values sought by customers in that segment, describe customer value commitments in the language of the customer, dialog regularly with their customers to understand what is important to those customers and what is changing in their value set, and lead change in their market offerings—they don't wait for change to overtake them.

CHECKLIST

Pentadigm demands a certain discipline.

❑ A discipline to understand the customer and the value set of the customer that drives their needs, their buying decisions, and buying behavior.

❑ A discipline to build customer value commitments for the customers in direct response to that value set that drives their buying decisions and behavior.

❑ A discipline to design and develop your organization, your people resources, and other infrastructure based on your customer value commitments to ensure the relevance of these elements to the creation of customer value.

❑ A discipline to regularly and rigorously obtain feedback from your customers about your customer value commitments and customer value creation.

❑ A discipline to measure your performance using the customer's scorecard rather than your own.

❑ A discipline to never rest on your laurels, to always be looking for ways to improve your understanding of the customer value segment's needs and expectations and your customer value commitments.

❑ A discipline to plan rigorously around the changing needs and values of customers and to manage and transform your business, business model, and your organization based on the changing needs and values of your chosen target customers.

PENTADIGM
ROAD MAPS

The Pentadigm Road Map

Step 1: Discover
1. Define and Map Market
2. Understand Customer Value Expectation
3. Discover Customer Value Segments
4. Assess Competitive Position
5. Select Target Customer Value Segments

Step 2: Commit
1. Define Customer Value Segment Strategy
2. Develop Superior Offering
3. Create the Right Organization
4. Communicate Internally and Externally
5. Define KPIs

Step 3: Create
1. Develop Customer Value Commitment Culture
2. Plan Customer Value Processes
3. Populate Customer Value Processes
4. Invest in Appropriate Infrastructure
5. Implement Customer Value

Step 4: Assess
1. Track Won and Lost Business
2. Proactively Seek Customer Feedback
3. Resolve Customer Complaints
4. Assess Performance Against Customer Expectations
5. Combine Analyses to Improve

Step 5: Improve
1. Spot Gaps and "Quick Hits"
2. Challenge Customer Understanding
3. Redefine Customer Value Commitments
4. Improve Customer Value
5. Anticipate Change

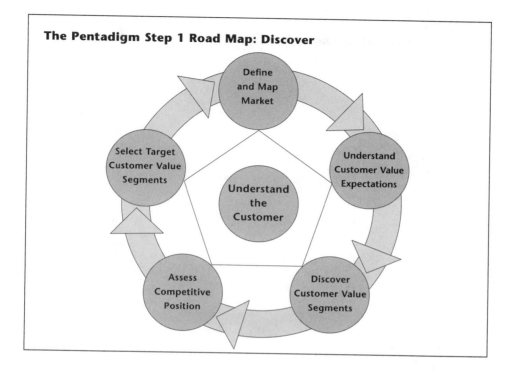

The Pentadigm Step 1 Road Map: Discover

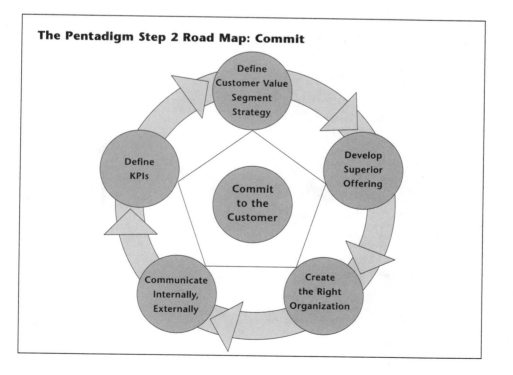

The Pentadigm Step 2 Road Map: Commit

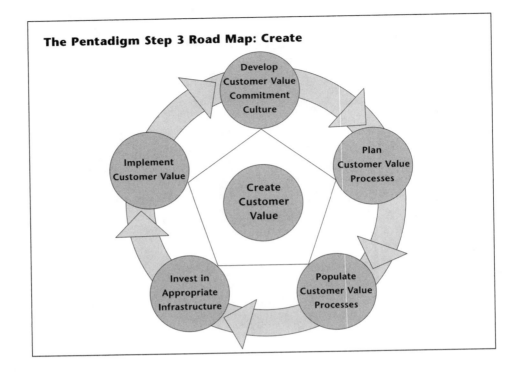

The Pentadigm Step 3 Road Map: Create

Develop Customer Value Commitment Culture

Plan Customer Value Processes

Create Customer Value

Implement Customer Value

Populate Customer Value Processes

Invest in Appropriate Infrastructure

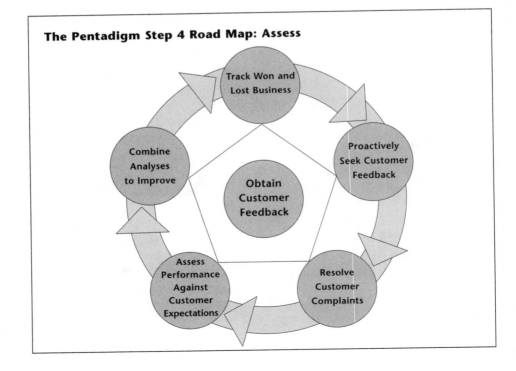

The Pentadigm Step 4 Road Map: Assess

Track Won and Lost Business

Proactively Seek Customer Feedback

Obtain Customer Feedback

Combine Analyses to Improve

Assess Performance Against Customer Expectations

Resolve Customer Complaints

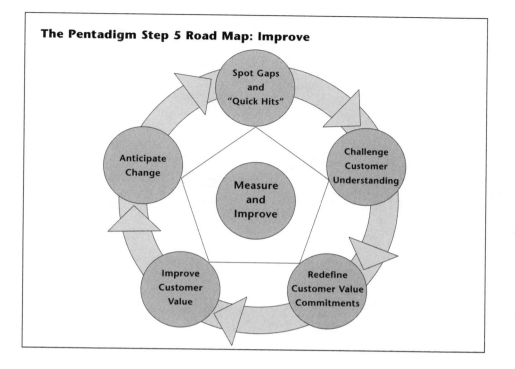

The Pentadigm Step 5 Road Map: Improve

Spot Gaps and "Quick Hits"

Anticipate Change

Challenge Customer Understanding

Measure and Improve

Improve Customer Value

Redefine Customer Value Commitments

TARGET CUSTOMER
VALUE SEGMENT
TRACER

The *Target Customer Value Segment Tracer* is a tool that helps qualify customer value segments to target. It's based upon your ability to fulfill the needs of specific customer value segments better than your competition and at a profit (see Exhibit A2-1).

There are eight basic steps in the process.

1. Define and identify a maximum of five criteria relevant to your business which reflect the attractiveness of a customer value segment to you.

2. Assess each customer value segment against these attractiveness criteria.

3. Assess your ability in the eyes of the customer to fulfill the key driving needs of the customer value segment relative to your competition. This means first identifying the unmet, poorly met, or determinant needs driving the supplier selection or preference decision, then measuring your customer's view of your performance and your competitor's performance against those criteria.

4. Plot the customer value segment using the score on each axis. The customer value segment attractiveness is plotted on the *y*-axis and the competitive advantage on the *x*-axis.

5. Scale the bubble to reflect the size of the customer value segment.

6. Show the customer value segment profitability in the inner circle.

7. Show your share of the customer value segment with a cutout.

8. Plot each customer value segment in terms of how you expect it to have evolved three years from now. The plot of the customer value segments in

EXHIBIT A2-1

Target Customer Value Segment Tracer

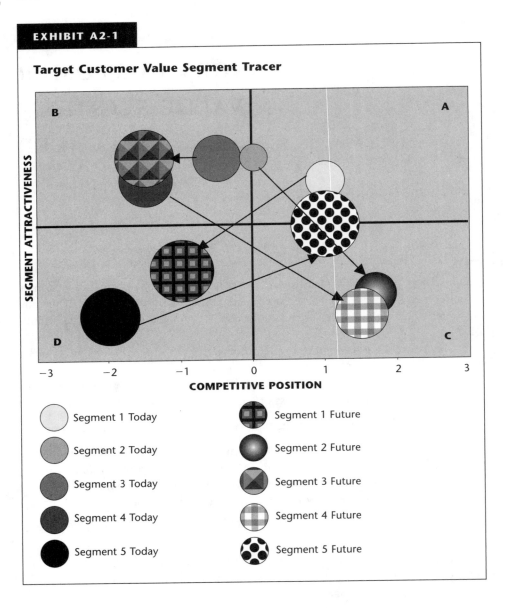

Exhibit A2-1 allows you to prioritize them in order of attractiveness and ability to compete over time.

- Highest priority is the upper right Quadrant A, which represents the highest attractiveness and the strongest competitive position.
- Second most important is the upper left Quadrant B, which is attractive, but where you need to strengthen competitive position.
- Third most attractive is lower right Quadrant C, where you have a competitive advantage, but in a less attractive customer value segment.

- Lowest priority is lower left Quadrant D, where you are competitively disadvantaged in an unattractive customer value segment.

Having selected your target customer value segments, you must evaluate the business potential represented by the target customer value segments against your business plans and your capabilities. If the total business potential exceeds what is in your plans, your plans might need to be reviewed upward. If the total business potential does not reach what is in your plans, your plans might need to be reviewed downward or you must include additional customer value segments. From a Pentadigm perspective, it's not advised to include any customer value segments that are evolving into Quadrant D.

CUSTOMER LIFETIME
VALUE (CLV)

Many companies talk about Customer Lifetime Value (CLV), but few have actually computed it for their own customers. Or, if they have, they don't know what to do with it as part of an overall marketing strategy once they have it.

Customer Lifetime Value—variously referred to as Net Present Value (NPV) or Life Time Value (LTV)—is the profit that can be anticipated from a customer or a customer value segment over a specified period of time, a financial metric that is relevant to corporate budget planning and forecasting. CLV answers the basic question about whether or not a customer or a customer value segment is worth selling to based on the anticipated profitability of the relationship. By knowing the worth of customers in terms of profitability, the acquisition cost of relationships can be calculated.

An Innovator customer value segment may represent an average CLV of $1,500 while the Hot Rush customer value segment may represent an average CLV of $1,075, for example. New customers derived from trade shows represent an average CLV of $1,375, while new customers derived from direct sales represent an average CLV of $1,835. Or the CLV could be analyzed by initial type of product or service purchased, the initial purchase investment, the customer value commitment which generated the buyer decision, or myriad other parameters.

Calculation of Customer Lifetime Value

Two approaches can be used for calculating CLV. One is to start in the current fiscal year with a customer sample and track the performance of the sample through future years. This computation could be for new products or services, new target markets, new sales, or channel management strategies, and so on. This is modeled in Exhibit A3-1; revenue, costs, and profitability are tracked for 2001 and 2002;

2002 is the current fiscal year. Based on these data, projections could be made for 2003 and beyond.

The second approach is to establish a historical baseline using two to three years of actual customer data and then make projections for a number of years forward based on the known or expected average lifetime of an account or a customer value segment. This works well for existing products or services, target markets,

EXHIBIT A3-1

Calculation of CLV Scenario 1

REVENUE	2001	2002	2003	2004	2005	AVE LT
Retention Rate		40%				1.29
Customer Sample	1,000	400				
Spending Rate	$4,000	$4,500				
Gross Revenue	$4,000,000	$1,800,000				

COSTS	2001	2002	2003	2004	2005	PCT
Acquisition Costs	$2,000,000					
SG&A Fixed Costs	$1,800,000	$810,000				45%
SG&A Variable Costs	$600,000	$270,000				15%
Retention Costs	$0	$90,000				5%
Total Costs	$4,400,000	$1,080,000				

PROFIT	2001	2002	2003	2004	2005
Gross Profit	($400,000)	$720,000			
Discount Rate	89.29%	79.72%			
Profit NPV	($357,160)	$573,984			
CLV = Σ Profit NPV	($357,160)	$216,824			
CLV/Customer	($357.16)	$154.87			

	2001	2002	2003	2004	2005
Value Ratio	−0.08	0.04			

and sales or channel management strategies. This is modeled in Projecting CLV. Data from 2001 and 2002 provide the ability to make projections for 2003-2005. This example presumes that 2002 is the current fiscal year.

CLV Calculation: Current Year

This scenario focuses on a customer value segment acquired in 2001 and tracked for the first two years of its existence.

Revenue Calculations

1. *Retention Rate.* There is no retention rate for the first year. The 2002 retention rate is the percentage of customers in the original 2001 sample of 1,000 who made a purchase in 2002.

2. *Customer Sample.* For the base year of 2001, this is either the total population of customers or a random group of 10–15 percent of customers from the base year. For this exercise, there were 10,000 customers acquired in 2001; 1,000 were randomly selected for the sample.

3. *Spending Rate.* This is an average based on actual buying behavior of the customers in the sample in 2001. It's calculated from sales (revenue) data, either by (1) totaling the purchases by each of the customers in the sample and dividing by the sample or (2) calculating the average customer spending rate for all customers that year.

4. *Gross Revenue.* This is the customer sample multiplied by the spending rate. Gross Revenue = Customer Sample × Spending Rate.

Costs Calculations

This will require data and support from accounting and finance.

1. *Acquisition Costs.* This is the amount of money that was spent acquiring business from the 1,000 customers in the sample. This money is easier to track with new products and services. For existing markets, use historical financial data, for example, use the sum of the total 2001 sales and promotions costs divided by the total number of customers acquired in 2001 and multiply that figure by the 1,000 sample size. Acquisition Costs = (Total Sales + Promotion Costs ÷ Total Number of Customers Acquired) × 1,000.

2. *SG&A Fixed Costs.* These data need to be provided from accounting. SG&A Fixed Costs are those that stay the same regardless of sales volume, such as advertising, R&D, salaries, office equipment, office space, and depreciation. In our example, the fixed costs are 45 percent of revenue; given that this percentage can change from year to year, an average was used. A more precise, adjusted percentage should be used for each year's calculations.

3. *SG&A Variable Costs.* These data need to be provided from accounting. SG&A Variable Costs are those that fluctuate with the increase or decrease of sales volume, such as sales, salaries, and commissions. In our example, the variable costs are 15 percent of revenue; given that this percentage can change from year to year, an average was used. A more precise, adjusted percentage should be used for each year's calculations.

4. *Retention Costs.* None in the first year. See Projecting CLV below.

5. *Total Costs.* This is the sum of what it costs to acquire, maintain, and retain the sample customers. Total Costs = Acquisition Costs + SG&A Fixed Costs + SG&A Variable Costs + Retention Costs.

Profit Calculations

1. *Gross Profit.* Gross Profit = Gross Revenue − Total Costs

2. *Discount Rate.* The Time Value of Money principle is based on the fact that a revenue dollar received the first day of the fiscal year has a different value than a revenue dollar received the last day of the year. To calculate the value of a year's revenue stream, a discount rate is used that creates an average value or net present value (NPV) for all of the dollars received during the year and provides a way to calculate total future revenue. The rate is based on interest rates and can be obtained from a Present Value or Discount Table. These scenarios use a 12 percent discount rate. In 2001, the discount rate is 89.29 percent, which means that the average value of each revenue dollar for the first year is $0.8929. A dollar received in 2002 has an average value of $0.7972.

3. *Profit NPV.* This is the discounted value of the Gross Profit. Profit NPV = Gross Profit × Discount Rate.

4. *CLV (Customer Lifetime Value).* This is the cumulative profit value of the sample 1,000 customers at the end of each year. After 2001 in Scenario 1,

it's calculated by adding the CLV equal to Σ Profit NPV from the previous year to the Profit NPV of the current year. CLV $= \Sigma$ Profit NPV.

5. *CLV/Customer.* This figure gives you an average of the Customer Lifetime Value in the sample or in a customer value segment, if calculations are being made that way. It's a cumulative number and is calculated each year by adding the Customer Sample for that year to the Customer Sample for each of the previous years. CLV per Customer $=$ CLV$\div \Sigma$ Customers.

6. *Value Ratio.* Your company's Value Ratio $=$ Desired Benefits $\div$ Relative Costs. The primary Desired Benefit of a market-focused, bottom-line driven organization is Customer Lifetime Value (profitability). The Relative Costs are what it takes to acquire, maintain, and retain that profitability. A Value Ratio is a quantified indication that value is being derived by your company from a customer or customer value segment. A value ratio of -0.08 means that value was not derived; for each $1.00 in cost to acquire, maintain, and retain the customer or customer value segment, $0.08 cents was lost. A value ratio of $+0.04$ means that $0.04 of profit was generated for each $1.00 in cost. Value Ratio $=$ Profitability $\div$ Total Costs.

CLV Calculation: Projecting CLV

This scenario (modeled in Exhibit A3-2) focuses on five years of a customer value segment for which two years of historical data are gathered—2001 and 2002—so that profitability projections can be made for the next three years. All of the numbers for 2003–2005 are projections or guesstimates.

Revenue Calculations

1. *Retention Rate.* For 2002, this is the number of customers from the original sample of 1,000 in 2001 which placed an order in the second year. Retention rates for 2003–2005 are projections or "guesstimates."

2. *Customer Sample.* This is the number of customers from the original sample of 1,000 which remain customers each year. Customer Sample $=$ Customer Sample from previous year $\times$ Retention Rate.

3. *Spending Rate.* In 2002, this is the same calculation as it was in the first year from sales (revenue) data. The numbers for 2003–2005 are projections.

4. *Gross Revenue.* Same calculation as in 2001.

EXHIBIT A3-2

Calculation of CLV—Projecting CLV

REVENUE	2001	2002	2003	2004	2005	AVE LT
Retention Rate		40%	50%	75%	90%	1.95
Customer Sample	1,000	400	200	150	135	
Spending Rate	$4,000	$4,500	$6,000	$9,000	$16,000	
Gross Revenue	$4,000,000	$1,800,000	$1,200,000	$1,350,000	$2,160,000	

COSTS	2001	2002	2003	2004	2005	PCT
Acquisition Costs	$2,000,000					
SG&A Fixed Costs	$1,800,000	$810,000	$540,000	$607,500	$972,000	45%
SG&A Variable Costs	$600,000	$270,000	$180,000	$202,500	$324,000	15%
Retention Costs	$0	$90,000	$60,000	$67,500	$108,000	5%
Total Costs	$4,400,000	$1,080,000	$720,000	$810,000	$1,296,000	

PROFIT	2001	2002	2003	2004	2005
Gross Profit ($1,000)	($400,000)	$720,000	$480,000	$540,000	$864,000
Discount Rate	89.29%	79.72%	71.18%	63.55%	56.74%
Profit NPV	($357,160)	$573,984	$341,664	$343,170	$490,234
CLV = Σ Profit NPV	($357,160)	$216,824	$558,488	$901,658	$1,391,892
CLV/Customer	($357.16)	$154.87	$349.06	$515.23	$738.40

	2001	2002	2003	2004	2005
Value Ratio	−0.08	0.04	0.09	0.13	0.17

Costs Calculations

This will require data and support from accounting and finance.

1. *Acquisition Costs.* None after the first year.

2. *SG&A Fixed Costs.* Same calculation as in 2001.

3. *SG&A Variable Costs.* Same calculation as in 2001.

4. *Retention Costs.* These are expenditures specifically intended to create or maintain customer retention and loyalty. This should be tracked.

5. *Total Costs.* Same calculation as in 2001.

Profit Calculations

1. *Gross Profit.* Same calculation as in 2001.

2. *Discount Rate.* Same calculation as in 2001 and 2002. In 2003–2005, the discount rates are 71.18 percent, 63.55 percent, and 56.74 percent, respectively.

3. *Profit NPV.* Same calculation as in 2001.

4. *CLV.* Same calculation as in 2001.

5. *CLV/Customer.* Same calculation as in 2001.

6. *Value Ratio.* Same calculation as in 2001.

Discussion

In these scenarios, the Value Ratio for the first year was negative, then became positive for each of the subsequent years. Without baseline data, projections about future profitability are difficult. And it's impossible to answer the question, "Should we be selling to these customers?" Even with projections, however, which are only as good as the judgment of the marketer, the spreadsheet is a helpful tool that provides the opportunity to do some "what if" analyses. This can help establish business objectives.

Changes in one or more parameters in the CLV Scenario as demonstrated in Exhibit A3-3 can produce some dramatic results. For example, a 5 percent increase in retention rate in the second year results in a 13.54 percent increase in CLV by 2005. Increasing the retention rates in 2002–2004 improves the 2005 CLV by more than 20 percent. Similarly, shifting the spending rate in 2003 from $4,000 per customer to $6,000 per customer boosts the five-year CLV of the sample by 12 percent. Not as dramatic as increasing the retention rate, but arguably easier to achieve.

What happens when retention and spending rates and the SG&A Fixed and Variable rates are all improved? Over five years from 2001 to 2005, the CLV increases by almost 55 percent. This tool permits you to not only play "what if," but can result in some tangible performance targets established with profitability results which can be quantified over time.

EXHIBIT A3-3

Calculation of CLV "What If" Scenario

REVENUE	2001	2002	2003	2004	2005	AVE LT
Retention Rate		40%	50%	75%	90%	
Customer Sample	1,000	400	200	150	135	1.95
Spending Rate	$4,000	$4,500	$6,000	$9,000	$16,000	
Gross Revenue	$4,000,000	$1,800,000	$1,200,000	$1,350,000	$2,160,000	

COSTS	2001	2002	2003	2004	2005	PCT
Acquisition Costs	$2,000,000					
SG&A Fixed Costs	$1,800,000	$810,000	$540,000	$607,500	$972,000	45%
SG&A Variable Costs	$600,000	$270,000	$180,000	$202,500	$324,000	15%
Retention Costs	$0	$90,000	$60,000	$67,500	$108,000	5%
Total Costs	$4,400,000	$1,080,000	$720,000	$810,000	$1,296,000	

PROFIT	2001	2002	2003	2004	2005
Gross Profit ($1,000)	($400,000)	$720,000	$480,000	$540,000	$864,000
Discount Rate	89.29%	79.72%	71.18%	63.55%	56.74%
Profit NPV	($357,160)	$573,984	$341,664	$343,170	$490,234
CLV = Σ Profit NPV	($357,160)	$216,824	$558,488	$901,658	$1,391,892
CLV/Customer	($357.16)	$154.87	$349.06	$515.23	$738.40

	2001	2002	2003	2004	2005
Value Ratio	−0.08	0.04	0.09	0.13	0.17

PENTADIGM
COMPETITIVE
ASSESSMENT

Begin with what you learned in your customer value segmentation. The segmentation objective was to figure out the things that mattered to customers or the things that will matter to your customers in the future. Look at what you determined were the strong economic drivers and behavior of your customers today or what will be in the future. Don't begin a competitive assessment until you understand the segmentation insights.

The next step is to compare your competitive intelligence with what you learned in segmentation. Who has the best position or who will have the most future impact on the customer's economics and behavior? Direct your thinking and data gathering on determining who is making the biggest difference to customers.

Reevaluating your understanding of your customer's expectations and the competitors' value offerings with your team is the critical step in developing and delivering a superior customer value commitment. Key questions your team needs to consider, debate, and fret over are as follows.

1. Review your assumptions, presumptions, points of view, and hypotheses about the market for your products/services.
   - Who are your targeted customers?
   - Describe the scenarios where you are bringing the most value to customers and explain why.
   - Describe the scenarios where you bring less value to customers and explain why.

2. Who are the competitors most closely competing against you on value offerings?
   - From your customer's perspective, which company(ies) do they believe provide superior value?
   - Explain why.

- How specifically are your target customers impacted when using your products compared to using competitors' products?
- What is the promise the customers obtain from you if they choose your customer value commitment or from your competitors if they choose theirs?
- What can/could customers do with you that they can't do with any-one else? Do you think this is meaningful to your customers? Explain how so.
- Where is your business vulnerable compared to competitors?
- Who is best at attracting and keeping customers? What's your rationale?

In cases where you have identified new or changing value expectations for customers, describe your new value position and answer these questions.

1. How does this new value provide superior value for customers over what any current companies provide?

2. How does changing your value position in the marketplace affect you or your competitors? Who would be affected, why and how?

3. Is it possible for you or a competitor to meet the new value expectations?

4. What would it take to launch the new value offering? Could anyone respond quickly?

Example of Competitive Analysis

For a supplier of engineering plastics (EP), a company we'll call Generic Plastics, a customer value segmentation analysis determined there were three primary target customer value segments—Innovation buyers, Optimizer buyers, and Operationalizer buyers.

Competitive Behavior in the Value Life Cycle

The overall market for this type of EP was maturing. Because of the maturity of the market, there were several dominant players for each of the three value segments.

For Generic Plastics, its customer and competitive positions were relatively weak compared to everyone else in the marketplace. The strategic challenge Generic Plastics struggled with was to determine where it could be successful with a value offering. Traditional competitive analysis showed very little promise of opportunity, especially considering the established and strong competitors. However, when the competitive assessment was completed from the customer value expectation perspective, one opportunity stood out. Roughly 70 percent of all customers were in the Operationalizers segment, but the competition was intense. Competitors were cost-cutting and restructuring operations to run more efficiently because margins were being squeezed. EP had become "commoditized"—customers no longer valued supplier innovations or differentiated products and services. It was a downward spiral in a zero sum game. No matter what a company improved operationally, the competition could quickly duplicate it. Price became the only variable in winning business.

Since the accounts in this segment represented large revenues, competitors committed the best sales, technical, and customer support to these accounts. But a customer driven by productivity doesn't value sales, technical, and customer support; and it's not profitable for the suppliers.

When Generic Plastics really studied the Operationalizer segment drivers, it became apparent that an Electronic Data Interface (EDI) with customers could dramatically improve the customers' productivity by reducing sourcing and purchasing costs. Developing new ways to do business more efficiently with customers in the Operationalizers segment became Generic Plastics' value offering. Options were researched to see if there ways to do this. In mid-1998, FreeMarkets.com was identified as the first competitor to focus on efficient transactions and lowered costs of transactions to customers in this segment.

This was great news for Generic Plastics. Its only potential competitor on the EDI value driver was still pre-IPO with little market reputation and an objective far broader than the EP market alone. Generic Plastics had in its sights a competitive offering that would have provided superior value to the productivity buyer segment. It had significant corporate support for the new value offering and could have launched a new customer value commitment to this segment before any traditional competitors in the segment understood the opportunity.

But Generic Plastics wasn't ready to innovate in E-commerce, even though the CEO had directed leadership to look at the implications. Generic Plastics' EP business unit leadership was trapped by a traditional perspective about its products and competition and couldn't get out of that box. It wanted a solution that fit its current business practices. The competitors launched E-commerce initiatives, negatively affecting Generic Plastics' EP performance even more.

The lessons from the Generic Plastics situation are intended to reinforce the Pentadigm competitive perspective.

1. First, revisit what the value drivers are for your customers within each segment that resulted in your segments in the first place.

2. Determine how your competitors are positioning themselves within the respective customer value segments.

3. Figure out who's going to win within the segment based upon the ability to deliver superior value.

4. If there's no apparent way you can win, look for the customer value segment or segment niche where competitors have become stale in their thinking and practices. What are the value drivers being overlooked or ignored in this segment?

5. There's no substitute for leadership that is committed to delivering superior customer value (regardless of how risky that may seem) and has the guts to do what is necessary to make the customer and business successful.

The opposite situation to Generic Plastics' case is when you're the segment leader in providing superior value. Would you conduct competitive analysis the same way? Obviously, the answer is no. First, a market leader who has held the position for a while is arguably weaker than it would appear to be in a traditional competitive analysis. It's the leader who may be the most blind to new customer value expectations. For example, in the data storage industry, IBM looked great on a traditional competitive analysis, both to IBM and its competitors. Nobody was likely to attack IBM because IBM was just too dominant in this market.

Enter EMC, which realized that, in a very mature data storage market, the customer value driver was more to gain productivity out of accessing data in their IBM systems. IBM missed the opportunity to lead a value offering that responded to this need, most likely because it didn't think it was vulnerable or didn't acknowledge or understand or believe customer values were shifting. While customer satisfaction may show favorable ratings for the leader, the leader needs to hypothesize what is happening to the customer's world at whatever point the customer is on the Value Life Cycle. Just like the EP market example, an updated segmentation analysis of the data storage market would have identified opportunities to provide innovative value offerings that met or exceeded customers' expectations.

Developing and Sustaining the Pentadigm

Using Pentadigm as your guide to competitive analysis reminds you that everything you do and every value you provide to customers has a potential value for customers and cost for you associated with it. Great value creators choose the most important meaningful value for their customer segments and embed in their organization how *not* to provide other benefits even when your competitors might be doing it. Customers are retained and you grow the relationships with customers versus your competition when you make it in the customer's best interest to do business with you. It's in the customer's best interest when you provide the best value in the marketplace. "One-upping" your competition may be ego gratifying, but it adds no value for customers. The companies who bring the most quantified impact to the customer's bottom line are in the best position to win the continued relationship with the customer regardless of how seductive a competitor's offer might sound.

The Threat of the Non-Generic

In Pentadigm we have urged you to define customer value segments and market opportunities defined by the customer value or benefit sought—for example, there is no market for buttons.

One of the reasons for this is to encourage you in your competitive analysis to think beyond the current technology solutions and to consider what else is out there that could be a threat, based on its ability to fulfill the defined customer value or deliver the benefit in a better way.

The makers of telex machines didn't recognize the threat of the fax because they were focused on competition from other telex machine producers. The makers of fax machines didn't recognize the threat of E-mail because they were focused on competition from other fax machine producers. The providers of postal and document courier services didn't recognize the threat of E-mail and the Internet because they were focused on competition from other postal and document courier service providers.

Where is your next competitive threat coming from?

VALUE COMMITMENT
RATING TOOL

One of the biggest challenges to discovering new value for customers is to be able to determine what value looks like or doesn't look like. More often, companies bundle a group of their best benefits and features, convincing themselves that it must be beneficial for the customer. Next, they present their offers to customers with broad strokes and flowery language. Sometimes, learning from others' success and mistakes is the best way to illustrate what customer value commitments should look, feel, and sound like.

This exercise is designed to help your team learn the characteristics of new value offerings, characteristics that will get a customer to respond to an offer or in some cases the characteristics that will make customers indifferent to a business's products and services. Customer value commitments that win the customers' business meet very clear criteria that are critical to customer success. These criteria include the following.

1. The *target customer* is clearly identified. The more specifically the customer can be described, the better.

2. There are clear and *specific* customer value *benefits* that can be quantified for the targeted customers.

3. For the targeted customers, the value identified really *matters* and will make a difference to them and what they are doing in life or business.

4. What really matters to customers can be *measured* for its *impact* on the customer.

5. There is a *clear* and obvious *connection* among the benefits, their impact and what the customer does or is looking to achieve.

6. The customer value commitment must be *feasible* for the business to deliver and the customer to buy.

Most companies struggle to discover a great value for their customers because they tend to define customer needs relative to the current point of view the business holds about its products, customers, and competition. Equally important is to be able to distinguish between true winning customer value commitments and those that are ill-conceived, vague, or fluff-filled sales pitches. This exercise has a variety of different customer value commitments in a range of products and services. As each example is worked through, it will become more apparent what truly constitutes a strong customer value commitment. This exercise, with the exception of one case, is taken from real businesses. The identity of each company has been hidden to respect the privacy of the business. Also, remember, before criticizing any company for not clearly articulating its value to customers, first try applying this exercise to your business.

Instructions: Rate each customer value commitment based upon the five-point scale. The following sample illustrates how to rate each value commitment on six attributes using the five-point scale.

Rate These Value Commitments

RATING KEY:

5 Outstanding, it's very clear	**3** I get it, I think	**1** They tried, but I'm clueless
4 I think it's clear	**2** I think I could guess	**0** No info, no clue

EXAMPLE:

Our customers are large manufacturers of consumer electronics. We promise JIT deliveries of lot-to-lot consistent products that increase your production throughput by at least 15 percent. We improve your inventory management by offering a limited selection of high-performance products that exceed all electronic manufacturing specifications. On average our prices are 20 percent lower than any comparable competitive product.

Target Customers	Specific Benefits	Really Matters	Measurable Impact	Clear Connection	Feasible	Total
4	4	5	5	4	4	26

After you have rated the twelve business examples, review the Insight section that follows the last business example to compare your answers to authors' perspectives.

Rate These Value Propositions

RATING KEY:

5 Outstanding, it's very clear   3 I get it, I think   1 They tried, but I'm clueless

4 I think it's clear   2 I think I could guess   0 No info, no clue

	Target Customers	Specific Benefits	Really Matters	Measurable Impact	Clear Connection	Feasible	Total

1. With our team of experts, we'll help you develop new business opportunities. We'll share the risks, the resources, the finances, everything you need. We are serious about getting you a return on your investments. We can take it further than other suppliers. We share responsibility for the ongoing development and the operations of your entire business direction and processes. We can also share responsibility for all your information-technology systems.

2. For short-distance travelers, less than 750 miles, we will provide the fastest point-to-point transportation. You will enjoy flying with our funny and friendly people for a cost, on average, 30 percent less than any other form of transportation.

3. For efficiency-driven businesses, we help you achieve your growth objectives and continuously reduce costs with our low cost-to-serve model to deliver low prices while leveraging leading-edge products and technology.

Rate These Value Commitments *(continued)*

	Target Customers	Specific Benefits	Really Matters	Measurable Impact	Clear Connection	Feasible	Total

4. For the car care buff who takes great delight in personally beautifying his or her car's finish, we provide a wax system that goes on and off 50 percent faster. Our unique applicator is also ergonomically designed to cut muscle strain in half, and reduce arm and hand fatigue to a minimum. The price is equal to the leading competitive wax systems, but has ASTD surface finish equal to a new car's finish.

5. To financially oriented contractors and developers in need of rock- and asphalt-based construction materials, we provide Six Sigma level quality, 24 hours a day, 7 days per week, 365 days per year. Our prices are typically at a 10 to 15 percent premium over our competitors.

6. We enhance technically innovative companies with our leading-edge technological breakthroughs. We provide information to identify market opportunities and support development on targeted research projects and offer competitive pricing with demonstrated value.

7. Our cutting-edge performance, blazing processor speeds, awesome graphics, and almost unlimited multi-media options are all in a stylish, streamlined notebook computer that you can carry anywhere your busy life leads you.

Rate These Value Commitments   *(continued)*

	Target Customers	Specific Benefits	Really Matters	Measurable Impact	Clear Connection	Feasible	Total

8. To businesses whose data warehousing expenditures exceed $5 million per year: We will reduce your system costs by 30 percent and provide a 75 percent improvement in the speed of accessing data, while improving reliability by 50 percent.

9. To technical buyers we provide dedicated, technical expertise and solutions allowing you to grow by differentiation. The benefits you receive are:
   1. Quick response and better resource utilization,
   2. Reduced production costs,
   3. Personal, knowledgeable expertise,
   4. Mutual success, and
   5. Growth, new products, and differentiation.

10. For businesses that drive their profitability by partnering with their suppliers, we will partner with you to grow your business by providing reliability of supply and predictable prices through long-term contracts. We work closely with you to understand and respond to your company's needs with knowledgeable commercial contacts, and engage management in committing to our mutual success. Your benefits are:
    - Up-to-date and reliable information resource
    - Simplified transactions and product qualification
    - Predictable prices and costs with supply guarantee
    - Improved understanding of customer wants and needs
    - Access to the organization, both globally and locally

Rate These Value Commitments *(continued)*

- Reduced quality-control costs
- Vendor consolidation, lowering admin costs
- Reduced inventory and working capital
- Keeping customers competitive in market-place
- Updated ordering information and reordering

Target Customers	Specific Benefits	Really Matters	Measurable Impact	Clear Connection	Feasible	Total

11. We exclusively run operations by ISO certifications and lean manufacturing standards. We don't start until we can finish, and we don't stop until we're done. The tangible benefits for you are significant:
    1. We will ship you assembled and tested products within five days of production start.
    2. Our quality is unsurpassed.
    3. We offer the fastest time-to-market in the industry.

12. We focus on serious golfers who are highly competitive with their friends, work colleagues, and business clients. The customers we are pursuing have handicaps in the 10 to 20 range and are driven to cut at least 5 to 10 more strokes off their game. Our systematic approach to improving the golf performance of our customers does this by:
    - improving their driving distance by 25 to 40 yards
    - improving the accuracy and placement of drives by 45 to 55%
    - enhancing a player's short game accuracy to achieve shots within a 10-foot radius of pin placement
    - reducing putting strokes by 15 to 20%
    - focusing concentration and confidence and increasing match wins by 33 to 50%

    If our customers do not achieve the results we promise in 4 to 6 months, we reimburse all fees.

Insight Section: Rating Customer Value Commitments

This exercise was intended to teach through the examples of a company's customer value commitments. This is often easier than judging our own. In reviewing the ratings, the users should ask, what were the common reasons why ratings for one customer value commitment were higher or lower? Answering this question teaches how to judge customer value commitments more accurately and realistically.

One of the critical points of *Value-Based Marketing for Bottom-Line Success* is to discover value from the customer's perspective and find out how that value positively or negatively improves their business. Promising to help customers to do things better and faster is not the same as specifically saying what better will mean to the customer. Our bias in rating customer value commitments therefore favors those commitments that are very specific and descriptive in what they will help customers be able to do better. Offering customer value commitments with broad global statements and few specifics usually means that a business is trying to throw its best ideas forward before truly understanding the customer's world.

Finally, customer value commitments are the business team's internal thinking and ideas about customers and its strategy. Unlike positioning and customer mission statements that make many companies feel they are customer-focused, the customer value commitment is where the business team is ready to bet its paychecks. It doesn't have to be a work of great literature; it just needs to state those things that the team will do in order to build a profitable business in each customer value segment it pursues.

Additionally, these are not advertising statements or sales pitches, although they form the basis of a promotional campaign to customers. Therefore, in rating customer value commitments, don't get hung up on how cleverly worded something is. Rather, spend time on figuring out what really matters to customers. ***Substance matters more than style in this case.***

Rate These Value Commitments

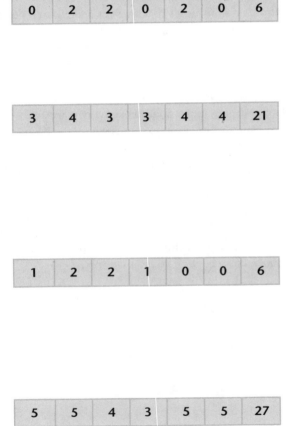

	Target Customers	Specific Benefits	Really Matters	Measurable Impact	Clear Connection	Feasible	Total
1. "Team of Experts"—In theory it sounds good and probably made this business feel they were very customer focused. But being vague and without any specifics, it's unclear what they will really do for customers.	0	2	2	0	2	0	6
2. "Short-Distance Travelers"—In truth, in disguising this value commitment, we made it weaker than it is in real life. This business has one of the best values for customers and is one of the best-run companies in the world. Lesson: It's about creating specific benefits that matter to customers, not creating fancy worded documents and internal slogans. Know who this is?	3	4	3	3	4	4	21
3. "Efficiency-Driven Businesses"—Which businesses are efficiency driven? There could also be some real conflicts in their implementation between being low cost-to-serve and offering leading-edge technology products. How will they achieve their return on investment in new technology? Many questions still need answering.	1	2	2	1	0	0	6
4. "Car Care Buff"—You've seen these people, haven't you? On a great-looking weekend they're cleaning their car—every detail of it. It sounds like the company has a staff who does the same thing on weekends!	5	5	4	3	5	5	27

Rate These Value Commitments *(continued)*

	Target Customers	Specific Benefits	Really Matters	Measurable Impact	Clear Connection	Feasible	Total
5. "Financially Oriented Contractors"—This is another case where the truth is better than what we describe. This company lives and breathes the lives of their customers and has reinvented an industry.	3	4	4	4	3	5	23
6. "Enhance Technically Innovative"—Vague, vaguer, and more vagueness. Need we be more vague?	0	2	0	0	1	0	3
7. "Cutting-Edge Performance"—From a market leader who tried to turn their value commitments into promotional copy. Lesson: value commitments are not ad copy. And people wonder why the advertising world gets a bad rap at times. And as one of us found out the hard way, you might look stylish carrying their machine, but don't have a serious technical problem on the road.	2	2	3	2	1	2	12
8. "Businesses Whose Data"—They have a clear criteria for their target customers and what they expect to do for them. The question we would explore is how much these benefits extend to the overall health and profitability of the customer's business.	5	5	3	5	2	4	24
9. "To Technical Buyers"—They are on the right track, but need to dig into specifics more of how they are going to make a difference with their customers.	2	3	2	1	2	0	10

Rate These Value Commitments *(continued)*

	Target Customers	Specific Benefits	Really Matters	Measurable Impact	Clear Connection	Feasible	Total
10. "For Businesses That Drive"—It's starting to get focused in a specific area of partnering, but needs more detailed work. The big question may be is it feasible to do everything they are suggesting they can?	2	2	2	1	2	1	10
11. "We Exclusively Run"—Without knowing who the target customers are, it's very difficult to judge what is the start of maybe a good value commitment. Identifying specific customers where this value matters is the next step.	0	3	0	2	0	2	7
12. "Focused on Serious Golfers"—You've seen the type-A golfer who is so driven to do well, fun is an afterthought. That is, after they play well. It's very clear what the golfer gets and knowing the type of golfer they are, it really does matter! And, results are guaranteed or your money back. Where do we sign up?	5	5	5	5	5	4	29

DEVELOPING CUSTOMER VALUE COMMITMENTS THAT ARE REAL AND SUPERIOR

Having a deep understanding of your customers and the market environment is the first critical step to discovering and developing customer value commitments that will make a business successful with its customers. It's necessary to gain new insight and understanding of the market dynamics and opportunities, and focus where you can provide the greatest value for customers. The following questions will guide the start of the discovery process to further help determine whether your value commitments are *real* and *superior*. We're suggesting ignoring evaluating profit at this point, since we have found too much concern for profit in early discovery can bias creating great breakthroughs.

Determining if Value Commitments Are Real

1. What are your business's assumptions, presumptions, points of view, and hypothesis(es) about the market you're trying to serve?
   - Think specifically about how your market(s) and industry are emerging.
   - What are the deeply held points of view and underlying assumptions about how your markets, customers, and competitors operate?
   - What are the factors that could change or influence current assumptions and tenets about how your marketplace competes?

2. How have you been targeting customers—by organization, consumer, or buyer type?
   - Why have you chosen to focus on these customers?
   - What is the basis of how you are selecting and focusing resources for customers?
   - Who specifically in the customer's organization are your customers?
   - Why do they buy from you?

- What would they say about what your product/service does for them?
- Could they provide quantified measurement of the results they achieve with your product/service?
- Could you provide quantified measurement of how you impact them?

3. What are your customers trying to do in their day-to-day lives?
   - Why are they trying to accomplish this?
   - Describe the scenarios where you bring things that are making a difference to these customers. Why is what you're doing working for them?
   - Describe the scenarios where you bring things that may not be making much difference to these customers. Why are they not working?

4. Are your organization's plans and actions consistent with helping your intended target customers? How so? Describe specific features/benefits and results that would appeal to target customers and your rationale.
   - Are there any features/benefits and results that do not align to your customer's needs?
   - Is your sales and marketing effort in line with your intended target customers? How so? How not so?
   - Are your resources focused in the best way to win customers' business? Specifically describe your viewpoint.

Determining If Value Commitments Are Superior

1. What are the relevant and meaningful results your business claims it is delivering to customers?
   - How specifically are your target customers impacted when using your products/services compared to using a competitor's?
   - How do you know this is meaningful to your customers?
   - Is this making a positive contribution to them?
   - How have you quantified the contribution?
   - What is the promise you're making to customers if they use your product(s)?

2. If you were in the shoes of the customers, what would be your assessment of your value commitment?
   - Is the *experience* you create with customers meaningful and compelling?
   - How so? Can this experience be quantified?
   - Is your customer experience equal to, less than, or greater than the experience they receive from a competitor?

- How could you strengthen the experience? What additional functionality, features/benefits, and results would you recommend as part of your offer? Why?
- Why would these improvements be valuable to customers? Would you be able to quantify the value of these improvements?

3. Should your business continue to focus on its current customers or new customers?
- Which specific new customers should the business target? Why?
- Would there be enough of these new customers to create a segment worth going after?
- Are any benefits missing that these customers would find important and pay for?

4. Who are the competitors most closely competing against you?
- Where is your business vulnerable compared to competitors?
- How good are you at attracting and keeping customers relative to competition?
- What would you improve?
- What kind of competitive situation(s) would make your business vulnerable with customers?

5. From your customer's perspective, which company(s) do you think they see as having the superior value and achieving the best customer results?
- How would/could you improve your value commitment to maintain and grow your customer base?
- Do you think you can realistically implement these improvements?

PENTADIGM VALUE–BASED MARKETING DIAGNOSTIC

As an outcome of developing the Pentadigm model and mind-set, we have developed also a tool to help readers assess the Pentadigm performance of their own organization: the *value-based marketing diagnostic*. This diagnostic is an objective, comprehensive, in-depth analysis of your value-based marketing processes and practices, including:

- A detailed examination of your practice on the five steps
- A detailed examination of your approach to value-based marketing
- A detailed examination of your implementation of value-based marketing
- An internal appraisal from customer-facing staff through the CEO
- An external appraisal with direct customer feedback

1: Discover — Understand the Customer

1.1 Define and Map the Market

Areas to Address
- How the organization collects and analyzes information on the market it operates in

Key Assessment Points
- How the organization collects and analyzes information on external forces in the marketplace
- How this information is used by the organization to drive marketing strategy

- How the organization analyzes costs incurred and value created and captured at each stage of the value chain

Examples
- Organization seeks proactively and maintains regularly customer/market data to analyze customer value segments and their value and benefits sought.
- The market has been defined around the key customer values and benefits sought, with particular attention to unmet and poorly met needs.
- Key players in the market have been identified as well as suppliers, channels, and influencers.
- Value is captured at each level of the value chain.
- All relevant customers in the value chain have been defined, including the ultimate end user.

Key Questions
- How do you gather information on the market?
- How frequently do you gather and update information on the market?
- What type of information do you collect?
- How objective is the information?
- How is this information stored, analyzed, and used?

Documentation/Evidence
- Market maps
- Value chain analysis
- Market force and environmental analysis
- Market research reports

1.2 Understand Customer Value Expectations

Areas to Address
- How the organization determines customers' value and benefits sought and expectations, and then uses these to shape its offering

Key Assessment Points
- How the organization collects and analyzes a variety of internal and external data to determine the value and benefits sought and the expectations of current and potential customers
- What processes the organization has for using this knowledge to review and enhance product and service features

- How the organization derives customer understanding from internal customer interfaces

Examples
- External research is supplemented by internal contact information, performance and complaint data, and correlated to customer satisfaction data.
- Organization has developed a customer information system to obtain and capture customer needs and expectations data, which drives a formal process to make regular enhancements to products and services.
- All customer-contact personnel have access to a customer information system providing a full history of transactions, contacts, value, and benefits sought and satisfaction of customers they deal with.
- Organization closely monitors losses and gains of customers to determine how product and service features can be enhanced to ensure customer loyalty.
- Fully integrated process to evaluate performance in meeting customer value and benefits is sought and a feedback system that demonstrates to the customer that their comments are being used to improve offering development is implemented.

Key Questions
- Which methods and sources does your organization use to identify customer value and benefits sought?
- How do you identify customer value segments and potential customers and distinguish among their value and benefits sought?
- How is information on customer value and benefits being sought, centralized, stored, and communicated across the organization?
- Can you provide evidence that you have improved your products and services over the last few years as a result of your identification of customer value and benefits sought and expectations?
- How do you collect and analyze internal feedback at customer interfaces?

Documentation/Evidence
- A systematic and effective process for collecting and analyzing a variety of market and customer data
- Documentation of customer value and benefits sought and expectations included in the organization's strategic plans
- Product and service features changed/designed to respond to customer value and benefits sought
- Summaries of customer research

- Customer research plan
- Examples of questionnaires

1.3 Discover Customer Value Segments

Areas to Address
- How customers' value and benefits sought and expectations are used to segment the market

Key Assessment Points
- How the organization makes use of market information to group customers into discrete customer value segments

Examples
- Organization proactively seeks and regularly maintains customer/market data to analyze customer value segments and their value and benefits sought.
- Customer value segmentation of the market/customer base
- How research drives customer value segmentation

Key Questions
- How do you identify customer value segments and potential customers and distinguish among their value and benefits sought?
- Can you group customers into discrete clusters based on similar value set?
- Can you profile and quantify each customer value segment?
- Have you identified unmet customer needs?

Documentation/Evidence
- A systematic and effective process for collecting and analyzing customer data
- Documentation of customer needs by customer type and/or behavior
- Grouping of customer need into clusters/customer value segments
- Profiling of customer value segments
- Summaries of customer value segmentation work

1.4 Assess Competitive Position

Areas to Address
- How the organization collects and analyzes information on its competitors' offering and their performance in the eyes of the customers

Key Assessment Points

- How the company identifies competition—both generic and non-generic, existing and potential
- How the organization collects and analyzes information on competitors' processes and the features of their products and services
- How the organization attempts to understand the driving forces in the market
- What processes the organization uses to understand its strengths and weaknesses relative to the competition
- How this information is used by the organization to improve its understanding of its own products, services, and processes

Examples

- Competition identified according to ability or potential ability to fulfill customer value set.
- Competitor information is gathered through customer contact, lost-order analysis, market research, and formal benchmarking.
- Analysis of competitor information is widely communicated and used to support customer-contact staff in targeting prospects and developing sales arguments.
- Competitors' and industry trends and standards are known by the organization.
- Products, services, and processes are regularly compared with competitors' and with customer information to ensure they fully reflect best practice and correspond competitively to customer value and benefits sought.

Key Questions

- How do you decide who your current and future competitors are?
- How do you gather information on your competitors?
- What type of information do you collect?
- How is this information analyzed and used?
- How do you verify the accuracy of the information?
- Do you understand the driving forces in the market?
- Do you understand the relative position of your offers with respect to competitive offerings from the customer's perspective?

Documentation/Evidence

- A systematic process to collect, analyze, and disseminate competitor information
- A process to benchmark and evaluate competitors' processes and incorporate appropriate features in the organization's own approach

- Typical information held on a key competitor
- Examples of changes to products and services based on improved customer understanding achieved through competitor comparisons
- Product/service comparison data
- Competitor information pro forma
- Evidence of SWOT analysis or similar
- Evidence of market analysis

1.5 Select Target Customer Value Segments

Areas to Address
- What processes the organization uses to select targeted customer value segments
- How the organization assesses the size, value, and relative attractiveness of each customer value segment
- What process is used to evaluate competitive position from the customer perspective

Key Assessment Points
- How the organization sets the criteria for evaluation of customer value segments
- How the organization evaluates its own performance and that of its competitors with regard to customer need fulfillment and critical success factors (CSFs)
- How this information is used by the organization to select targeted customer value segments
- How the organization defines the customer value segment attractiveness relative to its business goals and strategies

Examples
- A variety of external information is used to evaluate size, value, and relative attractiveness of each customer value segment and relative competitive position.
- Competitor information is gathered through customer contact, lost-order analysis, market research, and formal benchmarking.
- Analysis of competitor information is widely communicated and used to support customer-contact staff in targeting prospects and developing sales arguments.
- Competitors' and industry trends and standards are known by the organization.
- Products, services, and processes are regularly compared with those of competitors and with customer information to ensure they fully reflect

best practice and correspond competitively to customer value and benefits sought.

Key Questions
- Do you understand the relative size, value, and attractiveness of each customer value segment?
- Can you quantify the customer value segment attractiveness criteria?
- Can you prioritize the customer value segment attractiveness criteria?
- Can you measure the customers' perception (or actual rating) of your ability to fulfill their value set versus competitive offerings?
- Do you understand the relative competitive position in each customer value segment?
- How accurate is the information you have? Is it verified externally?

Documentation/Evidence
- Key market attractiveness criteria
- Weighting of attractiveness criteria
- Target Customer Value Segment Tracer
- Customer satisfaction research

2: Commit—Commit to the Customer

2.1 Define Customer Value Segment Strategy

Areas to Address
- How the organization develops and refines its customer value segment strategy
- How it develops its position in specific customer value segments
- How the portfolio will be balanced

Key Assessment Points
- How the organization defines its customer value segment strategy
- How the organization develops a position for the customer value segment (grow, maintain, harvest, exit)
- How the organization develops a marketing strategy for the customer value segment
- How the organization defines a brand strategy per customer value segment

Examples
- A clear strategy has been developed with clearly communicated goals and objectives.

- The business has a portfolio of strategies, ranging from growth, through maintain, to harvest.

Key Questions
- What is your customer value segment strategy?
- Do you understand the size and trends of the customer value segments?
- Do you understand your relative position in the customer value segment?
- Do you understand the position of your brands in each customer value segment?

Documentation/Evidence
- Internal and external research
- Market/product life cycle analysis
- Customer value analysis
- Brand tracking and positioning studies
- Customer value segment plans
- Local marketing plans

2.2 Develop Superior Offering

Areas to Address
- How the organization takes the information on customer values by customer value segment and builds differentiated customer offers based on value to the customer; how these offers are differentiated

Key Assessment Points
- How information gathered in Step 1 is summarized per customer value segment based on customer values
- What process the organization uses to develop distinctive customer value commitments
- What process is used to assess the value of customer value commitments to the organization and to the customer

Examples
- Customer value commitments are defined per target customer value segment.
- Customer value commitments are clearly defined with target audience, customer value, superior customer value, and profit.
- A clear and concise banner headline explains the customer value commitment (elevator test).

- Customer value commitments are distinctive, differentiated, and deliverable.

Key Questions
- Are the target audiences for each customer value commitment clearly defined?
- What is the compelling reason for the customer to buy?
- How is the value superior to the customer?
- How is the customer value commitment profitable?
- How can the customer value commitment be protected and for how long?
- What are the barriers to competitive entry?

Documentation/Evidence
- Target audience defined for each customer value commitment
- Customer values clearly defined for each main customer value segment
- Key differentiators defined for each customer value commitment
- Compelling reasons defined

2.3 Create the Right Organization

Areas to Address
- How the organization assesses its current capabilities and maps these against the capabilities necessary to deliver the customer value commitment, in order to establish the gaps
- How the organization plans to fill the capability gaps

Key Assessment Points
- How the organization defines the capabilities needed to deliver the customer value commitment competitively
- What process is used to assess the organization's current capabilities to deliver
- How the organization plans to fill the capability gap in terms of skills and competencies, service standards, warranties and returns, customer service, etc.

Examples
- A well-defined set of skills, capabilities, and competencies is defined for each key job in the organization.
- Each job in the organization contains an element of customer focus, customer value.

- A training and development program is offered to staff at all levels and is linked to career development.

Key Questions
- Have you defined what the key criteria are to deliver the customer value commitment?
- Have you assessed the organization's capability to deliver the customer value commitment?
- Have you identified any major shortfalls?
- Do you have an ongoing plan to fill the gaps?
- Is there a training and development program in place for all staff at all levels?

Documentation/Evidence
- Clear definitions of business criteria to deliver customer value commitments
- Capabilities audit
- SWOT analysis
- Skills and competencies defined and documented for all jobs in the organization

2.4 Define Key Performance Indicators (KPIs)

Areas to Address
- How the organization develops and maintains customer service standards, how they are deployed by customer service staff, how performance is tracked and improved
- How the organization benchmarks its performance

Key Assessment Points
- How the organization establishes key customer related measures
- How the organization defines a clear set of business rules and service standards to deliver the customer value commitment
- How performance against service standards is tracked
- How service standards are evaluated and improved to meet changing customer value and benefits sought and competitor offerings
- How the organization benchmarks its performance

Examples
- Standards are driven by customer expectations and key quality indicators, fully deployed throughout the organization, and these are compared to competitors' service standards.
- Employee customer contact performance is measured to these standards.

- Standards are reviewed on a regular basis with input from customer-contact personnel, customers, and management information systems, showing the consequences of past performance against standards.
- Organization embarks upon regular benchmarking exercises in key process areas.

Key Questions

- Which major customer service standards has your organization developed?
- Have they changed over the past three years?
- How do your service standards compare to those of competitors?
- How are the standards measured and tracked?
- What internal measures and standards do you have to ensure the support given by other units is timely and effective?
- How do you ensure service standards are competitive in the marketplace (benchmarking)?

Documentation/Evidence

- The organization's major customer service standards and the criteria by which they are measured
- Processes that demonstrate service standards are clearly derived from customer relationship criteria
- Trends in performance against service standards
- Examples of changes to service standards in response to internal evaluation and market value and benefits sought
- Reporting on performance versus service standards over time

2.5 Communicate Internally and Externally

Areas to Address

- How the organization defines and develops its customer value commitment communication process externally
- How the organization defines and develops its customer value commitment communication process internally

Key Assessment Points

- How the organization develops clear external communications of the customer value commitment
- How the organization plans the external communication of the customer value commitment to its customers
- How the organization develops clear internal communications of the customer value commitment

- How the organization plans the internal communication of the customer value commitment to its staff and channel partners

Examples
- Clear, well-written literature, brochures, technical documents (print and electronic) using customers' language and terminology are created.
- Regular communications programs target customers.
- Newsletters
- Regular communications programs to staff and channel partners are implemented.
- Publish clearly defined and documented business rules and service standards to each customer value segment.
- Plan regular updating.

Key Questions
- Does a set of business rules and service standards exist for each customer value commitment?
- Are they clearly defined and communicated to customers?
- Are they clearly defined and communicated internally?
- Has the customer value commitment been defined in terms meaningful to the customer?
- Has the customer value commitment been defined in terms relevant to the business?
- Has the customer value commitment been communicated to customers?
- How do you check customer understanding?
- Has the customer value commitment been communicated to staff and channel partners?
- How do you check staff and channel partner understanding?

Documentation/Evidence
- Customer value commitment guidelines and standards
- External customer value commitment communications
- Internal customer value commitment communications
- Newsletters, briefings, etc.

3: Create—Create Customer Value

3.1 Develop a Customer Value Commitment Culture

Areas to Address
- How senior executives' personal leadership and involvement, and the organization's leadership system, create and sustain a customer focus and promote performance excellence. Including senior executives' role in creating and reinforcing values and expectations throughout the entire

workforce, reviewing overall company performance, including customer-related and operational performance, using the leadership system and organization to focus on customer and high-performance objectives
- How the organization takes action to increase employees' authority to act (empowerment), their responsibility, and their ability to innovate

Key Assessment Points
- Management style as it impacts on customer value commitment and business performance
- The types of questions management regularly asks staff
- Commitment of leaders to improving customer value and supporting staff in delivering customer value
- How the organization takes action to increase employees' empowerment, responsibility, and innovation
- The organization's plans to prepare employees to take on increased responsibilities in day-to-day decision making

Examples
- Customer focus and commitment is part of corporate vision, mission, and values.
- Empowerment and innovation is stressed in organization's vision statement and in senior manager's day-to-day contact with employees.
- Practice of empowering leadership from top to bottom of organization is evident.
- Leaders regularly hold reviews on customer value aspects of the business and regularly meet to identify ways of improving customer focus.
- Organization has empowered customer-contact employees to resolve the majority of customer problems, including access to all relevant functions in the organization, considerable freedom to develop solutions, and authority to act.

Key Questions
- What are the key management concepts followed by your leaders?
- What types of contact do your leaders have with the staff?
- How do leaders set direction and monitor performance?
- What actions have you taken to increase the empowerment of employees in all functions?
- What is the perception of the customer-facing staff regarding empowerment?

Documentation/Evidence
- Visibility and accessibility of leaders to customer-contact personnel
- Examples of leaders' behavior as a role model in terms of customer value commitment

- Consistent reinforcement of the importance of customer value through management communications, decisions, actions, values, and expectations
- A leadership system that sets goals and directions to inspire performance excellence and reward increased focus on customers
- Change management programs in place and functioning
- Plans for increasing employee empowerment
- Evidence of increases in employee empowerment over the last 2–5 years
- Financial and other important powers granted to employees

3.2 Plan Customer Value Processes

Areas to Address
- How the organization defines and plans processes and subprocesses needed to deliver customer value
- How the organization implements those processes

Key Assessment Points
- How the organization plans customer value processes
- How the organization plans subprocesses
- Techniques used to ensure comprehensive process definition
- Linkage of processes to customer value

Examples
- Well-organized, rigorous system for planning customer value processes is in place.
- Formal and informal organizational structure that allows and encourages team building and team problem solving, cross-functional communications, contact with customers, and integration with suppliers is in place.
- Process planning and improvement teams that are empowered to help the organization change are in place.
- Innovative methods for opening lines of communication up and down the organization have been established.

Key Questions
- What are the key processes needed to deliver each element of customer value to which you have committed?
- Have you defined high-level processes and detailed subprocesses in a hierarchy down to individual activities?
- Do you know the value contributed by each process, subprocess, and activity?

Documentation/Evidence
- Process maps
- Linkages to customer value commitments at an item level
- Regular review and refinement of processes

3.3 Populate the Customer Value Processes

Areas to Address

- How the organization defines skills and competencies needed to implement customer value processes
- How the organization acquires, develops, and deploys these skills and competencies
- How the deployment of the skills and competencies is rewarded
- What process the organization uses to promote employee involvement, individually and in groups. Include how the organization gives feedback for achieving and maintaining motivation and involvement at all levels and functions
- What the key people management processes are, including how employees are managed, supported, and trained in order to be able to satisfy customer needs. How recognition, reward, and performance measurement for individuals and groups, including managers, supports the company's customer service objectives

Key Assessment Points

- How the organization defines skills and competencies needed to implement customer value processes
- How the organization acquires, develops, and deploys these skills and competencies
- How the organization deploys staff and external suppliers
- How the deployment of the skills and competencies is rewarded
- How employees are managed and supported in order to be able to deliver customer value
- How employees are trained and developed to be able to deliver customer value
- Techniques used to promote both team and individual contributions that will enhance customer value
- Ways in which individual employee ideas can be heard
- Systems that ensure timely feedback
- Programs to acquire and develop skills and competencies
- How the organization determines the training needs of employees, and if there is an ongoing method for reevaluating those needs
- Whether the organization has compensation systems in place linking a portion of employees' remuneration to the achievement of customer value goals

Examples

- Formal and informal organizational structure that allows and encourages team building and team problem solving, cross-functional communications, contact with customers, and integration with suppliers is in place.

- Process assessment and improvement teams that are empowered to help the organization change exist.
- Innovative methods for opening lines of communication up and down the organization have been established.
- Regular assessment of skills and competency needs against processes is used.
- Well-developed programs to acquire, develop, and deploy skills and competencies are in place.
- Customer value creation skills are the highest performance factor for hiring customer-contact employees.
- Policy, procedures, and management directives emphasize customer value.
- All functions in the organization are aware of customer value and benefits sought.
- Training is provided to all employees to improve job performance.
- A range of customer-value related reward schemes is in place to recognize individuals and teams.
- Performance (appraisal) is linked to customer value goals.
- Well-defined outsourcing and partnering programs are in place.

Key Questions

- What is the employee perception with regard to cooperation and teamwork in your organization?
- How do you measure employee perception?
- Are the skills and competencies needed for process implementation clearly defined for all processes, subprocesses, and activities?
- Have you defined an appropriate skills and competencies development strategy?
- Have you selected appropriate learning methods and providers?
- Do you know the value contributed by a set of skills and competence?
- Are the rewards for performance in skill and competency deployment well-defined, communicated, and clearly understood?
- How do you identify and select employees, in particular, customer-contact employees?
- To what extent do employees feel they are supported by management?
- To what extent are employees able to decide on the necessary course of action to meet customer requests?
- To what extent are employees able to improve their processes?
- To what extent does your organization have a strategic training and development plan to meet the training needs of new and existing employees? How are they developed?
- How do you assess employee training value and benefits sought and meet their needs?

- To what extent is compensation based on the achievement of customer value goals?

Documentation/Evidence
- Multiple avenues of employee access to management to propose ideas
- Well-defined skills and competencies for all processes, subprocesses, and activities, linked to job descriptions and levels
- Well-developed, communicated, and defined skill and competency acquisition and development programs
- Examples of customer value creation initiatives
- Customer value creation criteria used in recruitment and selection of employees
- The inclusion of service standards and measurement criteria in job descriptions, performance appraisals, promotion, and remuneration of employees
- Job descriptions and skill sets for employees
- Results of training needs assessments included in training plans
- Range of financial and nonfinancial mechanisms to recognize and reward good performance in customer value creation
- Records of routine employee meetings to review company progress
- Well-communicated reward and motivation system in place

3.4 Invest in Appropriate Infrastructure

Areas to Address
- Decisions about investments in infrastructure and outsourcing in line with customer values
- Decisions about system strategy, how systems are aligned with customer values
- Technology and channel support for employees to enable them to provide reliable and responsive service
- How customer data is stored and made accessible to all staff that have dealings with the customer.

Key Assessment Points
- How the organization decides upon investments in infrastructure and outsourcing in line with customer values
- How the organization decides upon its system strategy, how systems are aligned with customer values
- How the organization provides technology and channel support for employees to enable them to provide reliable and responsive service
- What processes exist to capture customer data, refine it, and store it in such a way that frontline staff has ready access to live information

Examples
- Well-developed investment programs for all key infrastructure elements, covering the long term and defining ROI exist.
- Management information system provides real-time support and insight to employees servicing customer inquiries and complaints.
- Employees are able to follow up on problem status in real time.
- Employees are involved in reviewing and developing systems to ensure they are easy to use and meet their business value and benefits sought.
- CRM database combines customer account data with customer sales and marketing data.

Key Questions
- Do you have an infrastructure and investment strategy that will enable realistic achievement of customer value commitments?
- Do you have a systems strategy that has been clearly communicated?
- How do you assess whether the level of technologies available to support employees is appropriate?
- To what extent do employees feel they are involved in developing an appropriate level of technology?
- Have you designed and implemented enterprise-wide knowledge management systems to share customer information?
- Is customer information accurate and up-to-date?
- How many different systems do employees need to use?
- Are all customer-facing systems user-friendly and efficient?
- Have you automated customer-facing interfaces?

Documentation/Evidence
- Infrastructure and investment plan are well-defined and clearly communicated
- Clearly defined partnering, channel, and outsourcing programs
- Systems strategy documented
- Management information systems and structures to provide information on performance against business and customer value creation
- Ease of access and use of customer and product databases
- Support available to staff based out of the office

3.5 Implement Customer Value

Areas to Address
- How the organization plans and prioritizes its actions
- How the actions are linked to the customer value commitment
- How the organization measures achievement of goals by successful completion of actions

- What processes exist for ensuring easy access for customers to seek assistance and to comment?

Key Assessment Points
- What process the organization uses to plan and prioritize its key actions
- What process the organization has to measure achievement of goals by successful completion of actions
- How effectively the organization sees that it is off track or off target
- How customers are provided with easy access to the organization for assistance, complaints, or other feedback
- Mechanisms available to customers that are both easy to use and responsive to their needs
- How quickly the organization responds to customer inquiries and resolves problems

Examples
- Transparent and well-documented action planning, linked to line items in the customer commitment, is in place.
- Regular reporting and assessment of actions, results, and achievements occurs throughout the company.
- Customer service and support is available and easily accessed.
- Company management can be accessed by the customers.
- A single point of contact enables rapid response to all customer needs.

Key Questions
- How do you set priorities?
- How do you ensure that customers know whom to contact when they have questions, comments, suggestions, or complaints?
- How do you evaluate your contact methods to see if they meet customer needs?
- How do you keep track of actions and their completion?
- How do you know if something is *not* going according to plan?

Documentation/Evidence
- Minutes of meetings where conflicting projects have been prioritized
- Documentation showing existence and patterns of use for the various contact mechanisms, e.g., free customer service numbers, product comment cards, etc.
- Effectiveness of contact channels as well as measures of their ease of use, e.g., how long it takes to get through on free phone numbers, how quickly questions are answered/problems resolved, etc.
- Results of research into how easy the organization is to do business with

- Reports showing numbers of contact by channel and by reason for contact
- Statistics showing waiting time, numbers in queue, etc.
- Regular documented reviews of action plans and commitments at all levels in the organization, with 360-degree assessment

4: Assess—Obtain Customer Feedback

4.1 Track Won and Lost Business

Areas to Address
- How the organization analyzes key customer-related data and information to understand why customers or orders are won or lost and potential sales achieved or not achieved

Key Assessment Points
- How the organization analyzes key customer-related data and information to understand why customers or orders are won or lost and potential sales achieved or not achieved
- How this data is used to develop an understanding of customer needs and to enhance products, services, and processes
- How independent and objective the analysis is

Examples
- Rigorous, systematic approach and structure are in place to identify the causes of lost customers or orders. Feed this into the overall understanding of customer value and benefits sought and drive improvements in products, services, processes, and behaviors.
- Rigorous, systematic approach and structure are in place to identify the causes of won customers or orders. Feed this into the overall understanding of customer value and benefits sought and sustain and reinforce the successful behavior.
- Through rigorous analysis, the organization understands the relationship between won and lost orders and the situation among all its customers.
- The organization translates this information into projections to determine the impact on its business.

Key Questions
- To what extent do you carry out follow-up to determine the causes of lost/won customers or the reasons why new customers/sales have been made/not made?
- To what extent does your organization measure and put a value on customer retention?

- To what extent does your organization analyze the cost of lost customers/business?
- How is data on won customers/business and successes used to sustain and/or reinforce marketing, products/services, pricing, or other strategies that will result in increased customer retention?
- How is data on lost customers/business and complaints used to change marketing, products/services, pricing, or other strategies that will result in increased customer satisfaction?

Documentation/Evidence

- Examples of data analysis that have resulted in action plans, new measures of performance, or reset priorities of product or service features
- Reports showing lost/won order analysis, with well-researched and documented reasons

4.2 Proactively Seek Customer Feedback

Areas to Address

- How the organization defines customer interfaces from awareness, through inquiry to ordering, services, after-sales contacts, and repeat business
- How the organization seeks feedback from customers, at all interfaces, to determine satisfaction with those interfaces and uses this to help build relationships and improve processes

Key Assessment Points

- How the organization identifies all customer interfaces
- How proactive and aggressive the organization is in seeking customer feedback that will help to build relationships and improve products and services
- How many different methods are used to gain customer input to ensure that the organization thoroughly samples its customer base on all types of transactions
- How easy it is for the customer to communicate with the organization on customer interfaces
- How well the organization responds to customer input and corrects the subject of customer complaints

Examples

- All possible customer interfaces (both passive and active) are defined and documented.
- Customer feedback is encouraged, respected, applied, and responded to.

- The organization routinely follows up on all, or a sample of, customer transactions to systematically determine satisfaction and gain information for improvement.
- Follow-up information is communicated throughout the organization for product and service improvements.
- Customers are informed of how their comments have been used by the organization to improve quality.

Key Questions
- To what extent do you carry out follow-up to determine if customers are satisfied with the contact they have had with your organization?
- To what extent do you gather data on new customers to determine why they selected your organization's products/services?
- Can you provide evidence that data obtained from feedback is used to improve existing products/services and to design new ones?
- What evidence can you provide to show the positive reinforcement of successful customer-facing behavior and the sharing of such successful ideas between different parts of the organization?

Documentation/Evidence
- Regular monitoring and reporting of all customer interfaces and their outcomes
- Reports showing inquiry levels and conversion rates of inquiries to customers
- Reports showing number of contacts by channel and by reason for contact
- Descriptions of a variety of methods of customer follow-up (e.g., phone calls, mail, surveys, and site visits)
- Customer retention reports and analysis
- Data showing the number and percentage of customers surveyed
- Evidence of the systematic analysis of survey data and linkages to process/product improvement activities
- Questionnaires and feedback cards
- Summaries of feedback findings

4.3 Resolve Customer Complaints

Areas to Address
- How the organization ensures that formal and informal complaints and feedback are recorded and aggregated for overall reporting and analysis
- How the organization ensures that complaints are resolved promptly and effectively

Key Assessment Points

- Whether the organization has a comprehensive yet simple process for collecting, summarizing, and reporting all formal and informal customer comments and complaints
- Whether customer feedback is analyzed, disseminated, and acted on quickly
- Whether the organization has a comprehensive process for tracking and resolving all formal and informal customer comments and complaints promptly and effectively

Examples

- Formalized system is in place to record, track, and give feedback on customer complaints to the overall organization and appropriate organization unit, regular reporting of complaint trend analysis at senior management levels.
- Employees in contact with customers have direct responsibility for resolving customer complaints.
- Indicators show a continuous improvement in response to customer complaints over time.
- Follow-up program is in place to inquire with customer that the customer-contact person acted in a responsive manner. This information is fed back to the customer-contact employee.
- Measurement indicators include: response time to complaint resolution; number of complaints per employee; cost impact of lost or gained business.

Key Questions

- How do you ensure that customer comments/complaints are quickly fed back to the appropriate units?
- What process exists to aggregate the overall level of complaints and communicate this to management?
- How does your organization keep track of customer complaints?
- To what extent do you record both formal and informal complaints?
- How do you ensure that all complaints are resolved?
- Can you demonstrate that the time needed to resolve customer complaints is continuously decreasing?
- Can you show that customers are satisfied with the way you handle complaints?

Documentation/Evidence

- A comprehensive system for managing complaints from initiation to resolution

- A comprehensive system for collecting and analyzing customer comments and complaints
- Customer complaint and feedback reports that are disseminated throughout the organization for information and/or action
- Methods to track complaints to ensure timely resolution
- Reports showing complaint resolution times and/or other related measures

4.4 Assess Performance Against Customer Expectations

Areas to Address
- How the organization determines customer satisfaction for customer groups, and how satisfaction relative to competitors is determined. Review of the process should include what information is sought, frequency of surveys, interviews, or other contact.
- How objectivity is assured, how the organization sets the customer satisfaction measurement scale to adequately reflect customer preferences; how the information is used

Key Assessment Points
- How the organization determines customer satisfaction for defined customer groups and customer value segments, covering the information sought, how measurement scales are set, and frequency of assessment
- How research partners are selected and managed to ensure objectivity
- How customer satisfaction data is analyzed, applied, and responded to
- How customer satisfaction relative to competitors is determined
- How results are communicated internally and externally

Examples
- Customer satisfaction indices are developed by customer group and customer value segment, drawing on a range of measures including regular satisfaction surveys, internal data, adverse indicators—such as complaints and returns—and transaction feedback.
- Processes exist to integrate customer satisfaction results into process reviews and overall customer understanding.
- Verification of data is performed through independent sources to confirm objectivity and validity.
- Satisfaction data is displayed relative to key competitors and benchmarked against best practices.

Key Questions
- How do you measure customer satisfaction?
- What are the different sources from which you obtain data on competitors' level of customer satisfaction?

- Do your methods vary for different customer value segments?
- How were the measures derived?
- What use is made of customer satisfaction research results?
- How do you ensure the data are objective, appropriate, and thorough?
- Do you measure satisfaction of current and potential customers?

Documentation/Evidence

- Selection criteria for independent provider of customer satisfaction research
- Formal process for measuring customer satisfaction and sources of data
- More than one source of customer satisfaction data
- Frequency and sample size when measuring customer satisfaction
- Examples of analysis and recommendations based on customer satisfaction data
- Systematic process for collecting and analyzing competitive satisfaction data
- Questionnaires used in satisfaction surveys
- Summaries of findings
- Details of actions taken and completed as a result of survey findings

4.5 Combine Analyses to Improve

Areas to Address

- Integration of key indicators and methods the organization uses to evaluate and improve its customer feedback processes, particularly addressing effectiveness, response time improvement, and translation of findings into improvements
- How the company identifies gaps in performance and translates them into new and improved processes

Key Assessment Points

- How the organization evaluates and improves all its customer feedback processes
- How the organization evaluates and improves its overall methods and measurement scales used in determining customer satisfaction relative to competitors
- How indicators and methods address effectiveness and the translation of findings into improvements
- How the organization identifies major gaps in performance
- What process is used to close performance gaps

Examples of Best Practice

- Policies and procedures supported by management information systems exist to improve the process for managing customer complaints.

- Focus groups are formed by the organization to compare internal perspectives of customer complaints with external groups.
- Customer complaints have decreased over time.
- Speed of complaint resolution has improved.
- Formal reviews of customer satisfaction measurement and analysis processes take place regularly.
- Independent sources are used to review and evaluate improvement of customer satisfaction processes.

Key Questions
- How have your complaint handling processes changed over the last three years? What has caused these changes?
- Can you provide evidence that changes in strategies have resulted in fewer complaints and fewer lost customers?
- What do you do when major adverse indicators show an upward trend?
- How do you review your processes for measuring satisfaction with your own and your competitors' products and services?
- How do you compare and contrast the results from different sources of customer interface and feedback?
- How do you validate results?
- What changes have been made to your processes over the last two to three years?

Documentation/Evidence
- Systematic processes to collect and analyze measurements of key criteria
- Examples of improvements made in methods to assess customer satisfaction or apply satisfaction data
- Evidence of cross-comparison and validation of data from different interfaces and sources
- Evidence of routine evaluation of the process
- Examples of changes and improvements made to the complaint-handling process

5: Improve—Measure & Improve Value

5.1 Spot Gaps and "Quick Hits"

Areas to Address
- What processes the company uses to understand customer and market trends and anticipate change. How that information is used to develop and analyze business scenarios

- How the organization identifies and monitors appropriate business measures (e.g., market share, average customer size) and seeks to identify the impact of improvements in customer service on the business results. Trends and results in appropriate key performance indicators (e.g., customer retention)

Key Assessment Points
- What processes the company uses to understand future customer needs
- How the organization establishes market trends
- Scenario development and analysis
- Trends in gaining (or losing) customers by customer value segment relative to competitor
- How the organization establishes and monitors links between customer satisfaction and business results
- Trends in key performance indicators relative to major competitors

Evidence Required
- Data that shows a positive trend in key performance indicators
- Customer profitability measured over time shows positive trend; losses of customers are lowest among industry.
- Evidence that these gains are due to improvements in customer satisfaction and were not the result of market factors

Examples
- Correlation analysis is performed to determine the impact of customer satisfaction on key measures such as market share, retention rates, and customer profitability.
- Positive trends exist for customer satisfaction and all key performance indicators, ahead of the competition.
- Organization demonstrates growth in market share for key customer value segments that is higher than competitors'.

Key Questions
- Can you demonstrate that you measure trends in gaining or losing customers by customer value segment?
- How does this trend compare with your competition?
- What are the key measures of performance for your organization? What are the trends in these key measures over the last two to three years?

Documentation/Evidence
- A systematic process to collect and analyze measurements of key criteria
- Evidence of routine evaluations of the process

- Reports linking customer satisfaction results with Key Performance Indicator
- Data that show a steady trend in gaining customers (beyond the rate of market growth)
- Data that show customer retention levels exceeding that of major competitors
- Reports showing trends in gaining and losing customers over time

5.2 Challenge Customer Understanding

Areas to Address
- How the organization evaluates the processes for gathering and analyzing data on customer value and benefits sought and expectations in order to continually improve
- How the organization shares customer data with all key contact staff
- What process the organization uses to review customer value segmentation in the light of new data

Key Assessment Points
- How the organization evaluates the process for gathering and mining data on customer value and benefits sought and expectations in order to continually improve
- The key criteria used to evaluate the processes for determining current and future expectations of customers and value and benefits sought
- How the organization shares customer data with all key contact staff
- What process the organization uses to review customer value segmentation in the light of new data

Examples
- The organization routinely and continuously evaluates the effectiveness of the processes used to determine customer expectations and improves the process as a result.
- The organization regularly updates key customer data and uses this to review and update customer value segmentation.
- The organization routinely assesses methods used to ensure they are effective; often outside experts are invited to do this.
- The organization reviews the collection methods for internal consistency.
- Summarized customer data is routinely shared with all departments so that they are aware of changing customer needs by customer value segment.

Key Questions
- How do you systematically evaluate your methods for gathering data on customer value and benefits sought and expectations?
- Can you provide evidence that you have improved the way you collect and use information on customer value and benefits sought as a result of the process evaluation?
- How do you share customer data?
- When did you last review your customer value segmentation?

Documentation/Evidence
- A systematic process to collect data on key criteria
- Evidence of routine evaluation of processes
- Examples of improvements made in the process
- Examples of increasingly successful market introductions of new products and services

5.3 Redefine Customer Value Commitment

Areas to Address
- The process for determining customers' future value and benefits sought and changes in the relative importance of product and service value to customers
- How changing needs have been reflected in new and updated customer value commitments
- Whether service standards and KPIs have been updated to reflect the change in customer value commitment

Key Assessment Points
- How the organization collects and analyzes customer and market data and other information to project future customer value and benefits sought
- How broad a range of information the organization uses from sources on competitors, technology, and social and economic factors to help the organization predict with confidence what customers will value
- What process is used to review and redefine customer value commitments
- Whether service standards are updated to reflect changes in customer value commitments

Examples
- Organization policies, procedures, and marketing communications stress that products and services are designed to meet changing customer values.

- Organization involves all appropriate functions in developing new products and services, and this is clearly driven by documented projections of customer value and benefits sought.
- Organization uses a mix of methods to identify and project value and benefits sought and features, such as surveys, focus groups, interviews, review of customer complaints and suggestions, etc.
- Customers are asked to rank benefits according to importance.

Key Questions
- How do you identify changes in customer value and benefits sought and project what they will be in the future?
- How do you incorporate future customer value and benefits sought in new-product development?
- Do you review past projections of customer value and benefits sought to see how accurate they were?
- When did you last review and update customer value commitments?
- How do you evaluate your customer value commitments against those of your competitors?
- How do you ensure that you are evaluating the true customer perspective (rather than your interpretation of the customer's perspective)?
- How do you ensure service standards are updated?

Documentation/Evidence
- A systematic process for obtaining, analyzing, and using multi-faceted data to project the future needs of customers and to determine which product and service benefits will be important to them
- Examples of previous projections that have proved timely and accurate
- Product and service benefits changed to respond to customer value sought
- Past projections versus reality
- Clear evidence of regular customer inputs obtained

5.4 Improve Customer Value

Areas to Address
- How the organization measures and improves leadership commitment and customer focus
- How the organization evaluates and improves its customer management strategies and practices. Including:
  1. how the organization develops a greater understanding with all customers or with key customers
  2. how evaluations lead to improvements in customer value creation
  3. how customer information is used in the improvement process

Key Assessment Points
- How the organization measures and improves leadership
- How the organization measures and improves its customer focus
- How the organization evaluates and improves its customer value management strategies and practices
- Criteria used to evaluate the customer value management strategies and processes

Examples
- Formal evaluation process is documented and institutionalized at all levels.
- Employee involvement teams at all levels are evaluating their processes to learn where they can improve customer value creation.
- Comparisons to competitors and best practices are performed to maintain leading-edge capability.
- Management reviews and directives continuously drive for improvement.
- Customers actively participate in improving services.

Key Questions
- How do you measure the organization's level of customer focus?
- How are managers' training and development linked to customer values?
- How does your organization measure the value it creates for customers?
- How is this evaluation used to drive training, technology upgrades, or customer value management practices?

Documentation/Evidence
- The key criteria used to evaluate the customer value management process
- Systematic process to collect data on key criteria
- Evidence of routine evaluation of processes
- Examples of improvements made in customer value creation

5.5 Anticipate Change

Areas to Address
- How does the organization track and anticipate changes in the market, customer needs and behavior, and competitor activity?

Key Assessment Points
- How the organization tracks and anticipates changes in the market, customer needs and behavior, and competitor activity
- How this information is used to change and improve customer value commitments, positioning at target customers, and differentiation versus key competition

Examples
- Clear evidence of changes in market position, planning, and strategy driven by anticipated changes to customer, market, and competitor conditions exists.
- New-product development is clearly linked to changing customer value and benefits sought supported by external research.
- Systematic analysis to determine root causes and processes to identify and implement corrective action is used.
- Repetitive customer complaints for the same problem have been reduced.
- Information is communicated to customers that improvements are reflective of customer complaints and processes are driven to control complaints.

Key Questions
- How are changes in market trends tracked and monitored?
- How are changes in customer need and behavior tracked and monitored?
- How are changes in competitor offerings tracked and monitored?
- How are these changes used to transform customer value segmentation, customer value commitments, differentiation, and competitive advantage?
- How does external customer feedback get fed into new-offering development?
- How are gaps in customer needs identified?
- What is the process for analyzing complaints to determine the underlying cause?
- Can you produce evidence that customer complaints analysis is used to drive changes in processes, products, and services?
- How do you ensure that appropriate actions are taken to prevent the recurrence of complaints?

Documentation/Evidence
- Reports on root cause analysis
- Improvements in processes and service standards resulting from this analysis (e.g., training of customer-facing staff or information to customers to help them make more effective use of products and/or services)

NOTES

Preface

1. Charan, Ram, and Useem, Jerry. "Why Companies Fail." *Fortune*, 27 May 2002, 50–52.

2. Collins, Jim. *Good to Great: Why Some Companies Make the Leap and Others Don't.* (New York: HarperCollins, 2001), 3–7.

3. Investing-CEO Speaks. "How Herb Keeps Southwest Hopping." *Money*, June 1999, 61, 62.

4. Ibid.

5. Conlin, Michelle. "Where Lay-Offs Are the Last Resort." *BusinessWeek*, 8 October 2001.

6. Ibid.

Chapter 1

1. EVA® (Economic Value Added) is a proprietary framework registered by Stern Stewart & Co.

Chapter 2

1. Day, G. S., and Reibstein, D. J. *Wharton on Dynamic Competitive Strategy.* (New York: John Wiley & Sons, 1997).

2. Judge, P. C. EMC: High-Tech Star. "The Inside Story of How Mike Ruettgers Turned EMC into a Highflier." *BusinessWeek*, 15 March 1999, 72–80.

3. Adapted from Schoell, W. F., and Guiltinan, J. P. *Marketing: Contemporary Concepts and Practices*, 4th ed. (Boston: Allyn & Bacon, 1990).

4. Lanning, M. J. *Delivering Profitable Value: A Revolutionary Framework to Accelerate Growth, Generate Wealth, and Rediscover the Heart of Business.* (Reading, MA: Perseus Books, 1998).

Chapter 3

1. Source: http://www.cybernation.com/victory/quotations/subjects/quotes_customers.html

2. Reid, P. C. *Well-Made in America: Scenes from Harley-Davidson on Being the Best.* (New York: McGraw-Hill, 1990), 102.

3. Kichen, S. "Thunder Road." *Forbes*, 18 July 1983, 92.

4. Krakauer, J. "A Hog Is Still a Hog, but the "Wild Ones" Are Tamer." *Smithsonian*, November 1993, 90.

5. Sun Tzu. *The Art of War.* James Clavell, ed. (New York: Dell Publishing, 1983), 18.

6. Hammonds, K. H. "Michael Porter's Big Ideas." *Fast Company*, March 2001, 150.

Chapter 4

1. Source: http://www.cybernation.com/victory/quotations/authors/quotes_drucker _peterf.html

2. Lanning, M. J. *Delivering Profitable Value: A Revolutionary Framework to Accelerate Growth, Generate Wealth, and Rediscover the Heart of Business.* (Reading, MA: Perseus Books, 1998).

3. Goldner, P. S. *Red-Hot Cold Call Selling: Prospecting Techniques That Pay Off.* (New York: American Management Association, 1995).

4. Among the sources: Frito-Lay at www.fritolay.com/company.html; The Baked Lays Addict Page at www.worldvillage.com/wv/feature/bakedlay.htm.

5. De Bonis, J. N., and Peterson, Roger S. *AMA Handbook for Managing Business to Business Marketing Communications.* (Lincolnwood, IL: NTC Books and the American Marketing Association, 1997).

Chapter 5

1. Porter, M. E. "What Is Strategy?" *Harvard Business Review* 74, 6 (1996): 61–78.

Chapter 6

1. Adapted from PIMS/TARP and other sources.

Chapter 7

1. Brady, D. "The Education of Jeff Immelt." *BusinessWeek*, 29 April 2002, 86.

2. Bridges, W. *The Character of Organizations: Using Personality Type in Organization Development*, Updated Ed. (Palo Alto, CA: Davies-Black Publishing, 2000).

3. In Mackenzie, R.A. *The Time Trap.* (New York: Fine Communications, 2002).

Chapter 8

1. Collins, J. "Best Beats First," *Inc.*, August 2000.

2. Ibid.

3. Rogers, E. M. *Diffusion of Innovations*, 4th ed. (New York: The Free Press, 1995).

4. Source: http:// www.dowcorning.com/content/announce/xiameter_background er.asp

5. "XIAMETER Dramatically Reduces Cost for Commonly Used Silicon-Based Materials," (Midland, MI: Dow Corning press release, March 5, 2002).

INDEX

ABOUT THE AUTHORS

J. Nicholas (Nick) De Bonis, Ph.D.

An experienced strategic marketing consultant and practitioner, Nick works closely with global companies and their business units and teams as a long-term strategic consultant, mentor, and coach. He helps clients identify their performance needs in business strategy and planning, global strategic marketing and leadership, and then coordinates the design and development of appropriate learning modes to achieve the desired behavioral outcomes. His client list includes Agfa Consumer Imaging, Akzo Nobel, AlliedSignal Plastics, BellSouth Telecom, Boehringer Ingelheim Vetmedica world-wide, Dow Chemical world-wide, Ericsson Telecom, GTE (now Verizon), Kodak Film & Advantix Camera groups in the U.S. and Kodak medical imaging in Europe, MediaOne International, QuebecTel, Roche Pharmaceuticals, Schlumberger world-wide, Sprint, and Celanese Ticona. Nick's diverse professional background includes successful careers in marketing and advertising, sales, sales management and sales training, management, and print and broadcast media. He has also owned and managed his own company. Nick coauthored *Top Dog* with J. David Pincus, published in 1994 by McGraw-Hill Business Books. His second book, coauthored with Roger Peterson, is *The American Marketing Association Handbook for Managing Business-to-Business Communications*, published in 1997. From 1992–96, he was a full-time adjunct associate professor at the Goizueta Business School at Emory University in Atlanta, where he resides. He has also been on the faculty at LSU, Texas A&M, California State University-Fullerton, and Pepperdine University. From 1980–96, he supported his teaching habit as a consultant in marketing strategy and integrated marketing communications for companies like Canon Copiers USA, IBM, MDS Qantel, and Sprint. Nick earned his doctorate in advertising and marketing from the University of Tennessee-Knoxville, and continues to conduct research and publish in the area of value delivery systems, relationship marketing and relationship communications.

Email: DeBonisMarketing@aol.com

Eric Balinski

Eric Balinski is principle of SYNECTION, a consultancy focused on performance improvement and achieving breakthrough business results. Eric has global expertise in enabling complex businesses to create highly motivated teams that deliver profitable growth and stretch goals. His specialty is in transforming an organization's customer and enterprise performance. Prior to starting SYNECTION, he held business leadership roles and was the Global Director of Business Education for two Fortune 100 firms, leading a variety of workforce practices that redefined how these companies competed in the marketplace. In leadership development, he has taught value creation worldwide to every business, function, and level. He has also held business leadership positions at GE, Dow Chemical, and Allied Signal. Eric is affiliated with Accelare, the pioneers in Enterprise Process Management, whose clients include Harvard Pilgrim Healthcare, Children's Hospital of Philadelphia, Fidelity Investments, and American Express.

Email: ebflycast@aol.com

Phil Allen

Phil Allen is an International Marketing graduate and career marketer. His marketing expertise has developed through hands-on experience at national, continental, and global levels in sales, market research, marketing, and key account management with multinational corporations including Albright & Wilson Ltd, Bayer AG, English China Clays, Hilti AG, and The Dow Chemical Company. Since 1997 Phil has run his own marketing excellence practice, MarketAbility—creating value for clients by helping them to apply marketing excellence to their businesses. MarketAbility delivers practical marketing for value growth, based on systematic market planning, creative segmentation, differentiated value propositions, and practical implementation. MarketAbility facilitates marketing strategy development and implementation working together with the client's team and offers training and education programs and new business development expertise. MarketAbility serves many clients in the chemicals, plastics, and energy industries. Phil's expertise ranges from customer research through new business development, market segmentation, market planning, and key account management to marketing strategy development and implementation. He has also developed and coined the new concept of Customer Value Management, a practical approach to creating and capturing customer value. He is a regular contributor to numerous marketing and industry journals and speaks at selected marketing conferences. Phil is a consultant and trainer for Cranfield Market Planning Centre and Management Centre Europe (MCE). A fluent German speaker, he lives near Zurich, Switzerland, and works around the world.

Email: phil.allen@marketability.org

The American Marketing Association is the world's largest and most comprehensive professional association of marketers. With over 45,000 members, the AMA has more than 500 chapters throughout North America. The AMA sponsors 25 major conferences per year, covering topics ranging from the latest trends in customer satisfaction measurement to business-to-business and service marketing, attitude research and sales promotion, and publishes nine major marketing publications.

For further information on the American Marketing Association, call toll free at 800-AMA-1150.

Or write to:
The American Marketing Association
11 South Wacker Drive
Suite 5800
Chicago, IL 60606-2266
Fax: 800-950-0872
URL: http://www.ama.org